The Rushdie Affair

Second Edition

With a postscript
by Koenraad Elst

Daniel Pipes

The Rushdie Affair

The Novel, the Ayatollah, and the West

Transaction Publishers
New Brunswick (U.S.A.) and London (U.K.)

Second printing 2004

New material this edition copyright © 2003 by Transaction Publishers, New Brunswick, New Jersey. www.transactionpub.com

Originally published in 1990 by Birch Lane Press.

This book is printed on acid-free paper that meets the American National Standard for Permanence of Paper for Printed Library Materials.

Library of Congress Catalog Number: 2003042683
ISBN: 0-7658-0996-6
Printed in the United States of America

Library of Congress Cataloging-in-Publication Data

Pipes, Daniel, 1949-
 The Rushdie affair : the novel, the Ayatollah, and the West / Daniel Pipes ; with a postscript by Koenraad Elst.—2nd ed.
  p. cm.
 Includes bibliographical references and index.
 ISBN 0-7658-0996-6 (alk. paper)
 1. Rushdie, Salman. Satanic verses. 2. Khomeini, Ruhollah—Views on literature. 3. Islam and literature—History—20th century. 4. Freedom of the press—History—20th century. 5. Censorship—History—20th Century. I. Title.

PR6068.U757S27355 2003
823'.914—dc21   2003042683

To the One
Who Makes Happy

A book is a product of a pact with the Devil that inverts the Faustian contract.... Dr. Faust sacrificed eternity in return for two dozen years of power; the writer agrees to the ruination of his life, and gains (but only if he's lucky) maybe not eternity, but posterity, at least.

—Salman Rushdie, *The Satanic Verses*

In the jungle of the cities, we live among our accumulation of things behind doors garlanded with locks and chains, and find it all too easy to fear the unforeseeable, all-destroying coming of the Ogre—Charles Manson, the Ayatollah Khomeini, the Blob from Outer Space.

—Salman Rushdie, July 1984

I am coming to the conclusion that privacy, the small individual lives of men, are preferable to all this inflated macrocosmic activity. But too late. Can't be helped. What can't be cured must be endured.

—Salman Rushdie, *Midnight's Children*

CONTENTS

ACKNOWLEDGMENTS

I have been helped by many people in researching and writing this book. Given just a weekend's time, Roger Donway came through with a typically virtuoso performance of editing. Khalid Durán and Bernard Lewis first provided me with press clippings, then carefully read and commented on the entire manuscript. Sasson Somekh and George Szamuely read portions of the book and offered insightful responses. Henri Barkey, Patrick Clawson, Adam Garfinkle, David Littman, Irene Pipes, Vladimir Tismaneanu, Howard Wiarda, and Eliot Weinberger collected materials for me on *The Satanic Verses* controversy from here and there around the globe.

My student assistants, Robert Baron, Daniel Cohen, Brayton Connard, and Paula Rasich provided valuable help with clippings, library research, and a host of other tasks. Saundra Bailey and Kelly Flanigan provided thoughtful and efficient help with logistics. Marvin Wachman, Alan Luxenberg, and Kevin McNamara willingly shouldered extra administrative burdens at the Foreign Policy Research Institute, giving me the time to write an unplanned book.

An invitation from Rasha Al-Sabah, Vice Rector for Community Service and Information at Kuwait University, fortuitously enabled me to sample opinions on the Rushdie affair in the Middle East exactly at the height of the controversy.

When the ayatollah posthumously induced the original publisher of this book to cancel the contract (on which, see the Appendix), I depended heavily on Floyd Abrams, Steven Emerson, Paula Roberts, and Judith Shapiro for counsel. Hillel Black showed the enthusiasm for this book that every author dreams of in an editor, but few actually find.

Materials that first appeared in *Commentary*, *The Philadelphia Inquirer*, *Reason*, and *The Wall Street Journal* are used here with the gracious permission of the publishers.

Finally, thanks are due to the wizards, mostly anonymous, who provide the computer hardware and software which make it possible to write virtually the whole of a book in three and a half months.

Unless otherwise noted, all references to radio and television broadcasts derive from the *Daily Report* put out by the Foreign Broadcast Information Service; the same source also provided a number of news agency items and newspaper articles. For reasons of style, I have slightly amended some FBIS translations. Dates without years refer to 1989.

Philadelphia   *D.P.*
September 1989

INTRODUCTION

Robert MacNeil, co-host of the "MacNeil/Lehrer NewsHour," leaned across the television studio desk and told me in mid-February 1989, "You know, I've been reporting the news for decades, but I've never before seen a novel as the lead item in the day's news." And he was right; not only had a novel never dominated the news before, but there was never before anything quite like the controversy surrounding Salman Rushdie and his novel *The Satanic Verses*.[1]

Together, Rushdie and Ayatollah* Ruhollah Khomeini stirred powerful emotions on a global level. Censorship, protests, riots, a death edict, a break in diplomatic relations, even a confrontation of civilizations—it all had a fantastical quality which made the incident more appropriate to the world of magical realism found in Rushdie's novels than to the sober world of politics. Or, to switch literary genres, the incident had the making of an international thriller. As Jean-Claude Lamy observed, it has all the elements: "At the center, a single man (sacrilegious apostate for some, innocent novelist for others) chased by a multitude of killers, a clash of civilizations, geo-strategic rivalries, and the wrath of God! And there is even blood, which has already flowed in Islamabad, Kashmir, and Bombay, and is more than likely to flow elsewhere."[2] But the event was real, not literary. More than that, it had a significance that went far beyond the actors directly

---

*Khomeini became known among his followers as the imam, an honorific of extraordinary power among Shi'i Muslims; but he remained known in the West as the ayatollah, and so we continue to refer to him in this way.

15

involved. The following pages attempt to explain what happened, why it happened, and what the implications of the incident are for East and West alike, for ayatollahs and novelists.

Though the event seemed to come and go in a moment, the full story actually lasted half a year, from September 1988 to March 1989. Small as it first appeared, the incident was actually far-reaching. The controversy began in India, moved to Great Britain, then traveled to the United States, South Africa, Pakistan, and Iran. It engaged thousands of individuals in protest, from renowned American writers to obscure Bengali rioters. It caused the deaths of over twenty people, disrupted billions of dollars in trade, brought profound cultural tensions to the surface, and raised issues about freedom of speech and the secular state that had seemingly been settled decades or even centuries earlier. The Rushdie controversy raised important questions about the many millions of Muslims now living in the West and their relationship to the civilization around them. On a more mundane level, it led to a church being destroyed, book store windows being smashed, movies not distributed, and musical records withdrawn. At least three persons lost their jobs: a radio talk show host, a comic book writer, and the editor of a religious monthly.

The reason for the incident needs explanation. Comparison between *The Satanic Verses* and other writings reveals that Rushdie's novel contains by no means the most blasphemous thoughts expressed by a Muslim in recent years. Why then was it the book that sparked a furor? Did Muslims in many countries find it a convenient vehicle for political protest? Or did the book have some feature, possibly one even unknown to the author, which sparked protests in such diverse places?

The complexity of the Rushdie incident makes it not possible in short compass to cover its every aspect. Writing primarily for a Western audience, I have therefore emphasized those events which are less likely to be familiar to it. The controversy prompted much discussion about freedom of expression, the nature of blasphemy, and the role of the literati. These issues have been treated at length by others, so I cover them lightly. Instead, I emphasize equally important topics which received less attention, including such matters as the Muslim understanding of *The Satanic Verses* and the Soviet response to the controversy. Most important, I hope to explain the long-term importance of this event for Muslims resident in West Europe and North America, and why it augurs the beginning of a new era for them and for their host societies.

Recounting the Rushdie incident presents one special challenge, especially for an analyst who writes when the events are still fresh. The tumult of February and March 1989 engaged the emotions of almost everyone who followed the news; it was one of those pure cases where ideologies and religions clashed, and when all concerned had strong feelings. The newspapers and magazines were full of glib comments about the Muslims' "return to barbarism," the "unquestioning, perhaps fanatical" faith of the East, and the like. For their part, Muslims answered with accusations of cultural imperialism and a new Crusading spirit. With such recriminations in the air, simple stereotyping became a real trap. Accordingly, the Westerner who would describe the controversy must take special care not to condemn without understanding. He need not sympathize with the Muslim rioters and Khomeini, but he must understand their motives and explain their views. As John Voll, a historian of Islam, requests, "Even scholars who personally condemn the action of the Ayatollah need to be able to present Khomeini's views in such a way that they would at least be recognizable to his followers."[3] I endorse Voll's approach and aim to present precisely such an understanding.

The pages that follow begin with a detailed account of the events that took place in the half year between September 1988 and March 1989. Part I then focuses on two texts, *The Satanic Verses* and Ayatollah Khomeini's edict, and attempts to explain why the one led to the other. After one layer and another has been peeled away, a conclusion emerges: the key to the controversy lies in a terrible misunderstanding about the book's title. Part II surveys the responses to the texts, from conspiracy theories in

Iran to petitions in the United States, then considers the implications of this controversy. Two issues receive special attention: the perennial problem of censorship (Is it justified if it saved dozens of lives? How extensive will the chilling effect be?) and the very new questions raised by millions of Muslims living in the West. It appears very likely that the Rushdie affair will have a lasting impact on relations between this Muslim diaspora and its host population, and not for the better.

NOTES

[1]Salman Rushdie, *The Satanic Verses* (New York: Viking, 1989).

[2]Jean-Claude Lamy, "Affaire Rushdie: Les deux scandales," *Jeune Afrique*, March 15, 1989. 29

[3]John Voll, "For Scholars of Islam, Interpretation Need Not Be Advocacy," *Chronicle of Higher Education*, March 22, 1989.

1.

HALF A YEAR OF UPHEAVAL

Controversy over *The Satanic Verses* started in late September 1988 and built up to a crescendo by mid-February 1989. Then, a month later, the issue dropped from sight, though its effects continued to be felt long after.

Protests and Riots

Protests against *The Satanic Verses* began even before the book's official British publication, on September 26, 1988. Surprisingly, the furor began not in Britain but in India, where Muslims learned about *The Satanic Verses* from two magazines, *India Today* and *Sunday,* which in their mid-September editions provided reviews of the book, excerpts, and interviews with the author. With prescience and understatement, Madhu Jain predicted in *India Today* that *The Satanic Verses* "is bound to trigger an avalanche of protests from the ramparts."[1]

It did not take long. Syed Shahbuddin and Khurshid Alam Khan, Muslim members of the Indian parliament, did not like what they had read of the book, so they began a campaign to have the novel banned in India. Their efforts met with almost instant success; under a ruling of the Indian Customs Act, the Finance Ministry prohibited the book on October 5. Shahbuddin had the honor not only of starting the controversy, but of laying down two of its most enduring traits. Addressing Rushdie, he wrote shortly after the banning:

You are aggrieved that some of us have condemned you without a hearing and asked for the ban without reading your book. Yes, I have not read it, nor do I intend to. I do not have to wade through a filthy drain to know what filth is.[2]

His defiant assertion, "Yes, I have not read it, nor do I intend to," foreshadowed the sentiments of almost all other Muslim leaders. Neither he nor they felt a need to read the book in its entirety, and precious few critics even bothered to read extracts. Second, Shahbuddin's nastiness ("I do not have to wade through a filthy drain to know what filth is") came to characterize the tone of the dispute to come. The debate would be an emotional one at the highest pitch, with no rhetorical prisoners taken.

Then the action moved to Great Britain. Word reached the Muslims there in a letter that arrived on the first day or two of October, from Aslam Ejaz of the Islamic Foundation in Madras to his friend Faiyazuddin Ahmad of the Islamic Foundation in Leicester, England. In the letter, Ejaz informed Ahmad about the impending ban in India on *The Satanic Verses*, and encouraged Ahmad to do God's work in Great Britain. Ahmad bought the book, read it, and was appalled. He then photocopied the offending passages and on October 3 sent these around to other Islamic organizations in the United Kingdom.

On October 7, more copies went out to the London embassies of all Muslim states. The Saudi government, which sees itself as the standard-bearer of orthodox Islam, took up the cause with alacrity. The next day, the Saudi-sponsored newspaper published in London, *Ash-Sharq al-Awsat*, featured a story on *The Satanic Verses* denouncing the book. Soon thereafter, the Saudi-backed weekly, *Impact International*, published a selection of the book's most controversial passages. Ahmad was invited to Jidda, Saudi Arabia, where he briefed officials about the novel and mobilized Saudi support for a campaign against it. Several Saudi-sponsored international organizations (including the Muslim World League and the U.K. Action Committee on Islamic Affairs) then took up the cause.

Overall, these efforts to bring international pressure to bear did not achieve much. Weeks passed and most Muslim states gave no response, not even bothering to ban the book. Indeed, as adverse publicity stimulated curiosity, importation of the novel to Muslim countries continued to be legal and, by all reports, to be done. The one gesture by the Muslim states was in late December, when they sent a delegation of three London-based ambassadors to meet the Home Office Minister, John Patten.

In the meantime, the effort within Britain picked up wide support among Muslims. Hesham El Essawy, chair of the Islamic Society for the Promotion of Religious Tolerance, wrote a letter to Viking Press on October 12: "I would like to invite you to take some kind of corrective stand, before the monster that you have so needlessly created grows, as it will do worldwide, into something uncontrollable."[3]

The publishers did little more than snicker; a society claiming to promote tolerance was requesting censorship! Also on the 12th, Trevor Glover, the managing director of Penguin, received a like letter from 'Ali Mughram al-Ghamdi, the Saudi who served as convenor of the U.K. Action Committee on Islamic Affairs, an umbrella group representing Saudi-backed Muslim organizations in Britain. A letter sent out by Ghamdi on October 28 to rouse British Muslims to action dubbed *The Satanic Verses* "the most offensive, filthy and abusive book ever written by any hostile enemy of Islam" and called for three measures: the retraction of all copies of the novel, an apology by the author, and a payment of damages by him to a Muslim charity in Britain.[4]

The Union of Muslim Organisations, another umbrella organization, hosted a crisis meeting on October 15 at which it was decided to get *The Satanic Verses* legally banned in Britain and Rushdie criminally prosecuted, both on the charge of blasphemy. The group pressed for such a ban in a letter of October 20 to Prime Minister Margaret Thatcher, but its efforts went nowhere, for British laws of blasphemy, as Muslims soon discovered, apply only to Christianity, and even then are hardly ever applied. The prime minister's answer came on November 11, and it turned the

Union down flat—"there are no grounds on which the government could consider banning" the book, she wrote.[5]

Further efforts to pursue the matter (with the attorney-general, the lord chancellor, and the home secretary) proved equally unavailing. Muslims even pushed their cause at the Conservative party's annual meeting in Brighton, without success.

By October, threats against Rushdie's life had already begun to affect his daily routine; in that month he cancelled a planned trip to Cambridge, England, because of death threats. He took an unlisted telephone number. On leaving the house, he was sometimes accompanied by a bodyguard, especially when attending public functions. By all accounts, these threats came from the grassroots, and were not sanctioned by the Muslim leadership in Britain, much less by the states behind them. Writing in *Impact International,* M. H. Faruqi called for the application of pressure "through all civilised and legitimate means. But please leave Mr. Salman Rushdie all to himself and to his charmed circle of 'literary critics.'"[6]

There had also been trouble during the fall in the United States and South Africa. An organized letter campaign in several cities (notably Houston, Detroit, Chicago, and the Queens borough of New York) inundated Viking Penguin in New York City with tens of thousands of menacing letters. Serious threats against the press began in December 1988, two months before the book was available locally, and were repeated at least seven times even before the ayatollah's edict. One anonymous caller announced that $50,000 would be paid to anyone who assassinated the firm's president. On two occasions in December alone, bomb scares forced the Viking staff to evacuate its offices. Rumor had it that several Viking executives wore bulletproof vests to the office.

In South Africa, two anti-apartheid institutions, *The Weekly Mail* and the Congress of South African Writers (COSAW), invited Rushdie to deliver the keynote speech at a conference they were cosponsoring on censorship. The title of Rushdie's talk came from a famous line of Heinrich Heine, "When you start by burning books you end by burning men too." No one in South

Africa having ever seen *The Satanic Verses*, the organizers did not realize what they were up against by inviting Rushdie. But it soon became clear, as the death threats against him proliferated, that the 500,000-strong Muslim community in South Africa had been alerted to Rushdie's blasphemies and would not suffer his presence. The editors of *The Weekly Mail* were particularly impressed by the fact that almost all the threats against him were signed, and even included return addresses, suggesting powerful emotions of a sort they could barely comprehend. Protest demonstrations followed, as did more threats to Rushdie himself, his sponsors, and bookstores that might carry his novel (not a single copy of which had yet reached South Africa, it must be emphasized). Under Muslim pressure, the government banned the book. Finally, on November 1, one day before Rushdie was due to arrive, COSAW withdrew his invitation. Ironically, the speaker invited to indict censorship by the state was censored by his fellows-in-arms.

Frustrated by the British government's lack of response, as well as by *The Satanic Verses* having been awarded the Whitbread monthly prize for fiction in November, the Muslim community in Bolton (near Manchester) decided to take action on their own, and they settled on a ritual burning of the book, which they did on December 2. Although the ceremony attracted a crowd of 7,000 Muslims, press coverage was virtually nil, so the event did not have the hoped-for impact.

Finally, the campaign took off when a second copy of *The Satanic Verses* was burned on January 14 in Bradford, northern England, a town whose large Muslim population won it the sobriquet of "capital of Islam in the United Kingdom." Although only 1,000 demonstrators rallied in Bradford, a fraction of those in Bolton, this time the Muslims found non-Muslim supporters (such as local politicians and the bishop of Bradford) and the presence of these figures helped bring out the media in force. Television news showed an *auto da fé*—the novel attached to a stake and set on fire—in loving, if horrified, detail. Further, pictures of the scene were splashed in the media for days, commentators opined at length on the event, and it became a major topic of discussion throughout the country. Subsequently, 8,000 fundamentalist Muslims (that is, Muslims who seek application of the Islamic law in its every detail) marched in London on January 29 to protest the book.

In reply to these attacks, Rushdie published a statement asserting his credentials as a good Muslim. In it, he called the Prophet Muhammad "one of the great geniuses of world history," but noted that Islamic doctrine holds Muhammad to be human, and in no way perfect. Rushdie also held that the novel is not "an antireligious novel. It is, however, an attempt to write about migration, its stresses and transformations."[7]

But book burnings were merely a warm-up for the violence that began in Islamabad, Pakistan, on February 12 and then continued for over a month. Controversial selections of Rushdie's book had been crudely translated into Urdu, then presented in public readings in the streets. Outrage spilled into violence when a crowd of some 10,000 persons took to the streets and marched to the American Cultural Center. Shouting "American dogs" and "God is great,"[8] the protesters set fires to the building. As the crowd surged toward the Center, five demonstrators died at the hands of the police and about a hundred were injured. While the police held the bulk of the mob at bay, a group of some two to three hundred protesters slipped to the back of the American Center and began throwing large rocks at the windows which, made of Mylar, withstood the assault. The protesters also tried pulling down the gate, but this too was well constructed and resisted their efforts. They set small fires around the building's perimeter and pulled down the American flag, which was burned. Although the rioters had fifteen minutes free reign at the peak of the demonstration to attack the Center, they did not succeed in breaching the defenses of the fortified building. They did, however, shoot a Pakistani guard at the American Center, making him the sixth casualty of the day.

The American Cultural Center resisted this assault so well because it was constructed with just such an attack in mind. The building had been put up after a similar riot in 1979 destroyed an earlier Center. Ironically, the 1979 riot also had its origins in an incident—the takeover of the Great Mosque in Mecca by extremist Muslims—in which the United States government had no role. Those riots had been caused by Khomeini's accusing the United States of instigating the Mecca incident, and Muslims around the world, including those in Pakistan, used the occasion to attack American diplomats. Several people lost their lives in that earlier Islamabad violence.

Demonstrators also broke into the offices of American Express, where they set fire to the furniture, causing extensive damage. The strong police response to rioting in Islamabad raised a further ruckus of its own, with bills submitted to parliament condemning the police and demonstrations taking place in several Pakistani cities to protest the deaths in Islamabad.

Although the events of the 12th are clear, their causes remain disputed. The odd thing was that although the novel had been out for months in the United Kingdom, and Rushdie was living in London, British property was not attacked. Staging an assault on the American Center may have had to do with the forthcoming U.S. publication of *The Satanic Verses*, scheduled for February 22. Or the violence may have been directed toward those in the opposition who wanted to exploit the opportunity to attack Prime Minister Benazir Bhutto. (Rushdie and Bhutto are long-standing political opponents, but they are nearly identical in fundamentalist Muslims' eyes, being about the same age, educated in the West, and hostile to a role for Islam in public life.) Indeed, this is the way the prime minister interpreted the riots.

The question that perturbs the present Government was whether the agitation was really against the book, which has not been read in Pakistan, is not for sale in Pakistan, and has not been translated in Pakistan. Or was it a protest by those people who lost the [November 1988] election, or those people who were patronized by martial law [i.e., the followers of the late President Mohammed Zia-ul-Haq] to try and destabilize the process of democracy?[9]

Similarly, Rushdie accused the leaders of the demonstration of exploiting religious slogans for political ends. Along parallel lines, the U.S. ambassador to Pakistan, Robert Oakley, suspected Iranian and Libyan money behind the demonstrations.

On the next day, February 13, rioting in Srinagar, India, led to the death of one person and injuries to sixty (including twenty policemen). That night, matters were taken out of the hands of street protesters and raised to the level of state policy. Only one man could have done this: Ayatollah Ruhollah Musavi Khomeini.

Khomeini Steps In

All accounts agree that Khomeini had never heard of *The Satanic Verses* before mid-February. Although this may at first seem unlikely, it should not be. All the initial protests were local affairs; Iranian authorities repeatedly chose not to get caught up in the controversy, and Khomeini himself was not likely to be closely acquainted with the latest developments on the London literary scene. (This obliviousness on Khomeini's part, incidentally, disposes of the many questions why he had not earlier issued an edict against Rushdie.)

Accounts differ as to exactly how Khomeini learned about the novel. According to one version, he was in his house on February 13, watching the evening news on Iranian television, as he did every night, when he saw pictures of the rioting in Pakistan. The scenes he witnessed moved him deeply. Indeed, it is hard to imagine news more affecting for someone with Khomeini's sense of Islamic solidarity than Muslims outside an American Cultural Center crying out "God is great," then proceeding to die at the hands of the police. A second account has him hearing about the rioting in Pakistan from a small transistor radio he took with him on his three daily half-hour constitutionals. The final version has him alerted to the existence of the book by a petition, accompanied by translated excerpts, sent to him in January by a group of British Muslims via the Iranian embassy in London. Ahmad Khomeini then brought the matter to his father's attention, and the latter was said to be "shaken utterly" on reading portions of the novel.[10] The testimony of Khomeini's daughter, Zahra Mustafavi, confirms the likelihood of the first or second scenario. According to her, Khomeini tuned in to the radio through the day for news broadcasts, both Iranian and foreign. "He listens to news all hours except when sleeping or praying. He has a portable radio which he carried even during the fast, believe me, and even during meals. He's careful that he himself hears the news rather than hearing it from others."[11]

However alerted to the events in Pakistan, Khomeini proceeded to summon a secretary and then took the single most important step of the entire incident. He dictated the following legal judgment (*fatwa*) against Rushdie and his publishers:

In the name of Him, the Highest. There is only one God, to whom we shall all return. I inform all zealous Muslims of the world that the author of the book entitled *The Satanic Verses*—which has been compiled, printed, and published in opposition to Islam, the Prophet, and the Qur'an—and all those involved in its publication who were aware of its content, are sentenced to death.

I call on all zealous Muslims to execute them quickly, wherever they may be found, so that no one else will dare to insult the Muslim sanctities. God willing, whoever is killed on this path is a martyr.

In addition, anyone who has access to the author of this book, but does not possess the power to execute him, should report him to the people so that he may be punished for his actions.

May peace and the mercy of God and His blessings be with you. Ruhollah al-Musavi al-Khomeini, 25 Bahman 1367.[12]

At that moment, in London (three and a half time zones behind), Rushdie was attending a book party for his wife in the elegant atrium of Michelin House. He then went to dinner with her and with friends at La Poissonnerie de l'Avenue. Apprehensive about the consequences of the riots in Pakistan, Rushdie and his wife had left their house in Islington, in northeast London, on the 13th and spent the night of February 13-14 with friends. The edict was broadcast just before the 2:00 p.m. news in Iran; Rushdie learned of its existence in a telephone call from the BBC

World Service. By lunchtime, he was discussing the threat in the media. That afternoon, senior police commanders decided to provide him with "grade one" protection by the Special Branch, the highest level of security (and the sort usually accorded visiting dignitaries). Rushdie's last public appearance was at a memorial service for Bruce Chatwin. Apparently the last words to him before his disappearance were spoken by Paul Theroux, the travel writer, who whispered on leaving the church, "Your turn next. I suppose we'll be back here for you next week. Keep your head down, Salman."[13] Rushdie laughed and entered a car, which then took him into hiding.

To make the task of killing Rushdie more attractive, the head of an Iranian charity organization, the 15th Khorbad [5th of June] Relief Agency, offered $1 million to a non-Iranian assassin and 200 million rials to an Iranian. (At the inflated official rate of exchange, 200 million rials equals almost $3 million, but on the parallel market, it equals only $170,000.) The next day, 'Ali Akbar Hashemi Rafsanjani, speaker of the Iranian parliament, joined in. Rafsanjani had been advocating improved relations with the West, and so, caught out by Khomeini's edict, he had to make up lost ground. He did this by asking the religious leader of his hometown, Rafsanjan, for help; the latter found another 200 million rials to offer to Rushdie's executioner.

Many other Iranians also endorsed Khomeini's action. Members of the Iranian parliament expressed their "divine anger" at Rushdie and their support for Khomeini. To show their eagerness to die a martyr's death, theology students offered to "wear their [funeral] shrouds in Europe and the United States to carry out Imam Khomeini's order."[14] The Iranian ambassador to the Holy See announced that he would pull the trigger and kill Salman Rushdie with his own hands. The Islamic Revolution News Agency representative in Spain promised likewise (and found himself instantly expelled from the country).

More to the point, a number of groups sponsored by the Iranian government declared their determination to execute Rushdie. Mohsen Reza'i, leader of the Islamic Revolution Guard Corps, announced that his forces were ready "to carry out the imam's decree."[15] This corps had had a major role in Iran's war with Iraq, so the statement carried real weight. Interior Minister 'Ali Akbar Mohtashemi called on Hizbullah (the Party of God) to carry out the execution. Mohtashemi had early served as Tehran's ambassador in Damascus, where he organized the Iranian-backed terrorist groups in Lebanon, so his appeal elicited a favorable response; leaders of the Lebanese branch of Hizbullah promised to do "all that's possible to have the honor" of carrying out Khomeini's sentence. A number of other Lebanese-based groups engaged in their country's civil war, some with a history of terrorism against Westerners, promised to find and kill Rushdie. These included Amal, the largest Shi'i group, and the Islamic Unification Movement, a Sunni organization. The Revolutionary Justice Organization went further than the others and vowed to attack the British police, if necessary, on the way to an assault on Rushdie. Several Palestinian groups joined the effort, such as the (fundamentalist) Islamic Jihad for the Liberation of Palestine and Ahmad Jibril's (quasi-Marxist) Popular Front for the Liberation of Palestine—General Command. Something of a rivalry developed between these groups—who would get Rushdie first?

To demonstrate the terrible solemnity of the moment, the Iranian government proclaimed a national day of mourning on February 15, to be immediately followed by a Day of Protest and Revulsion. The president of Iran, Seyyed 'Ali Khamene'i, characterized Khomeini's statement as "an irrevocable dictum."[16] On February 16, some 3,000 demonstrators gathered outside the British embassy in Tehran to listen to politicians call the United Kingdom "the enemy of the Qur'an and Islam and the manifestation of all things evil."[17] Leading Iranian religious figures cancelled their theology classes.

On the 17th, President Khamene'i announced that "the people might forgive him," if Rushdie repented.[18] Accordingly, the next day, Rushdie did offer an apology, though a minimal one.

As author of *The Satanic Verses*, I recognize that Muslims in many parts of the world are genuinely distressed by the publication of my novel. I profoundly regret the distress that the publication had occasioned to sincere followers of Islam. Living as we do in a world of many faiths, this experience has served to remind us that we must all be conscious of the sensibilities of others.[19]

The apology concerned the effects of his writings, not the writings themselves, and so did little to mollify his critics.

Still, confusion in Iran followed, as a news agency report suggested that the apology, "though far too short of a repentance, is generally seen as sufficient enough to warrant his pardon by the masses in Iran and elsewhere in the world."[20] Then the ayatollah weighed in, on February 19, with an absolute rejection of Rushdie's statement, and, indeed, of any act of contrition on his part. Khomeini denied foreign reports that repentance by Rushdie would lift the "execution order" against him.

Even if Salman Rushdie repents and becomes the most pious man of [our] time, it is incumbent on every Muslim to employ everything he has, his life and his wealth, to send him to hell. If a non-Muslim becomes aware of his whereabouts and has the ability to execute him quicker than Muslims, it is incumbent on Muslims to pay a reward or a fee in return for this action.[21]

The confirmation of the edict meant it would not go away; governments found they had no choice but to deal with the issues raised by Khomeini.

Diplomatic Crisis

In answer to Khomeini's second announcement, the European Community elevated the controversy to a diplomatic incident and put Tehran on warning. On February 20, the foreign ministers of the Common Market agreed on a statement about Rushdie and his publishers:

The Ministers of Foreign Affairs of the 12 member states of the European Community, meeting in Brussels, discussed the Iranian threats and incitements to murder against novelist Salman Rushdie and his publishers, now repeated despite the apology made by the author.

The ministers view those threats with the gravest concern. They condemn this incitement to murder as an unacceptable violation of the most elementary principles and obligations that govern relations among sovereign states. . . .

The 12 express their continuing interest in developing normal constructive relations with the Islamic Republic of Iran, but if Iran shares this desire, it has to declare its respect for international obligations and renounce the use or threatened use of violence.

Meanwhile, the ministers of the 12 decided to simultaneously recall their Heads of Mission in Tehran for consultations and to suspend exchanges of high-level official visits. [22]

The heads of mission were then recalled. In the highly charged atmosphere of the moment, no one really had an idea how long the recall would last or what would come next.

On February 22, President Khamene'i characterized the *fatwa* as irrevocable and inescapable. "An arrow has been shot toward its target and it is now traveling towards its aim." [23] The only violent incident against Muslims in the United Kingdom occurred that same day, when an assailant hurled a milk bottle filled with petrol against a wall of London's central mosque at Regent's Park. It exploded ineffectually and a culprit was quickly apprehended.

On February 24, 'Ali Akbar Hashemi Rafsanjani, speaker of the Iranian parliament, distanced the government from Khomeini's edict by noting that "any Muslim might carry out his duty [against Rushdie and his publishers]. That has nothing to do with the Islamic Republic." [24]

The British government withdrew all its personnel from Tehran and demanded that the Iranian representatives leave London. Oddly, it did not break diplomatic relations, but insisted on what it called "reciprocity at zero." Observers knew of no precedent for the maintenance of diplomatic relations without any personnel; the British move was understood as a way of expressing

strong displeasure and regret simultaneously—and thereby sig-
naling that normal relations could be rebuilt as soon as the edict
was retracted. But far from retracting, Tehran took the next step
in the diplomatic dance; on February 28, the Majlis, Iran's
parliament, passed a bill that stipulated a complete break on
March 7 unless the British government declared "its opposition to
the unprincipled stands against the world of Islam, the Islamic
Republic of Iran, and the contents of the anti-Islamic book, *The
Satanic Verses.*"[25]

Prodded by feelers from "pragmatists" in Tehran, British
leaders did what they could to satisfy Tehran. On March 2,
Foreign Secretary Sir Geoffrey Howe went on the BBC World
Service to show foreign listeners that the government wished to
distance itself from Rushdie.

> We understand that the book itself has been found deeply offensive
> by people of the Muslim faith. It is a book that is offensive in
> many other ways as well. We can understand why it could be
> criticized. The British Government, the British people, do not
> have any affection for the book. The book is extremely critical,
> rude about us. It compares Britain with Hitler's Germany.* We do
> not like that any more than the people of the Muslim faith like the
> attacks on their faith contained in the book. So we are not
> cosponsoring the book. What we are sponsoring is the right of
> people to speak freely, to publish freely.[26]

Two days later, Prime Minister Margaret Thatcher made similar
remarks, prompting Rushdie to call a Labour MP from his place

---

*Howe is wrong; the only passage that refers to Nazi Germany comes in
reference to New York City (quoted below, p. 45). Rushdie contested Howe's
characterization, challenging the foreign secretary to produce the offending
sentence. In addition, the British press jumped on Howe for his remarks, seeing
his behavior as "obsequious and cringing" (*Financial Times*, March 9, 1989),
calling the analogy with Nazi Germany "too foolish," and characterizing his
sympathy with Islam as "false" and "bogus" (*The Independent*, March 6, 1989).
It was also pointed out, correctly, that the British leaders had no mandate to
undertake literary criticism on behalf of the country.

of hiding and express his concern that the government might be changing its support for him.

The Iranians acknowledged these gestures but demanded practical measures as well, such as the legal prosecution of the writer, confiscation of copies of *The Satanic Verses*, and injunction against further publication of the book. These steps the British authorities did not even consider undertaking; so, as threatened, Tehran broke relations on March 7. Its statement included some of the most unusual language and reasoning to be found anywhere in international diplomacy. The announcement noted that "in the past two centuries Britain has been in the frontline of plots and treachery against Islam and Muslims," and it went on to provide details about perfidious Albion in Palestine, Iraq, Pakistan and elsewhere. It observed that London had suffered severe reverses at the hands of Islamic movements, and so it had dropped the old military tactics and adopted more sophisticated political and cultural ones—and that this led the British to sponsor *The Satanic Verses*. But the Islamic Republic would not abide this plot, and therefore broke off relations with the United Kingdom.[27] A Tehran daily suggested that the break could easily last "at least a decade."[28]

In retaliation, the British government closed down the Iranian consulate in Hong Kong and expelled nine Iranian residents from the United Kingdom. The Foreign Office also urged British nationals to stay away from Lebanon. Further, the foreign secretary, using his strongest language since the controversy began, called the Iranian government a "deplorable regime" and (for the first time) condemned its recent "mass exterminations."[29]

Two unusual features characterized these diplomatic moves. First, both the British and the Iranian governments could count on exceptionally wide domestic support for their actions, including nearly unanimous parliamentary backing. Second, for all the animosity between the two states, neither side made a single move to interfere with existing trade relations. The British continued to purchase Iranian crude oil, the Iranians continued to purchase a wide array of British goods, and such official British services as the Export Credits Guarantee Department (which provides short-term loans for British exports) witnessed a "fairly busy, regular market" even with regard to Iran.[30]

On March 10, Rafsanjani suggested that burning all copies of *The Satanic Verses* would defuse the crisis. That same day, a bomb exploded in San Diego, in the family car belonging to the captain of the U.S. naval ship that had downed an Iran Air passenger plane in July 1988. The incident suggested that the Iranians had the means to attack their enemies across long distances, and that they would wait as long as they had to. This conclusion was confirmed by mounting evidence that the Iranian government had been behind the December 1988 explosion over Lockerbie, Scotland, of Pan Am flight 103, in retaliation for the same Iran Air disaster.

The foreign ministers of the forty-four states belonging to the Organization of the Islamic Conference met on March 13-16, 1989 in Riyadh, Saudi Arabia, and adopted the Saudi position, not the Iranian one, on Rushdie:

> The conference declared that blasphemy cannot be justified on the basis of freedom of expression and opinion. The conference strongly condemned the book *The Satanic Verses*, whose author is regarded as an apostate (*murtadd*). It appeals to all members of society to impose a ban on the book and to take the necessary legislation to insure the protection of the religious beliefs of others.[31]

A British official responded a day later by attempting, again, to disassociate his government from Rushdie. Foreign Office Minister William Waldegrave went on the BBC's Arabic Service to explain:

> I would like to put on record that the British Government well recognizes the hurt and distress that this book has caused, and we want to emphasize that because it was published in Britain, the British Government had nothing to do with and is not associated with it in any way.... What is surely the best way forward is to say

that the book is offensive to Islam, that Islam is far stronger than a book by a writer of this kind.[32]

Tehran interpreted this statement as a British acknowledgment that the book included blasphemous passages, and counted this admission as a major step forward from the Howe and Thatcher statements. It made, however, no concessions in return.

Exactly one month after the decision to withdraw top diplomats of the EC from Iran, the foreign ministers met again and decided, under Greek, Irish and Italian pressure, to send them back. Only the British government objected. The Iranian foreign minister greeted the decision as a "return to realism" and "a realization of the importance of Islam."[33] Khomeini took enormous satisfaction from this about-face. He described the Europeans' returning "humiliated, disgraced, and shame-faced, regretful of what they did."[34] In answer, the French Foreign Ministry, while allowing that it did not usually comment on "statements made by religious figures," called Khomeini's description an "exaggeration."[35] At the same time, Foreign Minister Roland Dumas indicated that the French ambassador could be returning soon to Tehran. Of the twelve EC heads of mission, all but the British, French and West German were back in Tehran by late April. The latter two were back in place in June, just after Khomeini's death. Their Canadian counterpart, who had also been withdrawn, returned along with the majority of the EC representatives.

On March 22, the British expelled another nine Iranians from the country, bringing the total number to eighteen; this was followed by five more in mid-April. As the incident tailed off, British spokesmen made more and more concessionary statements. On March 27, during a visit to Pakistan, Foreign Minister Howe promised to "explore the possibility of taking necessary steps under British law to resolve the problem created by the publication of the book" and "expressed his deep sympathy with the Muslims over its publication."[36]

Just when the incident appeared to have abated, two Muslims living in Brussels were murdered on March 29, possibly in connection with the controversy. These were 'Abdullah Muhammad al-Ahdal, the Saudi imam of a mosque, and Salem el-Beher, the mosque's Tunisian librarian (who appears to have been killed only because he was in Ahdal's vicinity). The execution of Ahdal was apparently in retribution for his remarks on a Belgian television program, where he pursued the Saudi line: while *The Satanic Verses* was "gratuitously blasphemous," he made "a distinction between Islamic society and this country. Khomeini is responsible for his own country, but we are in a democratic country where everybody has the right to express his own thoughts and express themselves as they want." Further, Ahdal held that Khomeini's death sentence breached Islamic law; "you can't condemn a man to death like that."[37] Ahdal reported several verbal threats against his life and was given police protection; the police also issued him a weapon. Despite these precautions, one hour after meeting with a group of local Muslims angered by his moderate stance, he was shot dead. Soldiers of God (Jund Allah), a pro-Iran Beirut organization, claimed responsibility for the assassination.

But the connection of these murders to Rushdie was not fully established, for a leading Saudi religious figure, 'Abdullah 'Umar Nasif, director of the Muslim World League, disclosed that Ahdal had received threats even before the Rushdie book emerged as an issue.

With these deaths, the international incident about *The Satanic Verses* came to a close, at least temporarily.

NOTES

[1]Madhu Jain, "An Irreverent Journey," *India Today*, September 15, 1988.

[2]*The Times of India*, October 13, 1988. Later, Shahbuddin refused to get involved with Khomeini's edict, saying the matter was between the author and the ayatollah alone.

[3]*The Observer*, February 19, 1989.

[4]Quoted in Lisa Appignanesi and Sara Maitland, eds., *The Rushdie File* (London: Fourth Estate, 1989), p. 59.

[5]*Sunday Times*, February 19, 1989.

[6]*Impact International*, October 28, 1988.

[7]*The Observer*, January 22, 1989.

[8]Islamic Revolution News Agency, February 13, 1989.

[9]*The New York Times*, February 14, 1989.

[10]*Jeune Afrique*, March 15, 1989; *Vorwärts*, February 25, 1989; *The Times*, February 15, 1989 and *Tehran Times*, February 23, 1989.

[11]*The Washington Post*, February 18, 1989.

[12]*Kayhan Havai*, February 22, 1989. The Persian date equals February 14, 1989.

[13]*Sunday Times*, February 19, 1989.

[14]Radio Tehran, February 16, 1989.

[15]Islamic Revolution News Agency, February 15, 1989.

[16]Ibid.

[17]Ibid.

[18]Radio Tehran, February 17, 1989. Khamene'i added, ominously, "in that case, Americans themselves will kill him. They will not allow such a person to remain alive, to reveal their [conspiratorial] policies, and to bring disgrace upon them."

[19]Press Association, February 18, 1989.

[20]Islamic Revolution News Agency, February 18, 1989.

[21]Islamic Revolution News Agency, February 19, 1989. The last sentence repudiates President Khamene'i's statement of two days earlier, that "there is really no need for setting aside any money" for Rushdie's execution (Radio Tehran, February 17, 1989).

[22]*Daily Telegraph*, February 21, 1989.

[23]Reuters, February 22, 1989.

[24]Radio Tehran, February 24, 1989.

[25]Islamic Revolution News Agency, February 28, 1989.

[26]Press Association, March 2, 1989.

[27]Islamic Revolution News Agency, March 7, 1989.

[28]*Tehran Times*, March 1, 1989.

[29]*The Times*, March 9, 1989. Those 1,200 or so "exterminations" of opposition elements within Iran having taken place up to half a year earlier, many commentators found it unfortunate that the condemnation had to wait until diplomatic relations had been broken.

[30]*Financial Times*, March 9, 1989.

[31]Saudi Press Agency, March 16, 1989; *Al-Ahram*, March 17, 1989.

[32]Press Association, March 17, 1989. Only the Swedish government, whose ambassador to Tehran called *The Satanic Verses* "blasphemous," went further to meet Iranian demands.

[33]*The Times*, March 22, 1989.

[34]Islamic Revolution News Agency, March 23, 1989.

[35]Agence France Presse, March 23, 1989.

[36]Radio Islamabad, March 27, 1989.

[37]*The New York Times*, March 30, 1989. This text derives from the French translation provided by Ahdal's own interpreter; there is reason to think that the translation was faulty.

PART I: THE AUTHOR, THE NOVEL, AND THE EDICT

2.

RUSHDIE: A MAN OF THE LEFT

Salman Rushdie was born in June 1947 in Bombay, India, the only son of four children. His family had come originally from Kashmir (as had Khomeini's), so Urdu-Hindi was its first language, not Marathi, the main language of Bombay. Having limited command of the local lingua franca, the family relied heavily on English, a language Salman began learning at the age of five. During his childhood, the family was in decline. Salman's grandfather, a businessman, had made the family fortune; his father (who died in 1987) spent it. Nonetheless, Salman grew up in a commercial environment; as he later wrote in *Midnight's Children*, a quasi-autobiographical novel, the "family had espoused the ethics of business, not faith."

Salman attended the Cathedral School in Bombay, where he showed himself a serious and talented student. In 1961 he was sent to Britain to attend Rugby. The shock of transition to English school life and the difficulty of adjusting was very great, and it apparently colored all his subsequent experiences in Great Britain. Nonetheless, he excelled at school and in 1964 entered his father's alma mater, King's College, Cambridge University. At Cambridge, he read history (and wrote a paper on Muhammad which forms the factual basis of much of the Mahound account in *The Satanic Verses*). On his own, he studied English literature intensely. He also became involved in the theater and saw five or six films a week.

Upon graduation from Cambridge in 1968, Salman rejoined his family, who in the meantime had moved, quite against Salman's wishes, to Karachi, Pakistan. He spent an unsuccessful two years with his family there, working mostly at a television station. One of the problems he kept encountering was censorship, whether of plays he wished to produce or of articles he wished to write. Highly dissatisfied, Rushdie returned to London in 1970, where he has lived ever since. He then married a British woman, Clarissa, and became a British subject. A boy, Zafar, was born in June 1979, but the parents divorced in 1987. Rushdie married Marianne Wiggins, an American novelist living in London, in January 1988.

After returning to England in 1970, he worked for about a decade as an advertising copywriter, first at Ogilvy and Mather, then at Charles Barker, handling such accounts as the Milk Marketing Board. A story about a Muslim holy man, Rushdie's first attempt at a novel, was aborted. It was followed in 1976 by Rushdie's first published book, *Grimus: A Novel*, a science fiction account "based very loosely on a Sufi poem *The Conference of the Birds* by Farid-ud-din 'Attar.'"[1] Not suprisingly, this odd mix received poor reviews. A second book, *Midnight's Children*, was finished in 1979 and was a great success, winning the Booker prize in 1981 and selling a half-million copies. Indeed, *Midnight's Children* not only established Rushdie as a major novelist, it gave him the freedom, at a young age, to devote himself full-time to writing. His third book, *Shame*, about Pakistan, came out in 1981 and also won wide acclaim. A short travel book, *The Jaguar Smile*, chronicled Rushdie's brief trip to Nicaragua in July 1986 and his almost uncritical admiration for the Sandinistas. *The Satanic Verses* was published in September 1988 and earned widespread critical praise, including the 1988 Whitbread prize for fiction, worth £20,000.

At the time of the publication of *The Satanic Verses*, Rushdie had established himself as a leading member of the London intelligentsia. He had written best-selling books much acclaimed by the critics (an unusual combination); he was a fellow of the

Royal Society of Literature, a frequent contributor to the literary pages of such newspapers as *The Observer*, and an active participant in leftist causes. In short, he had made it in one of the most dynamic cultural centers in the world.

Great Britain and the United States

Although Rushdie had lived in Great Britain since childhood and had become a British citizen, he hardly embraced his adopted home. On the contrary, the more time he spent in England, the deeper his ambivalence seemed to become. In part, this had to do with the proverbial snobbism of the English toward a colonial; in part, too, it had an ideological base, for Rushdie absorbed the fashionable leftism of the late 1960s. "Like many of my contemporaries I spent my student years under the spell of Buñuel, Godard, Ray, Wajda, Welles, Bergman, Kurosawa, Jans,có, Antonioni, Dylan, Lennon, Jagger, Laing, Marcuse, and, inevitably, the two-headed fellow known to Grass readers as Marxengels."[2]

His experiences and outlook caused Rushdie's writings to bristle with hostility toward Great Britain. This is especially apparent in *The Satanic Verses*. Indeed, the passages about Indians in Britain are worth noting in detail, for they establish the political context of *The Satanic Verses*. When one of the book's two heroes, Saladin Chamcha, survives—in magical realist style—a fall of thousands of feet from an exploded jet airliner, he lands on a British beach, where British immigration officials arrest him. Carrying him off in a paddy wagon, they handle him with all the delicacy one expects of thugs in a police state. First he has to strip. "Opening time, Packy; let's see what you're made of," one of them orders. The pajamas are then "dragged off the protesting Chamcha, who was reclining on the floor of the van with two stout policemen holding each arm and a fifth constable's boot placed firmly upon his chest, and whose protests went unheard in the general mirthful din." Chamcha is then abused verbally ("You're a fucking Packy billy") and forced to crawl on the van floor to collect his own excrement. The officers abuse

him roundly all the while and begin pulling "the hair on his rump
to increase both his discomfort and his discomforture." Finally,
Chamcha's tormentors indulge in a bit of police fun:

> thumping and gouging various parts of his anatomy, using him
> both as a guinea-pig and a safety-valve, remaining careful, in
> spite of their excitation, to confine their blows to his softer, more
> fleshy parts, to minimize the risk of breakages and bruises; and
> when Jockey, Kim and Joey saw what their juniors were getting up
> to, they chose to be tolerant, because boys would have their fun.

When punks and skinheads attack Asian families, the police let
them go. Innocent Asians, however, feel the "full might of the
Metropolitan Police."

Racism is endemic in Rushdie's London. Here is an everyday
experience encountered by a Jewish woman:

> One Sunday not long after her father's death she was buying the
> Sunday papers from the corner kiosk when the vendor announced:
> "It's the last week this week. Twenty-three years I've been on this
> corner and the Pakis have finally driven me out of business." She
> heard the word p-a-c-h-y and had a bizarre vision of elephants
> lumbering down the Moscow Road, flattening Sunday news
> vendors. "What's a pachy?" she foolishly asked and the reply was
> stinging: "A brown Jew."

That Rushdie came to be seen by radical fundamentalist
Muslims as a stand-in for the United States is deeply ironic, for
he espouses the classic anti-Americanism of third-worldists.
Hints of his views can be seen in *The Jaguar Smile: A Nicaraguan
Journey*,[3] the vehicle for a broadside against "the stupidity of
U.S. policy" toward Nicaragua. Actually, the United States was
guilty not just of stupidity, but of dishonesty and greed. The book
is littered with casual references to "the great American fist,"
"the American empire," and the like. With regard to Central
America, he saw the U.S. government as "the bandit...posing
as the sheriff." As for the United Kingdom, he saw the problem

as no less serious. Discussing the possibility that Britons might decide to request the U.S. forces to leave their soil, Rushdie mused on the consequences: "But would the Americans leave? It's a real question. If the British government were to order the American bases out, would they go? And if not, what's the difference between being a member of NATO and being occupied?... But would the Americans leave? I have serious doubts they would."[4] Britain, in other words, is really a colony of the United States.

However, the full force of Rushdie's visceral anti-Americanism becomes apparent only in *The Satanic Verses*. Rushdie notes that American travelers overseas inhabit a perpetual fog, then observes: "It was a hard fate to be an American abroad, and not to suspect why you were so disliked." Perhaps the reason for that dislike lies in the commercialism Rushdie calls "the Coca-Colonization of the planet." Or their being too affluent for their own good. Thus, a rich Indian muses on selling what he owns of India's cultural heritage to American buyers, and is perversely tempted by the idea: "One day I will also take the dollars. Not for the money. For the pleasure of being a whore." Or these observations, uttered by an Indian Marxist: "What is Amerika for us? It's not a real place. Power in its purest form, disembodied, invisible. We can't see it but it screws us totally, no escape." (To be fair, another character contests this assessment, observing that "We [Indians] always forgive ourselves by blaming outsiders.")

But it is not just American influence that Rushdie hates, it is the United States itself. New York City he calls "that transatlantic New Rome with its Nazified architectural gigantism, which employed the oppressions of size to make its human occupants feel like worms." Even the country's vaunted immigration policy is a fraud. Rushdie castigates

the self-congratulatory huddled-masses rhetoric of the "nation of immigrants" across the ocean, itself far from perfectly open-armed. Would the United States, with its are-you-now-have-you-ever-beens, have permitted Ho Chi Minh to cook in its hotel kitchens? What would its McCarran-Walter Act have to say about a latter-day Karl Marx, standing bushy-bearded at its gates, waiting to cross its yellow lines?

The only good words Rushdie can find for the United States are for what he terms the black, gay, feminist, and socialist "dissident cultures."[5]

More broadly, Rushdie despises the entire West, which for him is a place "stuffed with money, power and things." Or, in the cruder terms of one of his characters, it reduces to "the motherfucking Americans" and "the sisterfucking British." One careful reader, Cheryl Benard of the Baltzman Institute in Vienna, denies that the Muslims come out on the bottom of Rushdie's hierarchy.

> It is Britons more than Moslems who might have cause to find the book "blasphemous." If Islam is portrayed as somewhat rigid and medieval, then the contemporary West, in his pages, is a nightmare out of [the movie] "Blade Runner." But it may be some time before Moslems realize that their black-sheep son, whom they believe to have written a Westernized pamphlet against Islam, has equally composed an Eastern diatribe against the world of the Unbelievers.[6]

There is much truth to this view.

The One Country Rushdie Likes

This does not mean that Rushdie loves his double homeland, India-Pakistan. He paints a profoundly unflattering picture of India in *Midnight's Children*.[7] That novel chronicles the life of a boy born on the exact moment of India's independence whose misadventures in friendship, love, and work serve as an allegory for the tribulations of his country. Rushdie is bitterly frank; India had failed the high expectations at the time of independence, becoming a country of extremes in wealth and poverty, of violence, and of ugliness and cynicism.

If possible, Pakistan comes off even worse, in *Shame*.[8] To begin with, the land itself is grossly deficient—a "few insect-nibbled slices" of India, "some dusty western acres and jungly eastern swamps that the ungodly were happy to do without." The efforts to build a new country had failed in ways small and big. The new capital at Islamabad is "in reality the biggest collection of airport terminals on earth, a garbage dump for unwanted transit lounges and customs halls." Pakistani society is nothing but "the peeling, fragmenting palimpsest, increasingly at war with itself, [and which] may be described as a failure of the dreaming mind."

Rushdie takes particular delight in insulting political leaders. *Midnight's Children* goes after the Nehru family, accused of wanting to make themselves hereditary kings. Not content with that, Indira Gandhi, the prime minister of India, aspired "to be Devi, the Mother-goddess in her most terrible aspect, possessor of the shakti of the gods, a multi-limbed divinity with the center-parting and schizophrenic hair." But Indira has feet of clay. Her son Sanjay, Rushdie writes, accused her, "through her neglect," of being responsible for his father's death; this passage prompted Mrs. Gandhi to file a law suit for libel against Rushdie, but she was assassinated before the case was resolved. Sanjay Gandhi himself is several times characterized as having lips like labia.

President Muhammad Zia-ul-Haq of Pakistan was so offended by the portrayal of him as Raza ("Old Razor Guts") Hyder in *Shame*, he prohibited sale of the novel in Pakistan. Having just been informed by his three aides that the Soviets have invaded Afghanistan, Hyder reacted to the news with glee. To the aides'

> astonishment the President had leapt from his chair, unrolled four prayer-mats on the floor and insisted that they all give thanks, pronto, fut-a-fut, for this blessing that had been bestowed on them by God. They had been rising and falling [in prayer] for an hour and a half...when he stopped and explained to them that the Russian attack was the final step in God's strategy, because now the stability of his government would have to be ensured by the great powers.

In a eulogy, Rushdie wrote that "Pakistan under Zia became a nightmarish, surreal land."[9]

Zulfikar Ali Bhutto is portrayed as a playboy-turned-power-mad politician whose cunning wins him undeserved popularity. And his daughter Benazir Bhutto, the subsequent prime minister of Pakistan, is nicknamed by Rushdie the famous "virgin Ironpants." He predicts that she will be "reborn into power," and that the result will be "arrests, retribution, trials, hangings, blood, a new cycle of shamelessness and shame." Needless to say, Benazir Bhutto did not enjoy the description of herself. "When I read Rushdie's book *Shame*, it made me feel very angry, very frustrated."[10]

Without actually mentioning his future arch-enemy Khomeini by name, Rushdie went after him too in *The Satanic Verses*. Not only is the Islamic Republic parodied, but Khomeini himself is devastatingly portrayed in an eleven-page vignette of an Imam. Rushdie has the Imam literally devouring his future subjects. Going beyond the ideological, the invective includes physical insults; at one point, the imam hoists "up his skirts to reveal two spindly legs with an almost monstrous covering of hair."

In typical fashion, Rushdie did not own up to his caricatures. He called the identification of virgin Ironpants with Benazir Bhutto "nonsense," despite a transparent connection.[11] And, in September 1988, he made it explicitly clear that the Imam of *The Satanic Verses* was Khomeini—three months later, he held that the Imam "is obviously not" Khomeini.[12] But these denials were in vain, for no one believed them.

In *The Satanic Verses*, one character "affectionately" refers to Prime Minister Margaret Thatcher as "Mrs. Torture" and "Maggie the Bitch." These sobriquets are hardly surprising, as Rushdie was an outspokenly hostile opponent of hers, having been a signatory of Charter 88, an anti-Thatcher manifesto and a founding member of the 20th June Group, organized by Antonia Fraser and Harold Pinter. The outlook of this group on Britain is summed up by the title of its publication: *Samizdat* (a Russian word meaning underground literature). In a passage typical of his political writings, he referred in 1984 to "the continuing decline, the growing poverty and the meanness of spirit of much of Thatcherite Britain."[13] When Mrs. Thatcher invited Rushdie to a lunch in honor of Mrs. Gandhi, he (not altogether surprisingly) declined.

Rushdie is a disaffected intellectual who criticizes or makes fun of nearly everything. One book attacks the Gandhis and modern India; another reviles the leadership in Pakistan; a third takes on American foreign policy; the fourth one blasts fundamentalist Islam and Britain. The assault comes easily, and it is glib. This incessant negativism made Rushdie a highly unpopular figure with politicians in several countries. Ironically, until *The Satanic Verses* came out, the only authorities who approved of Rushdie were those in Iran. The ministry in charge of publications had *Midnight's Children* and *Shame* translated into Persian; the translation of *Shame* subsequently received an award from an official jury appointed by the ministry!

Not unexpectedly, Rushdie had plenty of enemies in his own circles. Peter Jenkins of *The Independent* observed that Rushdie "may well be something of a sensationalist, certainly he can be a shrill and tiresome fellow, in his political utterances, abusing language and the meaning of words in preposterous hyperbole."[14] "Couldn't happen to a nicer guy," was what many in London could be heard muttering after the ayatollah's edict. Rushdie's British critics found it deliciously ironic that the man who accused Mrs. Thatcher of establishing a police state should then ask that same police state to protect him—and from his co-religionists, at that.

Ironically the author's last name (*rushdi*) is an Arabic word meaning "mature," "reasonable," or "proper"—characteristics quite the opposite of those displayed by Rushdie through his career as an immature and spoiled intellectual. It will be very interesting to see how his journey to the epicenter has affected him. Will the realization that he benefits from Western ideals cause Rushdie to drop his habit of easy cynicism? Will he regret having reviled Mrs. Thatcher after her government stood by him in his hour of need? In the final analysis, Rushdie can only make a home in the West. He could scorn it all he wanted, but when he needed a safe home, he retreated to it. Rushdie's views matter, for assuming he survives, he will be one of the world's most prominent writers and, at least for some time to come, his opinions will receive global attention.

But whatever the future holds, until now Rushdie has endorsed just one state. It may not be one that many would find appealing, but he found his place in Nicaragua under the Sandinistas. On a visit to Nicaragua in 1986, he discovered that the rule of law is more rigorously applied there than in the United Kingdom. "Nicaragua's constitution amounted to a Bill of Rights that I wouldn't have minded having on the statute book in Britain." For this and a host of other reasons, Rushdie found himself unable to resist the Sandinistas' charms:

> For the first time in my life, I realized with surprise, I had come across a government I could support, not *faute de mieux*, but because I wanted its efforts...to succeed. It was a disorienting realization. I had spent my entire life as a writer in opposition, and indeed conceived the writer's role as including the function of antagonist to the state. I felt distinctly peculiar about being on the same side as the people in charge, but I couldn't avoid the truth: if I had been a Nicaraguan writer, I would have felt obliged to get behind the Frente Sandinista, and push.

The Jaguar Smile was received scathingly by nearly everyone who knew something about the Sandinistas and Nicaragua. Howard Wiarda of the University of Massachusetts called the book "a fawning, laudatory, highly romantic portrait," and noted that Rushdie "knows no Spanish and got it wrong when he attempted to use some Spanish phrases in his book." Xavier Arguello wrote in *The New Republic* that the book fails because of its "remarkable superficiality," and called it "harmful."[15] Michael Massing scathingly categorized it as one of a new genre, the "snap book," wherein a fashionable writer parachutes into a troubled country and then writes up his experiences at too-great length. Massing reviled such books, where "war and revolution serve primarily as backdrops against which star writers can shine," as the epitome of self-indulgence.[16]

There was one area where Rushdie disagreed with his hosts, and it is an important one in light of subsequent controversies. Time and again during his short trip, he spoke up for freedom of expression and against the regime's practice of censorship. When one leader compared freedom of the press to cosmetics worn by the mother of a deathly sick child, Rushdie called this "the most chilling remark I heard in Nicaragua." He then pondered at some length the implications of this comment.

> The issue of press freedom was the one on which I absolutely parted company with the Sandinistas. It disturbed me that a government of writers had turned into a government of censors. Largely because of this issue, a kind of silent argument raged in my head throughout my stay. I would tell myself that something remarkable was being attempted here, with minimal resources and under great pressure. The land reforms, and the health and literacy campaigns... Then I would argue back: those campaigns are all very well; but they think that dissent is cosmetic.

Here too, Rushdie reveled in inconsistency. He called censorship in Nicaragua a "deep flaw," and regularly spoke up during his trip against the Sandinistas' reliance on this instrument. On meeting a secretary of the Soviet Writers Union, he grilled the man on Pasternak and Solzhenitsyn; when the conversation turned to Cuba, he brought up Padilla and Valladares. But later he endorsed the Sandinistas' repression, saying that "there is clearly the need to maintain a high level of control in the country."[17]

He was also inconsistent on the subject of newspapers. At first, Rushdie called the government's *Barricada*, "the worst paper I've seen in a long while" and praised the anti-Sandinista *La Prensa* as "the best paper in town." But in a subsequent interview, he reversed himself, calling *La Prensa* "a bit of a rag" and holding (falsely) that "quite a lot" of CIA money went into it.

Despite the profound political irresponsibility of his position as "a writer in opposition," Rushdie's record of concern for freedom of speech did make him a not entirely inappropriate symbol of this basic liberty.

NOTES

[1]Woodstock, N.Y.: Overlook, 1979; "An Interview with Salman Rushdie," *Scripsi* [Melbourne], August 1985, p. 125.

[2]Salman Rushdie, "On Günter Grass," *Granta*, Spring 1985, p. 180.

[3]New York: Elizabeth Sifton Books, Viking, 1987.

[4]Quoted in Bianca Jagger, "Central American Time: Salman Rushdie," *Interview*, March 1987, p. 85.

[5]Salman Rushdie, "Goodness—The American Neurosis," *The Nation*, March 22, 1986.

[6]Cheryl Benard, "Rushdie's Critique Is as Old as Islam," *The Wall Street Journal*, March 16, 1989.

[7]New York: Knopf, 1980.

[8]New York: Knopf, 1983.

[9]Salman Rushdie, "Zia Unmourned," *The Nation*, September 19, 1988.

[10]*Indian Express*, March 21, 1989.

[11]"An Interview with Salman Rushdie," *Scripsi*, p. 108.

[12]*The Observer*, September 25, 1989; Ameena Meer, "Interview: Salman Rushdie," *Bomb* [New York], Spring 1989, p. 35.

[13]Salman Rushdie, "Outside the Whale," *Granta*, Spring 1984, p. 129.

[14]Peter Jenkins, "Is Rushdie Just the Tool of Allah's Will?" *The Independent*, March 1, 1989.

[15]*The New Republic*, April 20, 1987.

[16]Michael Massing, "Snap Books," *The New Republic*, May 4, 1987.

[17]Quoted in Jagger, "Central American Time," p. 86.

3.

HOW IS THE BOOK BLASPHEMOUS?

Rushdie has undeniably great artistic talents, and *The Satanic Verses* is a crowded, elusive and sophisticated tale. But assessing the accusations against the book requires that it be looked at in a literal, and very unliterary manner, for this is the way it is understood by those who protest it. This means that every statement in the book must be taken as representative of the author's own thinking, even though that is clearly not always the case; on occasion, for example, two characters debate a point and hold contrary views. Intellectually deficient as it may be, such a narrow approach is unavoidable if one is to understand the novel's political meaning as understood by unsophisticated readers.

To take just one example: Rushdie's characters, even biblical ones, speak a slangy, street-wise dialogue; in the context of *The Satanic Verses*, it is entirely natural for Hagar to refer to Abraham as a "bastard" for abandoning her in a waterless valley. But the fundamentalist Muslim critics ripped this word out of context and turned it against Rushdie. "He insults Our Master Abraham (on him be prayers and peace) with a word—that does not bear repetition—that means born illegitimately."[1] Only by reading isolated quotes in such a literal and humorless manner can the book's effect be gauged. Indeed, to understand its impact fully, *The Satanic Verses* ideally should be read excerpted, out of

53

context, and preferably in translation—for that is how most of its critics became acquainted with it.

The Satanic Verses is a large and complex book, 547 pages long, containing three stories which at first glance may appear unrelated. The first (in chapters 1, 3, 5, 7 and 9) concerns two Indians, Gibreel Farishta and Saladin Chamcha, who fall out of a jumbo jet and miraculously survive. This tale, which deals with the two men's lives in England, their fantasy worlds, and their eventual return to Bombay, makes up the novel's central plot. The book is also a *roman à clef*, though few readers are likely to understand more than a fraction of the references.

The second story (in chapters 2 and 6) recounts some aspects of the story of Muhammad, the prophet of Islam. It relies partly on historical fact, partly on the novelist's imagination.

The third story (in chapters 4 and 8) concerns a Muslim village in India whose whole population follows, lemming-like, a holy woman into the Arabian Sea, expecting the waters to part for them so they can walk the whole way to Mecca. But the waters remain unparted, and virtually the whole village perishes. Although Rushdie has stated that the story is based on a true incident, its juxtaposition with a description of Khomeini's exile in Paris strongly suggests that it is an allegory for Iran and the Islamic Revolution. The holy woman transfixing the whole population of a village, then leading them to their deaths, represents the years since 1979 in Iran.

While the second and third stories both challenge the Islamic message and are obviously interrelated, they have only the slightest connections to the first story, which deals with the complex relationship of colonizer and colonized in the world of independent states. *The Satanic Verses* appears to comprise two distinct novels, and indeed, this seems to be its origins. In a 1984 interview, Rushdie indicated that he was working on two books— none other than the migration and religion elements yoked together in *The Satanic Verses*.

I am writing a novel which to my great surprise is set in India again. I had been working on a much larger project for a novel that wasn't, and that's just been elbowed out of the way for the moment by this other idea which seems to be insisting on getting written. It doesn't seem to be a political novel. It's a novel about God. A novel about religion.... I've wanted for some time to write a book about religion which was not simply a secular sneer. And I think I've got a story—I know I've got a story, only I'm not going to tell you about it. [*Laughter*] And then I do have a much larger project for a novel...a novel set in the West which deals with the idea of migration.[2]

Rushdie's nervous laughter, suggesting excitement mixed with apprehension, clearly had to do with the chapters on Islam that made the book so exceedingly controversial.

Although the three themes vary widely in time, space and subject matter, Rushdie tried to unite them. Thus, several names (Gibreel, Mishal, Hind, Ayesha) recur repeatedly in two or even three of the stories; in like manner, other names are played with (Allie, Al-Lat) and interposed. The notion of satanic verses also recurs; in addition to the Muhammadan incident (to be examined at length below), this term describes Saladin Chamcha's obscene and anonymous telephone calls to two lovers, causing them to break up. Also, the book is held together in that the subsidiary tales are dreams of Gibreel, one of the two Indians who falls out of the jet. He is said to be "moving through several stories at once." A film producer who hears Gibreel sleep talking "purloins" the dream-narratives about Muhammad and turns them into movies, in which Gibreel plays himself.

The dream about Muhammad is the source of all the controversy. It makes up two chapters of the book, "Mahound" and "Return to Jahilia," each thirty-six pages long. (Mahound is an archaic European name for the Prophet Muhammad; Jahilia, Arabic for "ignorance," is Rushdie's name for Mecca.) From the Islamic point of view, the single most offensive passages are those referred to in the book's title, those having to do with the Satanic verses. In addition, some other passages cause problems.

The Satanic Verses Incident

Before looking at the Satanic verses themselves, an important point must be made about the central feature of the Islamic faith. Each of the three major monotheistic religions has one feature which traditionally has defined it as a distinct body of faith. In Judaism, it is the covenant between God and Abraham; disavow this, and you cannot be a Jew. In Christianity, the central tenet is that Jesus is the Son of God. In Islam, the religion's irreducable core lies in the Qur'an (or Koran) as the exact Word of God. To doubt this is to deny the validity of Muhammad's mission and to imply that the entire Islamic faith is premised on a fraudulent base. At the very least, to be a Muslim means accepting on faith that God (or Allah) sent His message to mankind via the angel Gabriel who passed it along to Muhammad; and that the Qur'an is inerrant.

Put another way, a Muslim may question Muhammad's conduct as a political leader, criticize the caliphs (Muhammad's political successors) for impiety, blast the mullahs (religious leaders) for their greed, and ridicule the religious establishment for its hidebound ways. But a Muslim may not question the authenticity of the Qur'an. To do so is to raise doubts about the validity of the faith itself, and this is usually seen as an act of apostasy.

The Satanic verses episode should be analyzed at three levels: the historical record, Rushdie's treatment of the incident, and the Muslim response to Rushdie.

The Historical Record. Mecca, the city where Muhammad, the prophet of Islam, was born and lived, had long been a major center of the polytheistic Arabian religions. The Ka'ba, which now serves as the geographic center of Islam, was in pre-Islamic times the home of hundreds of idols. Indeed, the town's prosperity depended heavily on its role as a religious center, and the leaders of Muhammad's own tribe, Quraysh, counted especially on those shrines.

The emphatic monotheism of Muhammad's message therefore posed a direct challenge to the existing order in general and to the leaders of Quraysh in particular. For this reason, Muhammad's initial teachings met with a very poor response among the well-to-do in Mecca. The new faith did succeed in winning slaves, servants, non-tribal persons and other social riff-raff, but it made very little progress among the burghers. Winning these over became a major concern of Muhammad's; how was he to convert them? It is in this context that the Satanic verses issue took place in about A.D. 614, or one year or so after Muhammad began his career of public preaching. At-Tabari (d. 923), a historian and a commentator on the Qur'an who provides much of our historical knowledge about early Islam, recounts that members of Quraysh suggested to Muhammad that he take a flexible attitude toward their idols, and in return they would adopt a more friendly attitude toward his preaching. "If you make some mention of our goddesses, we would sit beside you [i.e., become Muslims]; for the nobles of the Arabs come to you, and when they see that those who sit beside you are the nobles of your tribe, they will have more liking for you."[3] In response, Tabari recounts, Muhammad "hoped in his soul for something from God to bring him and his tribe together."[4] Soon after, Muhammad recited the following verse of the Qur'an, making reference to three of the most prominent Meccan goddesses:

Have you thought upon Lat and Uzza,
And Manat, the third, the other?[*]

[*]Qur'an, Surat an-Najm, verses 19–21. The wording of the Qur'an translation used here comes from *The Satanic Verses*; Rushdie writes that he relied on the N.J. Dawood and Muhammad Ali translations, adding "a few touches" of his own.

At this moment, according to the account in Tabari, "Satan threw on his tongue" (*alqa ash-shaytan 'ala lisanihi*) the next words out of Muhammad's mouth.[5]

These are the exalted birds,
And their intercession is desired indeed.[*]

With these words, Muhammad accepted the three goddesses and confirmed the validity of their interceding between man and God. Naturally, Quraysh was delighted by Muhammad's acceptance of the goddesses. It meant that Islam was neither as monotheistic or as radical as it had first appeared; the traditional religions would live on, at least in an attenuated form; and the shrines of Mecca would retain their economic value.

But then the angel Gabriel (the nominal source of the Qur'an) came to Muhammad and bemoaned Muhammad's deed. "Muhammad, what have you done?" Gabriel now revealed to him that the devil had deceived him into uttering the last two lines. To be precise, in Tabari's accounts, Gabriel revealed that "Satan caused to come upon his tongue" the verse about the exalted birds. "Then God cancelled what Satan had thrown," abrogating these lines and replaced them with verses denouncing the cult of the three goddesses.[6] The complete Qur'anic text on this issue reads as follows:

Have you thought upon Lat and Uzza,
And Manat, the third, the other?
Shall He have daughters and you sons?
That would be a fine division!
These are but [three] names you have dreamed of, you and your
    fathers.

[*]These two lines, which lie at the center of the incident, are found in a wide range of Muslim sources. These include, other than Tabari, the biographer Ibn Sa'd (d. 845), the collector of hadith al-Bukhari (d. 870), and the geographer Yaqut (d. 1229). The precise wording of the two lines differs in each of their accounts.

Allah vests no authority in them.
They only follow conjecture and wish-fulfillment,
Even though guidance had come to them already from their Lord.[7]

What happened to the two lines, "These are the exalted birds,/ And their intercession is desired indeed"? Had Satan leaped onto and then off of Muhammad's tongue? Or had the Prophet tried to ingratiate himself with the city leaders, then regretted the effort and recanted? Or, worse, had the Prophet tried to win their favor, been rebuffed, and changed the text accordingly?

Obviously, this incident is one of the most delicate in Muhammad's mission. Many writers do their best neither to endorse an unlikely story nor challenge the premises of the Islamic faith. Here is how W. Montgomery Watt, a leading modern biographer of Muhammad, steers a neutral course in his summary of the incident:

> Muhammad must have had sufficient success for the heads of Quraysh to take him seriously. Pressure was brought to bear on him to make some acknowledgement of the worship at the neighbouring shrines. He was at first inclined to do so, both in view of the material advantages such a course offered and because it looked as if it would speedily result in a successful end of his mission. Eventually, however, through Divine guidance as he believed, he saw that this would be a fatal compromise, and he gave up the prospect of improving his outward circumstances in order to follow the truth as he saw it. The rejection of polytheism was formulated in vigorous terms and closed the doors to future compromise.[8]

The phrase "as he believed" is Watt's way to avoid judging the issue. In other words, this is the territory of faith where the historian dares not tread. But the novelist does.

Rushdie's Treatment. Rushdie is a skeptic. He treats the incident as one of deceit. The prophet spoke the false verses not because Satan put them in his mouth, but because he saw an opportunity to advance his cause. In *The Satanic Verses*, Mahound returns to the city as quickly as he can, to expunge the foul verses that reek of brimstone and sulphur, to strike them from the record for ever and ever, so that they will survive in just one or two unreliable collections of old traditions and orthodox interpreters will try to unwrite their story, but Gibreel [Gabriel], hovering-watching from his highest camera angle, knows one small detail, just one tiny thing that's a bit of a problem here, namely that *it was me both times, baba, me first and second also me.* From my mouth, both the statement and the repudiation, verses and converses, universes and reverses, the whole thing, and we all know how my mouth got worked.

This last point ("and we all know how my mouth got worked") refers to Gibreel's being forced to say what he does by Mahound. Gibreel explains Mahound's "old trick, forcing my mouth open and making the voice, the Voice, pour out of me...made it pour all over him, like sick." In another passage, Gibreel is said to have been "obliged to speak by the overwhelming need of the Prophet, Mahound." Gibreel even resorts to a bit of doggerel:

Being God's postman is no fun, yaar.
Butbutbut: God isn't in this picture.
God knows whose postman I've been.

To cover his deception, Mahound later comes up with the notion that the devil made him do it. Actually, it is not the prophet but one of his followers, Khalid, who puts this idea into his head.

Awkwardly, he says: "Messenger [of God], I doubted you. But you were wiser than we knew. First we said, Mahound will never compromise, and you compromised. Then we said, Mahound has betrayed us, but you were bringing us a deeper truth. You brought us the Devil himself, so that we could witness the workings of the Evil One, and his overthrow by the Right. You have enriched our faith. I am sorry for what I thought."

Mahound moves away from the sunlight falling through the window. "Yes." Bitterness, cynicism. "It was a wonderful thing I did. Deeper truth. Bringing you the devil. Yes, that sounds like me."

Mahound's response makes it clear that he found this *ex post* explanation useful, and that he would adopt it.

Rushdie's offense goes beyond the charge that Muhammad weaved and bobbed as his interests changed; his story implies that the entire Qur'an derived not from God through Gabriel, but from Muhammad himself, who put the words in Gabriel's mouth. If this is true, then the Qur'an is a human artifact and the Islamic faith is built on a deceit. There is nothing left.

But, of course, the sequence is all part of a dream. The dreamer, Gibreel Farishta, is a man who suffers from "paranoid delusions" of being the Archangel Gibreel (Gabriel). This delusion follows in part from his own name, which means "Gabriel Angel," and in part it has to do with his falling 29,000 feet from a jet plane, and surviving. Even if the dream quality does not absolve Rushdie of responsibility for the story, it does place him at considerable distance from it.

The Muslim Reaction. Because the Satanic verses incident derives from Tabari and several other impeccable sources of information about the life of Muhammad, Muslims must deal with it. They can neither ignore the story nor dismiss it as a non-Muslim calumny intended to discredit Islam. And there is a long tradition of contending with this difficult issue. In recent times, Muhammad 'Abduh (1849-1905), the key modernizing thinker of Islam, laid down the main lines of an Islamic defense.[9] Then, in a 1936 book titled *The Life of Muhammad*, Muhammad Husayn Haykal (1888-1956) elaborated on 'Abduh's thinking and, devoting a whole chapter to the issue, developed the standard Muslim position. After noting that orientalists had made much of the incident, Haykal argued that the Satanic verses were "fabricated," and called them "a fable and a detestable lie." He based this judgment on four arguments: the medieval sources provide different wordings of the two lines; the lines betray internal contradictions; the word "birds" (*gharaniq*) has nothing to do with deities; and the honesty of Muhammad's whole career proves he could not have engaged in such dubious activities.[10]

'Abduh and Haykal's argument carried the day in the Muslim world; to the extent that people even know of the incident, which is very little, there is wide consensus that the Satanic verses are apocryphal. The matter having been settled, two consequences follow. Anyone who has the temerity of raising it is seen as a provocateur intent on discrediting Islam. This assumption is ubiquitous in the Middle East, and has even reached the West. Thus, a *New York Times* account reported that Rushdie tried "to revive a blasphemous story" that was "discredited by later experts on the Koran."[11] Second, the Muslim decision to close the debate on this topic meant that almost no one—whether Muslim or Westerner—was familiar with the Satanic verses issue. The only exception was a very small number of specialists on early Islam.

More on the Qur'an and Muhammad

In addition to the Satanic verses incident, Rushdie finds many other occasions to raise doubts about the divine source of the Qur'an. For one, a character in the book named Salman, who serves as Mahound's scribe, starts making alterations in the text of the Book.

> Mahound did not notice the alterations. So there I was, actually writing the Book, or re-writing anyway, polluting the word of God with my own profane language. But, good heavens, if my poor words could not be distinguished from the Revelation by God's own Messenger, then what did that mean? What did that say about the quality of divine poetry? Look, I swear, I was shaken to my soul.

Eventually, however, Mahound caught on and berated Salman for his impudence. The episode ends ambiguously, for while Mahound did not catch on for some time, he did eventually discover

---

Besides being the given name of the novel's author, Salman here refers to one of Muhammad's closest companions and a major figure in Islamic history, Salman al-Farisi ("Salman the Persian"). To make matters yet more complex, some fringe Islamic sects hold that he was actually the angel Gabriel in disguise.

Salman's trickery. While it is not clear that Mahound is a fraud, it is also not clear that the words were anyone's but his own.

This incident, like most of those recounted in *The Satanic Verses*, was not made up by Rushdie out of whole cloth, but is grounded in the historical sources. According to the most authoritative Muslim sources on the life of Muhammad, a Meccan convert by the name of Ibn Abi Sarh emigrated to Medina, where he served as Muhammad's secretary. As the revelations came to Muhammad, Ibn Abi Sarh transcribed the texts. On one occasion, however, he slightly altered the words of the Qur'an and then saw, to his surprise, that the prophet failed to notice the change. This event disillusioned Ibn Abi Sarh, causing him not to believe in the divine source of Muhammad's revelation, so he apostacized from Islam and fled Medina.

Second, Rushdie points out that Mahound had a way of receiving revelations that suited his purposes, and not just once but repeatedly. The character named Salman pointedly observes:

> Mahound himself had been a businessman, and a damned successful one at that, a person to whom organization and rules came naturally, so how excessively convenient it was that he should have come up with such a very businesslike archangel, who handed down the management decisions of this highly corporate, if non-corporeal, God.
>
> After that Salman began to notice how useful and well timed the angel's revelations tended to be, so that when the faithful were disputing Mahound's views on any subject, from the possibility of space travel to the permanence of Hell, the angel would turn up with an answer, and he always supported Mahound.... It would have been different, Salman complained to Baal, if Mahound took up his positions after receiving the revelation from Gibreel; but no, he just laid down the law and the angel would confirm it afterwards; so I began to get a bad smell in my nose.

Ayesha, Mahound's favorite wife, made the same point to him. "Your God certainly jumps to it when you need him to fix things up for you." The implication of these comments hardly needs to be drawn out. Again, that Mahound just happened to receive revelations suiting his needs suggests the human origins of the Qur'an.

This criticism, incidentally, recalls the polemics of medieval Christian writers. They made much of Muhammad happening to get revelations at convenient moments. Norman Daniel notes the triple reproach at the heart of their accusations against Muhammad: "Muhammad was promiscuous, and he justified himself by pretending to revelations, which he then erected into general laws for the benefit of his followers."[12] Rushdie offended Muslims even more than otherwise by reviving archaic calumnies against Islam.

Indeed, there is much in the two chapters about Mahound that seems intentionally to revive the wording, tone and spirit of medieval Christian attacks on Islam. The very name Mahound harks back to the polemics of that era. Deriving from the name "Mahomet," it had, according to *The Oxford English Dictionary*, four meanings in the medieval period: the false prophet Muhammad, often vaguely imagined to be worshipped by Muslims as a god; any false god or idol; a monster or hideous creature; or the devil. In the seventeenth century Mahound also took on the meaning of Muslim or heathen. With the exception of some literary archaisms, Mahound has not been current in English for centuries. Until Rushdie resurrected the word, it had been as obscure as the Satanic verses episode.

Rushdie's use of this name, with its heavy baggage of Christian medieval polemics, smacked of rancour. But, as usual, Rushdie has to be read carefully, for he is a subtle writer. He explains his reason for adopting the name Mahound by referring to other cases of insults being turned into names of proud identification:

Here he is neither Mahomet nor MoeHammered; has adopted, instead the demon-tag the farangis [Franks] hung around his neck. To turn insults into strengths, whigs, tories, Blacks all chose to wear with pride the names they were given in scorn; likewise, our mountain-climbing, prophet-motivated solitary is to be the medieval baby-frightener, the Devil's synonym: Mahound.

Rushdie signals here that he intends nothing derogatory by the name Mahound. What is one to believe, the medievalism or the justification? As usual, Rushdie is too elusive to be pinned down.

Using the name Mahound instead of Muhammad had another consequence: almost all the British book reviewers, unaware of this name's meaning or the Prophet Muhammad's biography, completely missed *The Satanic Verses'* connection to Islam. It was as though Rushdie was writing a covert message to his Muslim readers.

Other passages too seem to be based on medieval polemics, if only because they insistently probe the most vulnerable or the most easily ridiculed parts of the Islamic tradition. Thus, Mahound's companions complain about the laws he brought down, and Rushdie provides a partial inventory of them.

> Rules about every damn thing, if a man farts let him turn his face to the wind, a rule about which hand to use for the purpose of cleaning one's behind.... They learned that sodomy and the missionary position were approved of by the archangel, whereas the forbidden postures included all those in which the female was on top.... [Gibreel] required animals to be killed slowly, by bleeding.

This listing mixes the Islamic law with its opposite and with the author's whimsy—and only a specialist in those laws can tell which is which. This catalogue purposefully confuses the sacred with the coarse, and the true with the false; Muslims who read it invariably concluded that Rushdie intended to ridicule, even sabotage, the faith.

But no part of *The Satanic Verses* has been so much cited or distorted as the story about a brothel in Mecca called The Curtain. Every detail of this tale seems to be imbued with sacrilege and impiety. The very name of the brothel, The Curtain, is a translation of *al-hijab*, Arabic for the veil a woman uses to cover her face. The twelve prostitutes at The Curtain take on the names, and even the personalities, of Mahound's twelve wives. And what could exceed this vision in sacrilege?

The men of Jahilia flocked to The Curtain, which experienced a three hundred per cent increase in business. For obvious reasons it was not politic to form a queue in the street, and so on many days a line of men curled around the innermost courtyard of the brothel, rotating about its centrally positioned Fountain of Love much as pilgrims rotated for other reasons around the ancient Black Stone.

In other words, the same men who by day circumambulated the Ka'ba, the holiest shrine of Islam, by night mocked this act of piety by circling the Fountain of Love waiting their turn with a prostitute.

Yet these offenses are not entirely gratuitous. Rushdie tries to show what happened as the Meccans converted to a radically different religion, and The Curtain, the scene of the deepest and most incorrigible anti-Islamic sentiments among the Meccan population, makes this point tellingly. Thus, Rushdie introduces the story of the prostitutes taking the names of the Prophet's wives by observing, "Where there is no belief, there is no blasphemy." The implication is clear: only because the men of Mecca had entered the Islamic faith could they derive salacious pleasure from imagining the prostitutes to be the Prophet's wives. In a perverse way, he is highlighting the religiousness of the new Muslims.

The final sacrilege comes at the scene of Mahound's death, when he sees a mysterious figure and inquires, "Is it Thou, Azraeel," the angel of death. But the voice that comes back is that of a woman. Mahound immediately knows whose it is. "Is this sickness then thy doing, O Al-Lat?" (This is the same as Lat, the paramount female diety and one of the three mentioned in the Satanic verses.)

And she said: "It is my revenge upon you, and I am satisfied. Let them cut a camel's hamstrings and set it on your grave."

Then she went, and the lamp that had been snuffed out burst once more into a great and gentle light, and the Messenger murmured, "Still, I thank Thee, Al-Lat, for this gift."

Not long afterwards he died."

This closing incident to Mahound's life can be read in either of two ways, one inimical to Islam, the other not. If Al-Lat turns out actually to be a diety, and not just a stone idol, Mahound was therefore justified in paying obeisance to her. But if her presence at Mahound's bedside was a product of his imagination, this implies that he believed in her at the time of the Satanic verses episode as well. Retroactively, we seem to be told, almost including Al-Lat in the Qur'an was a sincere mistake on Mahound's part. Here as elsewhere, the author leaves the alternatives open.

But Rushdie's Muslim critics ignored these nuances. In their view, Rushdie purposefully sought to denigrate the core of the Islamic faith, and nothing else.

Other Affronts

In addition to the Prophet and his companions, Rushdie ridicules other aspects of Islam, including the notion of a Lord Almighty and contemporary Islamic figures. Here is Rushdie on God's presence:

> Gibreel's vision of the Supreme Being was not abstract in the least. He saw, sitting on the bed, a man of about the same age as himself, of medium height, fairly heavily built, with salt-and-pepper beard cropped close to the line of the jaw. What struck him most was that the apparition was balding, seeming to suffer from dandruff and wore glasses.

In another passage, describing the role of religion in India, Rushdie calls God "the creature of evil." The speaker is a movie producer: "Fact is, religious faith, which encodes the highest aspirations of human race, is now, in our country [India], the servant of lowest instincts, and God is the creature of evil."[13]

Coming down to earth, Rushdie caricatures Khomeini's extremist views. In his earlier writings, it is true, Rushdie had had some good things to say about the Islamic Revolution. (He wrote in 1984, "We may not approve of Khomeini's Iran, but the revolution there was a genuine mass movement"—high praise coming from this author). But his sympathy had disappeared by the time of *The Satanic Verses*, in which the picture of contemporary Iran was reduced to trenchant parody: "After the revolution there will be no clocks; we'll smash the lot. The word clock will be expunged from our dictionaries. After the revolution there will be no birthdays. We shall all be born again, all of us the same unchanging age in the eye of Almighty God." Then, two out of *The Satanic Verses'* nine chapters sketch an allegory which severely disapproves of Iran under the ayatollahs.

Nor is that all. Rushdie has this to say about the imam of the cathedral mosque of Delhi, the Juma Masjid:

> The Imam, a loose-bellied man with cynical eyes, who could be found most mornings in his "garden"—a red-earth-and-rubble waste land in the shadow of the mosque—counting rupees donated by the faithful and rolling up each note individually, so that he seemed to be holding a handful of thin beedi-like cigarettes—and who was no stranger to communalist politics himself, was apparently determined that the Meerut horror [a massacre of Muslims] should be turned to good account.

It comes as no surprise to learn that the imam in question, Syed Abdullah Bukhari, endorsed Khomeini's *fatwa* and played a leading role in stimulating protests against *The Satanic Verses*.

Is *The Satanic Verses* blasphemous? To use Rushdie's favorite locution, it is and it is not. While the book contains many elements of high sacrilege, the author is usually careful to place them in frames—dreams, ambiguous wordings, and the like— which mask his intent. In other cases, he carefully avoids specific mention of historical names such as Muhammad, Qur'an or Islam. The sum of the novel, then, is far less sacrilegious than its parts. Photostats of offending pages make it look more outrageous than does a reading of the book as a whole. Thus, Rushdie has reason when he protests that his critics, by taking passages out of context, distort their meaning.

NOTES

[1]*Ayat Shaytaniya am Ahqad Shaytaniya* ([London: n.p., [1989]), p. 13.

[2]"An Interview with Salman Rushdie," *Scripsi*, p. 122.

[3]At-Tabari, *Jami' al-Bayan fi Tafsir al-Qur'an* (Cairo, 1321/1903), vol. 17, pp. 119-21.

[4]At-Tabari, *Ta'rikh ar-Rusul wa'l-Muluk*, ed. M.J. de Goeje et al. (Leiden: E.J. Brill, 1879-1901), vol. 1, p. 1192.

[5]Ibid.

[6]Ibid.

[7]Qur'an, Surat an-Najm, verses 19-23.

[8]W. Montgomery Watt, *Muhammad in Mecca* (Oxford: Oxford University Press, 1953), pp. 108-09.

[9]Muhammad Rashid Rida, *Tafsir al-Fatiha* (Cairo: Az-Zahra' li'l-A'lam al-'Arabi, 1405/1985), pp. 129-30.

[10]Muhammad Husayn Haykal, *Hayat Muhammad*, 9th edition (Cairo: Maktaba an-Nahda al-Misriya, 1965), pp. 164-67.

[11]Michiko Kakutani, "'The Satanic Verses': What Rushdie Wrote," *The New York Times*, February 23, 1989.

[12]Norman Daniel, *Islam and the West: The Making of an Image* (Edinburgh: At the University Press, 1960), p. 100.

[13]This sentence in the original includes stuttering sounds which are eliminated here.

4.

BLAME RUSHDIE FOR THE FUROR?

Opinion falls into two camps on the question of Rushdie's culpability. Some blame him for the controversy, arguing that he knew he was stirring up a hornet's nest, and that he chose to do so for his own aggrandizement or profit. This argument assumes that the furor was virtually foreordained. The counterview holds the Muslim response far out of proportion to anything that Rushdie wrote, and therefore unpredictable. Which case is the more compelling?

The Case Against Rushdie

Wise after the fact, some observers insist that Rushdie had to have foreseen the trouble in advance. The leading assertion of this argument was made by the British writer, Roald Dahl.

Clearly he has profound knowledge of the Muslim religion and its people, and he must have been totally aware of the deep and violent feelings his book would stir up among devout Muslims. In other words he knew exactly what he was doing and he cannot plead otherwise.

This kind of sensationalism does indeed get an indifferent book on to the top of the best-seller list...but to my mind it is a cheap way of doing it.[1]

Dahl advised Rushdie to "throw the bloody thing away. It would save lives." Writing in the *Financial Times*, Edward Mortimer held that Rushdie "clearly courted such a reaction" as he in fact got. Jimmy Carter held that the author "must have anticipated a horrified reaction throughout the Islamic world."[2] John Esposito, an Islamic specialist at Holy Cross University, said he knew "of no Western scholar of Islam who would not have predicted that [Rushdie's] kind of statements would be explosive."[3]

Others even held the author and publisher to account for the damage caused by the publication of *The Satanic Verses*. A British commentator, Nicholas Ashford, wrote that "they cannot avoid shouldering some of the blame for what has happened."[4] The most extreme position was taken by S.K. Islamabadi of Chittagong, Bangladesh, who held that "Rushdie should have foreseen that his inflammatory book could provoke a violent reaction among the believers of Islam of such magnitude that it could lead to violence and death. He and his publishers are, therefore, directly responsible for these deaths."[5]

The case for blaming Rushdie is a good one. To begin with, many of the passages noted in chapter 3 seem intended to provoke. And the title too; why, in a novel primarily about Indians between their homeland and England, take the title from one of the two sub-plots? And why from the most delicate incident within the sub-plots? The Qur'anic reference was utterly obscure to all but a few orientalists; to everyone else, it was dramatic but meaningless. Why make it the title?

At the beginning of the controversy, Rushdie acknowledged that he hoped *The Satanic Verses* would ruffle feathers, though denied that he expected an uproar.

I knew that the very theocratic, medievalist Islam that is being pushed out through the mosques was not likely to take very kindly to the book I was writing, but I didn't foresee a reaction on this scale. If you don't believe—and I don't—that some kind of disembodied supreme being sent an angel to dictate a book to a seventh-century businessman named Muhammad, you're in trouble.[6]

Then, as the furor mounted, he back-peddled from this challenge to Islam. In September 1988, when there seemed to be no need to hide his purposes, Rushdie freely admitted to what his book was about. "One of my major themes is religion and fanaticism," he acknowledged. "I have talked about the Islamic religion because that is what I know the most about."[7] But a month later, when the heat was on, he denied it all. The book "isn't actually about Islam, but about migration, metamorphosis, divided selves, love, death, London and Bombay."[8] Rushdie weakened his claim of innocence by being less than truthful about his motives.

Further, Rushdie gave away his true colors as the crisis mounted around him. On February 14, the day of Khomeini's edict, he spent the day in television studios, spouting defiance. "Frankly, I wish I had written a more critical book," he told the BBC. But then off-camera he smoked his first cigarette in six years and talked about taking a "very long holiday" in what he facetiously called an MFZ, an acronym for "Muslim-free zone."[9]

The most damning case against Rushdie, however, bears on the fact that he knew well what he was getting into with *The Satanic Verses*. Perhaps more than any other major novelist, he is preoccupied with the twin issues of religious sensitivities and censorship. These themes permeate his work, both fiction and non-fiction. In a 1984 essay, "Outside the Whale," he called for more engaged writing:

We live in a world without hiding places.... What I am saying is that politics and literature, like sports and politics, do mix, are inextricably mixed, and that that mixture has consequences.... There is a genuine need for political fiction, for books that draw new and better maps of reality, and make new languages with which we can understand the world.

Rushdie reiterated this view in *The Satanic Verses*, demanding that the poet involve himself in the world: "'A poet's work [is] to name the unnamable, to point at frauds, to take sides, start arguments, shape the world and stop it from going to sleep.' And if rivers of blood flow from the cuts his verses inflict, then they will nourish him." His position is clear: write the truth and consequences be damned.

But Rushdie rarely takes just one position in an argument. In *Shame*, he claimed license to do as he pleased, on the grounds that he was engaged in fantasy:

> But suppose this were a realistic novel!...The book would have been banned, dumped in the rubbish bin, burned. All that effort for nothing! Realism can break a writer's heart.
>
> Fortunately, however, I am only telling a sort of modern fairy-tale, so that's all right; nobody need get upset, or take anything I say too seriously. No drastic action need be taken, either.
>
> What a relief!

The contrast between these passages anticipates the ambivalence that characterizes Rushdie's response to the furor set off by *The Satanic Verses*. They also point to the immaturity of his thought; yes, he wants to shake up the world, but, no, he will not accept responsibility for what he has wrought.

Rushdie returns repeatedly to the matter of censorship in India, confirming that he knew precisely what trouble he would encounter. He wrote about this matter in *The Satanic Verses*: "The days when he [Gibreel Farishta] could do no wrong were gone; his second feature [film], *Mahound*, had hit every imaginable religious reef, and sunk without trace." A character in the novel commented on Gibreel's efforts: "'Looks like he's trying deliberately to set up a final confrontation with religious sectarians, knowing he can't win, that he'll be broken to bits.' Several members of the cast had already walked off the production, and given lurid interviews accusing Gibreel of 'blasphemy,' 'satan-ism' and other misdemeanors." We also read of an Indian producer who "had just finished a documentary film about communalism, interviewing Hindus and Muslims of all shades of opinion. Fundamentalists of both religions had instantly sought injunctions banning the film from being shown."

These passages make it clear that the author was acutely aware of the sensitivies and the dangers connected to his subject matter. Indeed, in a bizarre foreshadowing of Rushdie's own predicament, he has the Mahound character address the Salman character in *The Satanic Verses*: "Your blasphemy, Salman, can't be forgiven. Did you think I wouldn't work it out? To set your words against the Word of God."

Rushdie's exquisite awareness of religion and censorship meant that he knew that writers dealing with religious subjects routinely get into trouble in the Middle East. He often spoke about the troubles faced by authors such as Naguib Mahfouz and Tahar Ben Jelloun.[10] Further, as a well-informed student of history and politics, he realized exactly what Muslim sensibilities he was offending, and what this would mean. He himself observed after the furor began, "the orthodox Islamic world is somewhat behind the attitudes of the other great world religions."[11] Or, in more personal terms: "If Woody Allen were a Muslim, he would not live very long."[12] Rushdie's point is correct, and the long record of twentieth-century Muslim authors who have gotten into trouble is another reason to hold him culpable for the passions of early 1989. Even a brief recapitulation of some major controversies points to similarities between their works and his.

'Ali 'Abd ar-Raziq, a shaykh at Al-Azhar University in Cairo, published a book in 1925, *Islam and the Principles of Government*,[13] which argued that, properly understood, the Islamic religion calls for the separation of religion and politics. The suggestion that Islam has no role in public life provoked such an uproar, the other sheikhs of Al-Azhar put 'Abd ar-Raziq in a tribunal and unanimously found him guilty of impiety. He lost his diploma, was dismissed from the university, and was banned from holding religious office.

The next year, Taha Husayn, a leading Egyptian belle-lettrist, published a book called *On Pre-Islamic Poetry* in which one passage laid open to doubt the historical veracity of the Qur'an. That the Torah and Qur'an mention the names of Abraham and Ishmael, he wrote, "is not sufficient to establish their historical existence."[14] Under attack for apostasy, Husayn was put on trial, lost his university position, and was compelled to withdraw his book.

Skipping ahead to April 1967,[15] the Syrian army magazine *Jaysh ash-Sha'b* published an article which condemned God and religion as "mummies which should be transferred to the museums of historical remains."[16] Large demonstrations in all the major Syrian cities followed, leading to widescale strikes, the arrest of many religious leaders, and considerable violence. The Syrian regime attempted to mollify public sentiment by condemning the article as an American and Israeli plant. This did not suffice, so the authorities sentenced the article's author, Ibrahim Khalas, and two of his editors at *Jaysh ash-Sha'b* to life imprisonment. Eventually, they were released.

In 1969, Sadiq al-'Azm, a radical professor connected to the PLO, published a book in Lebanon called *A Critique of Religious Thought*. In it, he launched a general offensive against the role of Islam in the life of Muslims. He also revised some Islamic dogmas. Perhaps the most controversial of these came in the chapter, "The Devil's Tragedy," in which 'Azm ascribed to God the ultimate responsibility for evil and portrayed Satan as a tragic figure.[17] The Sunni establishment in Lebanon brought charges against 'Azm and confiscated copies of his book. Newspaper editorials called for him to cool off in jail for five years. The author went before a trial in January 1970, paid bail, and was nearly expelled from the country.[18]

In the Sudan, a theologian of distinction and originality, Mahmud Muhammad Taha, differentiated between those passages in the Qur'an that Muhammad received before his taking power (the Meccan verses) and those that followed his taking power (the Medinan verses). According to Taha, the former defined eternally valid principles of Islam whereas the latter were intended only for Muhammad's own instruction, and therefore do not serve as a model for subsequent Muslim life. As nearly all the Qur'an's many precepts are contained in the Medinan verses, this approach virtually eliminates the Qur'an as a source of commands. Further, if Qur'anic precepts do not apply to Muslims after Muhammad, obviously Muhammad's personal actions and statements have no wider applicability—and yet these form one of the key bases of Islamic law. Instead, Taha stressed the spiritual and ethical qualities of the Qur'anic message. Taha held that, to the extent that Muslims need a new law, they can write one in keeping with the needs of the present era.[19] Taha founded a movement, called the Republican Brethren, which forwarded his principles. These efforts to secularize Islam caused the High Shari'a Court of Khartoum in 1968 to find Taha guilty of apostasy. In consequence, the government collected and burned his writings.[20] Taha eventually won back his freedom, only to lose it again, this time permanently. On January 18, 1985, following a hasty, ill-prepared trial, this 76-year-old practicing Muslim was hanged in a public ceremony in Khartoum. The hearing itself and then the events leading up to the hanging make for particularly poignant reading; indeed, perhaps more than any other state persecution of a writer in modern times, this case echoes the trial of Socrates.[21]

A final example, a small one, comes from Rushdie's own experience. During his brief stay in Pakistan, he produced Edward Albee's *Zoo Story* for television, only to have it censored before it could be shown. Why? Because of a single reference in a monologue to "pork," the forbidden meat of Islam. And to make matters more surprising, Albee refers to pork in an extremely negative way: "six perfectly good hamburgers with not enough pork to make [them] disgusting." Rushdie appealed the ruling but, as he explained years later, no one accepted his claim that this constituted very sophisticated antipork propaganda. To the censors, as he put it, "pork was simply a four-letter word." At a later date, a documentary Rushdie made for the BBC about

religious tensions was banned in India. The authorities' cen-
sorious ways stemmed less from their fragile sensibilities than
from an awareness of the dangers of provoking communal
disturbances in the highly charged atmosphere of the Indian
subcontinent—an awareness Rushdie fully shared.

With such a record, one might ask how Rushdie could expect a
response other than what he got. But there is another argument to
consider, this one in Rushdie's favor.

The Case for Rushdie

The key point in Rushdie's defense is that the response to his
book was arbitrary in nature; therefore, he could not possibly
have anticipated the furor it would arouse. How could Rushdie
have imagined what response his book would provoke? Since no
novel had ever before become the centerpiece of an international
incident, he could hardly have expected this fate for his own.
Rushdie could hardly have expected that rioters would be sacrific-
ing their lives to protest his novel, much less that diplomatic and
trade relations would hinge on the exact wording in his fantastical
account of events that took place over thirteen centuries back.
Further, plenty of other books have been published that matched
or even exceeded Rushdie's in impiety toward Islam—without
rousing anything like the controversy his did. In other words, *The
Satanic Verses'* becoming the center of a storm was to some
extent a random event.

Any number of examples, by non-Muslims and Muslims alike,
can be cited to make this point. Take the 1983 novel by Richard
Grenier, *The Marrakesh One-Two*, which contains passages no
less blasphemous than those in *The Satanic Verses*. Grenier has
the would-be Hollywood producer of a film about the Prophet
Muhammad vent his views:

> Mohammed struck me as a kind of a gamey figure for a religious
> leader, I mean for a man God spoke to personally. I didn't know
> what to make of him really, sort of a blend of Saint Teresa of

Avila, Jane Addams of Hull House, William the Conqueror, and Casanova.... When he has his midlife crisis Mohammed gets the Call, and has visions, and goes into a trance and Allah dictates all these *Suras* [chapters] to him, which together make up the Koran. And either Mohammed is plagiarizing the Bible like mad and is a hysterical plagiarist or it's one hell of a coincidence.... He's always praying to Allah for guidance and if Mohammed really wants something bad enough you get the impression Allah is going to tell him it's okay. I mean Allah can't seem to say no to him.[22]

Although Grenier did receive some late-night callers whispering "Death to the enemies of Allah," no governments banned his book or called for his murder.

As for scholarship, nothing could challenge Islam more completely than two books published in 1977. John Wansbrough's *Quranic Studies* makes the following points about the Qur'an: that it was written by many human hands (and not by God); that the compilation took place over a period lasting perhaps as long as three and a half centuries (rather than twenty-three years); and that Muhammad was merely a prophet figure—real or imaginary, it hardly matters—who had nothing at all to do with the composition of the Qur'an (rather than being its sole source).[23]

Drawing on Wansbrough's efforts, *Hagarism*, a historical study by Patricia Crone and Michael Cook, ignores information on Muhammad and the Qur'an deriving from the standard sources—the Arabic literary accounts. Instead, the authors rely entirely on Aramaic, Armenian, Coptic, Greek, Hebrew, Latin and Syrian sources, as well as Arabic papyri, coins and inscriptions. This re-examination leads Crone and Cook to turn the normal account of Islam's origins upside-down. In their version, Muhammad was not elevated "to the role of a scriptural prophet" until the year A.D. 700 or so, seventy years after his death;[24] and the Qur'an was compiled only under the auspices of al-Hajjaj ibn Yusuf, the governor of Iraq in 694-714. To put it mildly, these assertions are at odds with what Muslims believe. Although Wansbrough, Crone and Cook raised a small tempest in academic circles, their books, with the implied charge that Islam was a fraud from the first, were altogether ignored by Muslims.

Muslims themselves have written books in Arabic, Turkish and Persian that challenged Islam more than *The Satanic Verses*. Indeed, Islamic society has traditionally tolerated some blasphemy. To take three examples, the renowned poet, Abu Nuwas (who died about 813), specialized in writing about wine and pederasty, and boasted of writing about virtually everything that displeases God. Al-Mutannabi (915-55) wrote of "droplets sweeter on the lips than the declaration that God is one."[25] Similarly, Abu'l-'Ala al-Ma'arri (973-1058) penned some very daring statements:

> Although your mouths hymn Allah One and Peerless,
> Your hearts and souls from that ye owe Him shrink.
> I swear your Torah gives no light to lead us,
> If there 'tis found that wine is lawful drink.[26]

Ironically, therefore, the charge that Muslims are acting "medieval" misses the point; in fact, they are not medieval enough.

Modern books challenging Islam can be found for sale in the Middle East and other parts of the Muslim world, and some of them have become best sellers. Indeed, they constitute what Khalid Durán calls the Muslim "tradition of free thinking,"[27] a tradition that historically was especially strong in Iran. With regard to Turkey, Ismail Nacar, a specialist on the subject, observed that "there are native Salman Rushdies in Turkey. There is no need to look for them outside the country."[28]

In the Arabic-speaking countries, Mu'ammar al-Qadhdhafi, the Libyan leader, provided a remarkable instance of sustained public blasphemy. He changed the Islamic calendar so that it begins in 632, the year Muhammad died, instead of the standard date of 622, the year he moved to Medina. Like Mahmud Muhammad Taha, he held that Islamic law governs only the private sphere, touching on such matters as personal morality and the afterlife, but offers no guidance in public matters. Qadhdhafi then replaced many of the Islamic laws with his own precepts, published in *The Green Book*. He ridiculed pilgrims to Mecca as "guileless and foolish," rejected as invalid reports about Muhammad's life (whose authority in Islam is second only to the Qur'an), criticized the Prophet Muhammad, and even expressed doubts about the veracity of the Qur'an's contents.

By the mid-1970s, Qadhdhafi saw himself almost as a new prophet, so he felt free to denigrate the Prophet Muhammad: "What has Muhammad done that I have not? It is I who liberated you [Libyans] and gave you international standing."[29] To Oriana Fallaci, an Italian interviewer, Qadhdhafi characterized *The Green Book* as a new scripture:

> *Qadhdhafi:* The Green Book is the guide to the emancipation of man. The Green Book is the gospel. The new gospel. The gospel of the new era, the era of the masses....
> *Fallaci:* Well, then, you're a kind of messiah. The new messiah.
> *Qadhdhafi:* I don't see myself in those terms. But the Green Book is the new gospel, I repeat. In your gospels it's written "In the beginning there was the word." The Green Book is the word. One of its words can destroy the world. Or save it...My word. One word and the whole world could blow up.[30]

Qadhdhafi also funded an American-based Jesus movement, the Children of God. In return, the group acknowledged him as a messianic figure and described him as "one of God's chosen ones...the only world leader who is talking in the name of God, and...chosen by God to be a world leader."[31] In short, by the late-1970s, Qadhdhafi's Islam bore little relation to the mainstream religion.

Qadhdhafi's singular views did not go unnoticed. In November 1980, the Supreme Council of the Ulema of Saudi Arabia considered Qadhdhafi's notions about Islam and labeled him a "deviator from the principles of Islam and the brotherhood of Believers." It condemned his "perjury and lies" and accused him of striving "to abrogate the Shari'a [sacred law of Islam]."

Declaring Qadhdhafi "to be completely anti-Islamic," it recommended combatting his ideas and ostracizing him from Islamic activities.[32] But the condemnations stopped there. No government banned Qadhdhafi's writings or called for his death. Quite the contrary, the Saudis later buried the hatchet, and the Iranians joined with him in a political alliance.

Obviously, Qadhdhafi's position as a head of state makes him a special case, but his prominence and influence should have made him more, not less, subject to criticism. Islamic law requires that the apostate who publicly broadcasts his actions and beliefs, and therefore can do more harm to Islamic beliefs, be punished more urgently than the one who acts in private. A king, a religious leader or a novelist therefore receives special attention. Along these lines, the Iranian authorities justified the harshness of their actions against Rushdie on the grounds that public acts are far more threatening to the faith.

> There is a fundamental difference between crimes committed in secret and those done in public and prejudicial to public sentiments, codes, and beliefs. The retribution for committing sins in secret may be limited in scale and the act ignored or even pardoned. Yet the public violation of the divine laws is very serious and calls for severe punishment.[33]

The twenty-year near-silence about Qadhdhafi makes the quick response to Rushdie appear unpredictable, even capricious.

In the Persian language too, blasphemous writings are available on the subject of Muhammad and the Qur'an. For example, when an Iranian exile, the pseudonymous Dr. Roushangar, asked, "Is the God of Muhammad deceitful and trick-playing, or is he loving and compassionate?" he implied directly that it was Muhammad who wrote the Qur'an.[34] But one of the most extraordinary examples in Persian, a case worth looking at in some depth, is the widely-distributed book by the intellectual 'Ali Dashti, *Twenty-Three Years* (the title refers to the period of

Muhammad's prophecy).[35] Dashti submits Muhammad's entire career to a close and critical inspection, and comes up with some exceedingly blasphemous conclusions.

On the question of the origins of the Qur'an, Dashti takes a somewhat different tack from Rushdie. He notes that Muhammad held the proof of the Qur'an's divine inspiration in the book's miraculous quality. Muslims universally consider two features of the Qur'an miraculous: its eloquence and its subject matter. Dashti challenges this view, holding that it "clearly stems from zealous faith rather than impartial study."

On the matter of eloquence, he finds more than one hundred mistakes in language, including errors in grammar, wrong vocabulary, and "confusion between the two speakers, God and Muhammad." As for content, Dashti argues that the Qur'an "contains nothing new." Its precepts are "self-evident," while its stories derive from Jewish and Christian lore. The notion of abrogating verses of the Qur'an strikes Dashti as an almost dead giveaway for its human composition—for if God is perfect, then how can He make mistakes which later need to be corrected? "This incongruity can only be explained as the product of an inextricable confusion between God and Muhammad.... The verses of the Qur'an are outpourings from both parts of his personality." This last sentence virtually states that Muhammad made up the Qur'an. Nor can he hide surprise at finding "illusions and irrational ideas...in a book deemed to be God's word." Dashti suggests the obvious: it is not that God shares the beliefs of seventh-century Arabians, but that these beliefs "were spread and perpetuated by the Prophet Muhammad"s utterances. Finally, Dashti comes right out and says what is on his mind: "The Lord who made observance of ancient Arab lunar time-reckoning compulsory everywhere and for ever must have been either a local Arabian god or the Prophet Muhammad."

Dashti has other criticisms of the Qur'an. He finds it amazing that a moral code intended for all time includes in it so many verses addressed only to Muhammad—and that many of those had to do with issues arising from the "astonishing range" of his marital privileges. Verses dealing with God's ideas about punishment leave Dashti appalled: "Reading these verses makes the hair stand on end."

Looking beyond the Qur'an, Dashti condemns many aspects of Muhammad's behavior. The prophet relied on "every sort of expedient . . . regardless of consistency with the spiritual and moral precepts" he was teaching. In some cases, killings motivated by Muhammad's boastfulness or his personal grudge "were passed off as services to Islam." About ninety percent of those professing Islam by the time of Muhammad's death in A.D. 632 did so "from either fear or expediency." Looking ahead a few years to the Arab conquests, the quest for booty was "an important factor in the implantation of Islam and consolidation of the Muslim community." Indeed, "the history of Islam is indisputably a record of violence and power-seizure."

Despite these passages, and many more, Dashti's book was sold in Iran, in the Persian language, for some time after the Iranian revolution. Although Dashti lived in Iran, Ayatollah Khomeini never issued a *fatwa* against him. It is therefore entirely not true, as Iranian parliamentarians wrote in a letter to Khomeini, that Rushdie's insults "are unprecedented since the inception of Islam."[36] A review of these other examples of blasphemy shows, rather, that it fits into a long tradition of criticism from within; and Rushdie's work was far from being the most critical of that tradition.

The very most extraordinary example of Muslim free thinking came from the pen of none other than Rushdie's tormentor, Ayatollah Khomeini. Very soon after issuing his edict, Khomeini composed a poem which read:

I have become imprisoned, O beloved, by the mole on your lip!
I saw your ailing eyes and became ill through love.

Delivered from self, I beat the drum of "I am the Real!"
Like Hallaj, I became a customer for the top of the gallows. *
Heartache for the beloved has thrown so many sparks into my soul
That I have been driven to despair and become the talk of the
    bazaar.
Open the door of the tavern and let us go there day and night,
For I am sick and tired of the mosque and seminary.
I have torn off the garb of asceticism and hypocrisy,
Putting on the cloak of the tavern-haunting shaykh and becoming
    aware.
The city preacher has so tormented me with his advice
That I have sought aid from the breath of the wine-drenched
    profligate.
Leave me alone to remember the idol-temple,
I who have been awakened by the hand of the tavern's idol.[37]

Although experts quickly pointed out that allusions to lovers and taverns were strictly allegorical, the fact remained that the seemingly puritanical ruler of Iran had also indulged in some obviously profane and un-Islamic sentiments.

The point of all this is simple: despite the evident sacrilegious content of Dashti and the others' writing, none of their works attracted Khomeini's ire. Rather, they continued quietly to be sold and read. This contrast with *The Satanic Verses* points to the absence of a predictable connection between the writing of sacrilege and retribution by Muslim authorities. These examples confirm the experience of all those who live with censorship; there is no way to guess in advance when the pot will be stirred. Some Muslims have done more than Rushdie and been punished less; others have done less and been punished more. According to strictly logical criteria, the demonstrators and Khomeini could have picked on any number of other books, or ignored Rushdie's. So, while it is true that Rushdie knew what he was doing, he

---

*Hallaj was executed in 922 for announcing "I am the Real" (by which he seemed to imply, "I am God"). This statement has outraged pious Muslims ever since.

could not have predicted what the Muslim response would be, for ultimately it was capricious.

Why, then, did they pick on *The Satanic Verses*? Why did this book provoke (among others) the Muslims of England, the Saudi authorities, mobs in Pakistan, and Ayatollah Khomeini? These actors are so diverse that a single coordinated effort is out of the question. Nor could it have been coincidence that so many Muslims in so many places responded to this novel with like outrage. Why was this book received so very differently from other attacks on the Prophet? The question is particularly pressing because: (1) the book was not in a principal mother-language of Muslims, but in English; (2) it was never published or even sold in a country with a Muslim majority; and (3) it is a work of fiction, not of scholarship or polemics, and is a sophisticated, densely-written novel at that.

Why, then, pick on Rushdie? Was it because he is an apostate?

NOTES

[1]*The Times*, February 28, 1989.

[2]Jimmy Carter, "Rushdie's Book Is an Insult," *The New York Times*, March 5, 1989.

[3]*U.S. News & World Report*, March 6, 1989.

[4]*The Independent*, February 18, 1989.

[5]*Far Eastern Economic Review*, March 30, 1989.

[6]*Newsweek*, February 6, 1989.

[7]*India Today*, September 15, 1988.

[8]*The New York Times*, October 19, 1988, reprinted on February 17, 1989.

[9]*The Washington Post*, February 15, 1989.

[10]For example, *L'Express*, February 24, 1989.

[11]*Far Eastern Economic Review*, March 2, 1989.

[12]*Der Spiegel*, February 27, 1989.

[13]'Ali 'Abd ar-Raziq, *Al-Islam wa-Usul al-Hukm* (Cairo: Matba'at Misr, 1925).

[14]Taha Husayn, *Fi'sh-Shi'r al-Jahili* (Cairo: Matba'a Dar al-Kutub al-Misriya, 1344/1926), p. 26.

[15]For the 1946 murder of Ahmed Kasravi, in which Khomeini was directly involved, see below, pp. 101-102.

[16]Ibrahim Khalas, *Jaysh ash-Sha'b*, April 25, 1967. Quoted in Jabir Rizq, *Al-Ikhwan al-Muslimun w'al-Mu'amara 'ala Suriya* (Cairo: Dar al-I'tisam, 1980), p. 111. Rizq quotes other provocative material on the same page.

[17]Sadiq Jalal al-'Azm, *Naqd al-Fikr ad-Dini* 5th ed. (Beirut: Dar at-Tali'a, 1982), pp. 55-87.

[18]Stephan Wild, "Gott und Mensch im Libanon: Die Affäre Sadiq al-'Azm," *Der Islam* 48 (1971-72): 229-34.

[19]Mahmoud Muhammad Taha, *Ar-Risala ath-Thaniya min al-Islam*, trans. by Abdullahi Ahmed An-Na'im, *The Second Message of Islam* (Syracuse, N.Y.: Syracuse University Press, 1987).

[20]Richard P. Stevens, "Sudan's Republican Brothers and Islamic Reform," *Journal of Arab Affairs* 1 (1981): 135-44.

[21]For details of the case, see Na'im's introduction in Taha, *Ar-Risala ath-Thaniya*.

[22]Richard Grenier, *The Marrakesh One-Two* (Boston: Houghton Mifflin, 1983), pp. 5-7. The movie *Ishtar* is loosely based on the story in *The Marrakesh One-Two*.

[23]John Wansbrough, *Quranic Studies* (Oxford: Oxford University Press, 1977). It is noteworthy that Wansbrough's index does not even list the name Muhammad.

[24]Patricia Crone and Michael Cook, *Hagarism: The Making of the Islamic World* (Cambridge, Eng.: Cambridge University Press, 1977), pp. 18, 29.

[25]"Verses Composed in the Poet's Youth," in A.J. Arberry, *Arabic Poetry: A Primer for Students* (Cambridge, Eng.: At the University Press, 1965), pp. 18-19.

[26]R. A. Nicholson, *Translations of Eastern Poetry and Prose* (New York: Greenwood Press, 1969), p. 110.

[27]Khalid Durán, "Fiktion oder Provokation? Auch Rushdie steht in einer Tradition," *Schweizer Monatshefte*, May 1989, p. 357.

[28]*Milliyet*, March 8, 1989.

[29]*Jeune Afrique*, November 22, 1978.

[30]Oriana Fallaci, "'Iranians are our Brothers': An Interview with Col Muammar el-Qaddafi of Libya" *The New York Times Magazine*, December 16, 1979.

[31]*Events*, January 12, 1979.

[32]*Majallat Rabitat al-'Alam al-Islami*, December 1980.

[33]Editorial, *Tehran Times*, February 16, 1989.

[34]Dr. Roushangar (pseud.), *Bazshinasi-e Qur'an* (San Francisco: Pars, 1985), pp. 205, 308-09.

[35]'Ali Dashti *Bist o Seh Sal* (Beirut, 1974). Trans. F.R.C. Bagley, *Twenty Three Years: A Study of the Prophetic Career of Mohammad* (London: George Allen & Unwin, 1985).

[36]Radio Tehran, February 22, 1989.

[37]*The New Republic*, September 4, 1989.

5.

KHOMEINI'S EDICT

Although Khomeini's *fatwa* of February 14 was not phrased in legal terms, the charge against Rushdie and "all those involved in its publication who were aware of its content" is clear; those among them who were Muslims are now apostates (*murtadd*). In effect, Khomeini's edict declared them *mahdur ad-damm*, "he whose blood is invalid or forfeit." The life of an individual whose blood is forfeit no longer enjoys the protection of the authorities; he can be killed without penalty.

The edict raises several questions. In pronouncing a death sentence, was Khomeini acting in accordance with the sacred law of Islam, the Shari'a? From an Islamic point of view, is there a justification for his singling Rushdie out? If the book had precedent, why did he go after the novelist with unprecedented fury? And what justification did he have for condemning the publishers too?

Was the Edict Legal?

According to the sacred law of Islam, apostasy is a "turning away from Islam" or "severing ties with Islam."[1] The law recognizes two kinds of apostasy: *irtidad*, which is apostasy to heresy or to unbelief, and *ridda*, which is leaving Islam for some other religion, such as Christianity. In other words, an apostate is a Muslim (either by birth or through conversion) who renounces his faith; it is not necessary for him to take up another one in its place. Conversion to another religion is an obvious sign of apostasy; but if this does not take place, apostasy is a more subtle matter. It is then manifested through "expressions of unbelief"— which may be words, deeds or even intentions.

A listing of such expressions includes not just the obvious ones (denying the existence of God, denying the Qur'an as the word of God, denying Muhammad as the last prophet, claiming Jesus to be the son of God, prostrating before an idol), but also some that are distinctly of a lesser sort (throwing the Qur'an in the trash or invoking God's name while drinking wine). Some of the expressions are so trivial, they have hardly ever been applied: translating the Qur'an, ridiculing the Muslim men of religion, or celebrating Nawruz, the Iranian New Year. For the Rushdie case, it is of special importance to note that insulting the Prophet, his wives or his companions is an act of apostasy.

According to schools of law in the majority Sunni branch of Islam, the apostate must be invited to repent and return to Islam before capital punishment is applied, and should he do so, he is then reinstated in the faith, without punishment. The Shi'i school of law to which Khomeini belonged, however, does not normally permit such repentence.

How do these regulations apply to Rushdie? Khomeini's edict did not say, so others were left to draw their own conclusions. Rushdie had not converted to another faith, so his apostasy could only be established through his expressions of unbelief. It was said that he had insulted the Prophet Muhammad, that his writings placed him "outside the pale of Islam," and that he was "a self-confessed apostate."[2]

The evidence for these assertions is ambiguous. Rushdie's style is one of indirection and allusion, not bald statement—as in the Mahound sequence of *The Satanic Verses*. Even when speaking about himself, the words are usually open to alternate interpretations. "Where God lived inside of me, there is now a hole. I am no longer a practicing Muslim. And this hole is what I wanted to explore. And exploration, isn't that suitable for a novel?"[3] But sometimes he comes right out and says what is on his mind. "I do not believe in the existence of an external Supreme Being.... I do not believe in supernatural entities, whether Christian, Jewish, Muslim, or Hindu."[4] As for deeds, he breaks Islamic regulations by drinking alcohol, and he even writes about his drinking. (This, from the account of his trip to Nicaragua: "I drank a toast in the best rum in the world, Flor de Caña Extra Seco. Mixed with Coke, it was called a Nica-libre, and after a few glasses I was ready to take on the salsa champions and knock them dead.") In short, Rushdie is a lapsed Muslim. Judged by a strict interpretation of the traditional rules, there is no doubt that he is an apostate.

But several considerations vitiate this conclusion. First, it is clear that, according to the classic definitions, a great many Muslims today are apostates. Their number includes communists (whose credo is atheistic), Muslim rulers (who do not apply the Shari'a), Iranians (who celebrate Nawruz), Muslims living in the West (who prefer to reside in countries where the Shari'a does not hold sway), and even the fundamentalists (who scorn the professional men of religion).

While no one flings the net quite this widely, some fundamentalists do deem rulers to be apostates, figuring that these have a special responsibility to apply the law. This was the charge put forward by the assassins of President Anwar as-Sadat of Egypt in 1981 to justify his murder.[5] Along similar lines, the mufti (religious leader) of Jerusalem declared in a June 1983 *fatwa* that the actions of the Syrian government made it "the duty of every Muslim to kill [President Hafiz al-]Asad, the worst enemy of the Muslims."[6] More recently, the Iranians raised the question whether the leaders of Turkey can be considered believers so long as they prevent female students from dressing in a pious fashion.[7] In addition, most Muslims consider members of two religions that broke away from Islam—Baha'is (in Iran and elsewhere) and Ahmadis (in Pakistan)—really to be apostates from Islam. From time to time Muslim true-believers will launch a pogrom against

Baha'is or Ahmadis. For the most part, however, impious rulers, Baha'is, and Ahmadis are left in peace.

Other apostates are also generally left alone. In Egypt, Christian men have been converting to Islam in recent years to take advantage of the Shari'a's favorable rules of divorce, then, once the divorce is effected, they drift back to their original Coptic faith. While this practice upsets Muslims, the apostates are not physically assaulted. Carlos Saúl Menem, the Peronist president of Argentina, may be the leading apostate of recent years. The son of Syrian immigrants, Menem (according to public statements by his Muslim wife) abandoned Islam solely for political reasons—because Argentinian law requires the president to be Catholic. The point is, there are quite a few Muslim apostates, and almost all of them are left in peace. Therefore, merely to deem Rushdie an apostate does not explain why he should be picked out for such spectacular condemnation.

Additionally, many sophisticated Muslims, especially those who have lived in the West or are Westernized, share Rushdie's skepticism about Muhammad, the Qur'an, and God. Many of them would understand exactly what Rushdie meant when he described his situation: "I am a lapsed Muslim, which is to say you still define yourself by the thing you've lapsed from. I am not a believer in any formal sense but I am shaped by that thing, and I am interested in Islam and its history, which I've studied. In that sense, yes, I'm a Muslim."[8] Few others dared express in public, however, even a fraction of what he said and wrote. Still, the Iranian government does not proclaim a bounty on the heads of those, like 'Ali Dashti, who did do so. Why was Rushdie singled out for punishment?

As many Muslim critics have pointed out, there is also a procedural problem. Properly to condemn Rushdie of apostasy, he must be subjected to a trial and found guilty. This is not easy, for Islamic law protects the defendant with extensive and detailed rules for procedure. Unless every requirement is scrupulously fulfilled, judges are directed not to condemn. For example, to take a different sort of violation, the fact that an unmarried woman is pregnant is not sufficient grounds to find her guilty of fornication; pregnancy is merely circumstantial evidence. For its part, Islamic law lays down very precisely the requirements for a conviction of fornication: the woman must be witnessed *in fragrante delicto* by no less than four Muslim men of established virtue, and all of them must be willing to say so in court, even though a mistrial will lead to their being punished instead.ˉ The strictness of Islamic laws is designed precisely to avoid the 1001-nights style of justice that prevailed in early Muslim courts, whereby rulers decided issues of life and death on the basis of whims. By similar token, apostasy must be established through careful legal inquiry. It cannot be decided on the basis of television news or even a few passages from a book read out of context. In short, Khomeini ignored all the procedures set up to prevent abuse of the laws.

There are more problems, having to do with the condemnation of "all those involved in its publication who were aware of its content." Islamic law cannot justify sentencing this group of people to death, for several reasons. The Shari'a clearly establishes that disseminating false information is not the same as expressing it. "Transmitting blasphemy is not blasphemy" (*naql al-kufr laysa kufr*). Also, those "involved in publishing" *The Satanic Verses* at Viking were non-Muslims, so they cannot possibly be sentenced under the Islamic laws of apostasy. Should there be another ruling under which they fall, Khomeini failed to provide a justification. Finally, the phrasing "all those involved in its publication who were aware of its content" is too vague, and must be defined by a court before it can serve as the basis for executions.

ˉThe previous major attempt by Muslims to censor a work of art in the West involved non-Islamic legal procedures on just this point. The 1980 television movie, *The Death of a Princess*, told the story of a Saudi grandfather who condemned his granddaughter to death for fornication, without her having the benefit of a trial. Although entirely against the precepts of Islam, the senior member of the royal family could get away with this form of Arabian tribal justice.

In brief, Khomeini played fast and loose with the laws of Islam, and it was not the first time he had done so. No reading of Islamic law can justify the taking of the U.S. embassy in Tehran and the holding of American diplomats as hostages, nor the hostage-taking in Lebanon,[9] nor executing prisoners of war, nor summary trials of political opponents, nor criminal trials based on hearsay. Further, Khomeini's very grounding in the Shari'a caused him to violate it in ways which would never occur to someone not versed in the law. By far the most important example was his assertion in January 1988 that *raison d'état* takes precedence over the laws of Islam. "For Islam, the requirements of government supersede every tenet, including even those of prayer, fasting and pilgrimage to Mecca. The government is authorized unilaterally to abolish its lawful accords with the people and to prevent any matter, be it spiritual or material, that poses a threat to its interests."[10] This pronouncement runs counter to one of the deepest assumptions of Islam, that God's will bends before no man. (In the eyes of not a few Muslims, this makes Khomeini an incomparably greater danger to Islam than Rushdie.)

Khomeini might have veiled his actions with Islam, but he repeatedly took steps far outside the bounds of Islamic tradition. Sepehr Zabih put the case mildly when he observed, "Many Moslem scholars are convinced that there is simply no congruence between true Islamic precepts and practice and the vengeful ferocity of the pro-Khomeini Shia clerics."[11] Khomeini, whose rise in the Islamic heirarchy of Iran owed much to his mastery of Islamic doctrine, often failed to meet its requirements. Instead, he arrogated to himself a host of new prerogatives. As Malcolm Yapp has written,

> Khomeini's claims are quite staggering in their scope. To an outsider, the oddest feature is the way in which Khomeini's controversial pronouncements are taken by Muslims to be authoritative statements of law.... Muslim law appears to have undergone a dramatic change. The opinion of one man appears to have replaced all the elaborate mechanisms by which opinions were formed and consensus achieved.[12]

It is ironic that Khomeini, the first legal scholar of Islam ever to hold power in a major state, reverted to an archaic habit of personalized statecraft, ignoring the fourteen centuries of procedures he had so carefully learned and then taught to others.

Criticism of Khomeini

The breach of Islamic law involved in the Rushdie *fatwa* did not go unnoticed. Many Muslim critics disagreed with Khomeini in a respectful manner, not wanting to rouse the wrath of radical fundamentalists. Muhammad Hussam ad-Din, a theologian at Al-Azhar, Egypt's leading religious institution, decried the non-legal quality of Khomeini's act. "Blood must not be shed except after a trial, [when the accused has been] given a chance to defend himself and repent."[13] The head of Azhar's Fatwa Council, 'Abdallah al-Mushidd, rejected Khomeini's call to assassination: "We must try the author in a legal fashion for Islam does not accept killing as a legal instrument."[14] Or, another Azhar figure: "Killing someone is not that easy. There are laws to be implemented."[15]

In far off Senegal, the so-called Ayatollah of Kaolack, Ahmed Khalifa Niasse, condemned the edict, in part because Rushdie had not been properly tried, in part because he lived in a country not ruled by Muslims.[16] The Islamic Jurisprudence Academy in Mecca urged that Rushdie be tried and, if found guilty, be given a chance to repent. Even some Shi'is kept cool. Ayatollah Mehdi Ruhani, head of the Shi'i community in Europe and Khomeini's cousin, criticized Khomeini for acting too quickly. Khomeini "has respected neither international law nor that of Islam."[17] Ruhani pointed out that Islamic law cannot be implemented when it interferes with the sovereignty of a foreign state.

For the most part, the Iranian leaders suffered these taunts in silence. One ayatollah, Mohammed Emami Kashani, made a game effort at a defense. He held that Rushdie's sacrilege was so gross and obvious that a trial was not necessary. To justify this position, Kashani referred to the incidents in the Prophet Muhammad's life when he ordered the execution, without trial, of poets who lampooned him.

Indeed, Islamic tradition records at least three cases of poets who opposed Muhammad having been assassinated under his orders. A Muslim killed 'Asma' bint Marwan by driving a sword through her as she slept in her house, surrounded by her children, with the youngest of them lying in her arms. Likewise, Abu Afak was murdered in his sleep. The third of them, Ka'b ibn al-Ashraf, was lured out of his compound by his own foster-brother, who had enrolled him in a mock conspiracy against Muhammad. Once on the street, five men jumped Ka'b and killed him. The murderers cut off his head, carried it triumphantly to the prophet, and flung it at his feet.

Despite these precedents, Kashani's was a singularly weak defense, and for two reasons. Muslims have always recognized that the prophet engaged in a variety of activities that were his prerogative alone, and not available to the Muslim community generally. To take one obvious example: the prophet married twelve women, but Muslim men are permitted but four. The same exceptionalism applies to the prophet's approval of the assassination of hostile poets. Second, Muhammad acted before Islamic law had been elaborated and systematized, so he had to trust his own judgment. Over the course of nearly fourteen centuries, however, a vast corpus of laws was developed to deal with the whole range of human problems, from menstruation to commercial contracts. The majesty of Islamic law lies in its universal applicability and its attention to detail—aspects which Khomeini brazenly and willfully disregarded in pronouncing his edict.

But no matter how valid these Muslim criticisms of Khomeini, they concerned differences of procedure, not of substance. They implied that the *fatwa* would be acceptable if it adhered more scrupulously to the routines of Islamic law. To non-Muslims, these intra-Muslim disputes appeared merely legalistic, for both sides agreed that Rushdie had to die, and the only question was whether his death should precede or follow a trial. The Western view of this dispute was summarized by a cartoon in *Le Monde* showing Khomeini raising his arm to signal three mullahs to shoot at Salman Rushdie, who is tied to a stake (an oversized quill). Just as Khomeini is about to give the go-ahead, a figure whispers to him, "Er, the stake does not meet regulations."

Only one Muslim religious leader stood up for free speech. Jalal Ganje'i, a dissident ayatollah based in Europe and associated with the Mojahedin-e Khalq, the main Iranian opposition group, held that "there is nothing in Islamic precepts or laws which calls for the killing of a person only because he expressed his own ideas." Ganje'i called Khomeini "not a Muslim" and appealed to foreign states to go beyond withdrawing their heads of mission from Tehran, and to break off diplomatic ties with Iran to isolate that regime.[18]

Why Khomeini Took This Step

Why did Khomeini turn *The Satanic Verses* into an international incident? If the book is not unprecedented in its skeptical view of Muhammad, and Rushdie is only one of many apostates, why make this the centerpiece of Iranian foreign policy?

Critics vs. Supporters. Curiously, critics and supporters of the ayatollah offered almost diametrically opposed motivations for the ayatollah's action. Critics were nearly unanimous in seeing it primarily in political terms. Former Iranian President Abolhassan Bani-Sadr characterized the event as "a political affair and not a religious one,"[19] with which Mas'ud Rajavi of the Mojahedin-e Khalq agreed.

Some critics emphasized domestic political tensions in Iran. Amir Taheri saw controversy over *The Satanic Verses* as "an issue likely to stir the imagination of the poor and illiterate masses."[20] Harvey Morris considered it a "revolutionary *coup de théâtre*" intended to replace the Iraq-Iran war as a focus of national unity.[21] Alireza Jaffarzadeh of the Mojahedin-e Khalq argued that Khomeini took "this suicidal action out of desperation. The crisis he has created is the only thing that is keeping him in power."[22] That was also the Soviet view ("The commotion over this book is a pretext used in the struggle to consolidate power within the country")[23] as well as of officials in the Bush adminstration.

Others saw the controversy mostly in terms of foreign policy. Youssef M. Ibrahim explained it as Khomeini's bid "to reassert his role as spokesman and protector of Islamic causes."[24] *The Wall Street Journal* editorial writers stressed that the ayatollah's "real enemy is not *Satanic Verses* but the old Great Satan itself— America, whose influence today hangs in the balance in such strategically important countries as Pakistan and Afghanistan."[25] William Waldegrave of the British Foreign Office blamed the incident on "radical elements in Iran, which do not want their country to have normal relations with the West and the Gulf states."[26] Not content with one explanation, John Pearson of *Business Week* came up with two: it was a way "to head off a push by pragmatists" to end Iran's diplomatic isolation, and it was Khomeini's method "to whip up a new wave of fanaticism."[27]

Supporters of the ayatollah saw his move very differently, as a primarily religious response to a religious offense. They believed the book was reason enough in itself to call for Rushdie's death, and did not feel compelled to find ulterior motives. The Iranian *chargé d'affaires* in London stated unequivocally that Khomeini saw the punishment of Rushdie as "much more important than relations between two countries."[28] The top Iranian diplomat in Cyprus told a local audience that "the verdict issued by the Iranian leader is a purely religious one and based on religious considerations."[29] An Iranian editorialist explained that Khomeini's verdict of a death sentence "is not a political issue. It is simply a religious edict."[30] Rafsanjani deemed the *fatwa* "a religious edict," nothing more.[31]

In brief, while nearly all critics saw Khomeini's act as a political ploy, nearly all supporters interpreted it as an act of religious piety. This contrast offers a suggestive insight. Critics analyzed the event in terms of political gain for the Iranian leader; supporters explained it as an emotional response to a blasphemy. The one perceived gain; the other defense. Which side is correct?

The political argument rests on two main points: the timing and method of Khomeini's action. *The Satanic Verses* appeared in September 1988, but Khomeini responded to it only five months later—and three months after the book had been reviewed in the Iranian press. For those advocating a political interpretation, the timing is no accident; Khomeini chose the precise moment to intervene when months of spadework by Iranian diplomats (following the cease-fire with Iraq) to improve relations with the outside world was about to pay off. As for methods, had Khomeini really wanted to have Rushdie murdered, nothing would have been easier than to have quietly dispatched a terrorist squad. Broadcasting his intentions allowed Rushdie to take cover, so Khomeini's real goal must not have been the elimination of Rushdie but something quite different.

Convincing as they appear, both these points can be readily explained. On the matter of timing: Khomeini did not respond to *The Satanic Verses* earlier because he had not heard of the book's existence until the riots which took place in Islamabad on February 12. As for a public edict rather than a discreet suicide squad, the explanation lies in Khomeini's modus operandi. When he considered someone an enemy—the shah, Jimmy Carter, Saddam Husayn—he attacked them through intensely personal public denunciations. Clandestine methods have their utility, to be sure, but public figures required denunciation as well as death. It is plainly inconceivable that Khomeini would abandon so heinous a criminal as Rushdie to the anonymity of Iranian hit squads.

Significantly, Khomeini did not assign the duty of killing Rushdie to the Iranian government but relied on the media to carry his words to the ears of potential assassins. This had two main implications: the duty to kill Rushdie transcended Iranian state interest; and all who wrote or commented on the edict, even critically, were made potential accomplices to Khomeini's crime.

Religious Motives. The weakness of the political case is matched by the strength of the case for religious motives. Prima facie, there is strong evidence to accept the verdict of Khomeini's supporters. When all who are horrified by the book say their own motives stem from religious sentiments, their unanimity carries considerable weight. Equipped with the same information as Khomeini, they consistently respond as he did. Surely they have a keener access to the ayatollah's thinking than do jaded political analysts, most of whom are entirely impervious to the power of faith.

Second, what about the many Muslims in Great Britain, South Africa, Pakistan and India who took to the streets before Khomeini spoke up? In the United States, the publisher received 100,000 letters of protest before Khomeini's edict (or even the book's publication). Such activities had no connection to the struggles of Iranian political life and cannot be attributed to tensions within Iran. It was ordinary Muslims, not the politicians, who made the book an issue. The cause against Rushdie began as a populist one, with the leaders joining in only later. Of course, it is possible to dredge up a political explanation for each country where disturbances occurred—a revolt against oppression in Britain, Rajiv Gandhi's electoral calculations in India, the frustration of the fundamentalist Muslims in Pakistan—but the sheer multiplicity of this argument renders it unpersuasive.

Third, the sequence of events on the night of February 13 precludes the possibility of Khomeini's being influenced by his politically-motivated advisers. A debate between pragmatists and extremists could not have taken place for logistical reasons. While some accounts tell of a crucial meeting at which "two of the key figures in Tehran's faction-ridden government sought to influence Khomeini,"[32] there was, in fact, no time for such a meeting. Khomeini watched television, saw Muslims being martyred in Pakistan, called his secretary, and dictated the edict. Skirmishing factions simply lacked the time to battle for Khomeini's soul.

Fourth, the argument that Khomeini sought a way to weaken the people he later castigated as liberals, or to impede relations with the West makes no sense. Khomeini alone decided the Iranian government's major policy orientation. Should he have chosen to rupture relations with the West, he could have done so by fiat, as he had done before. He had no need to place a bounty on a novelist's head to enforce his views. By the same token, Khomeini had the ultimate voice in deciding between the competing factions in Iran; a politician in his position of authority did not have to resort to tricks to get his way.

As for the idea that Khomeini sought to whip up fervor in Iran by attacking Rushdie, this too is implausible. After exactly a decade's worth of Islamic revolutionary life, with all its travails— the imposition of a radical new order accompanied by much violence and instability, eight years of brutal war, a steady economic decline—he could hardly think that Iranians would drop their many immediate concerns in the excitement over a magical realist novel published thousands of miles away in a language very few of them understood.

Fifth, the *fatwa* closely conforms to Khomeini's ideology. Like other leaders with a revolutionary message, he despised state boundaries. He was the self-appointed guardian of Islamic interests, not just Iranian ones, and so too was his regime. The Iranians regularly refused to allow their interests to determine their international posture. "Economic and diplomatic ties are not the only standard by which Iran maintains ties with foreign countries. Creating an opportunity for Muslims to comply freely with Islamic principles and act in accordance with the provisions of Islam is far more important than economic relations."[33] This was no idle theory but an operational tenet. The Iranians felt they had a revolutionary right to involve themselves wherever Islam was endangered; the usual restrictions did not apply to them. Indeed, they openly declared that such terms as "internal" affairs and "freedom of expression" were used as "a pretext for implementing evil plots against Muslims and the oppressed people of the world."[34] The attack on Rushdie and his publishers fit this much larger context. Justifying its involvement against

The Satanic Verses, the Foreign Ministry of Iran portrayed itself as "the executor and supporter of Islam's foreign policy against blasphemy."[35]

Sixth, non-fundamentalists tend to miss the fact that, for all their belligerent activities, fundamentalist Muslims feel beseiged and defensive. In the words of a thoughtful analyst, Emmanuel Sivan, the "Islamic revival—while activist and militant—is thus essentially defensive; a sort of holding operation against modernity. And though it has no doubt a sharp political edge, it is primarily a cultural phenomenon."[36] Indeed, as chapter 7 shows, Khomeini's edict should properly be seen more in terms of its cultural defensiveness than its political offensiveness.

Seventh, the emphasis on a political motivation points to a persistent problem in Western analyses of Khomeini: the unwillingness to take his assertions at face value. The received wisdom is extremely reluctant to accept that a Hitler or a Khomeini really intends to apply the outlandish ideas he articulates. In 1978, as Iranians and others tried to foresee what kind of government he would impose in Iran, Khomeini's writings tended to be ignored for the simple reason that they were eccentric. The notion of mullahs running the show was too strange to believe; along with James Bill, an American specialist on Iran, many analysts overlooked the evidence and concluded that the religious leaders "would never participate directly in the formal governmental structure."[37] In fact, of course, they have dominated the state apparatus for over a decade.

Bill was hardly alone in this error. Indeed, as two Washington authors, Michael Ledeen and William Lewis, explain, this blindness to Khomeini's unorthodox thinking afflicted Iranians no less than foreigners:

Since the National Fronters [in Iran] and their many American friends and supporters in the bureaucracy and the academy had expected Khomeini to abstain from political activity once the shah had been overthrown, they were systematically outmaneuvered, surprised, and finally humiliated by the ayatollah. True modernists all, they could not seriously entertain the notion that the Iranian "revolution" would prove to be a regression to a medieval model.[38]

Gary Sick, formerly of the National Security Council staff, confirms that "Khomeini's ideas were no secret, and it is no use to complain after the fact that politicians and intellectuals inside and outside Iran refused to take them seriously."[39]

One would think that the lessons of 1978-79 would have convinced Khomeini-watchers not to try to interpret this man as though he were a British MP or an American cabinet officer. But the lessons have not sunk in. Reducing Khomeini's *fatwa* to politics-as-usual indicated that, once again, they ignored the true originality of Khomeini's thinking. In the process, of course, they also overlooked its power.

Eighth, Westerners are too reluctant to take religion—any religion—seriously. In part, this is due to secularization, the "process whereby religious thinking, practice, and institutions lose social significance."[40] Secularization makes it hard to believe that anyone would allow religious considerations actually to determine his actions—there must be some other motive. In part, it is due to the legacy of modernization theory, which holds that the whole world is developing in the West's shadow, and therefore must be secularizing. In part, it is due to the philosophic doctrine of materialism, which places great stress on material conditions, especially economic ones, while scorning the role of ideas, seeing these as mere cover for economic interests. Together, secularism, modernization theory, and materialism create a bias against taking any religion seriously, including Islam.

Many Precedents. Finally, the attack on Rushdie and his publishers squares with a host of other actions taken by Khomeini. Three stand out.

Forty-five years earlier, when Khomeini was an obscure mullah, he took almost exactly the same step against an author. In a 1944 book, *The Exposure of Secrets*, Khomeini wrote an indirect polemic against Ahmed Kasravi, a prominent writer whose anti-clerical views (Shi'ism, he said, is a "perversion whose origin lay neither in ethics nor in theological issues, but in a sordid struggle for power")[41] had gained a significant following in Iran. Without explicitly naming Kasravi, Khomeini addressed him in highly abusive language:

> The commandments of Islam do not provide a cure for your diseases, which are: the worship of lust, faithlessness, lying compulsively, and charlatanism. The law of Islam declares that your blood can be shed with impunity, and that your thieving hand can be cut off.[42]

With this blast, Khomeini pronounced Kasravi *mahdurr ad-damm*, permitting a Muslim to execute him without fear of punishment. The pamphlet was read by Mohammed Nawab-Safavi, who went on to found a terrorist group, the Fedayin-e Islam. In 1946, Kasravi was its very first target. Inspired by the Khomeini tract, Sayyed Husayn Emami and three others attacked Kasravi with knives, murdering him in his office in front of a half dozen witnesses. Though Khomeini's response to the execution is not known, his close friend, Sheikh Sadeq Khalkhali (known decades later in the West as the "hanging judge"), remembered the moment as "the most beautiful day in my life."[43]

A second incident occurred just two weeks before the *fatwa* against Rushdie and his publishers, when Khomeini passed an almost identical sentence on the producers of Radio Tehran. On January 28, 1989, the radio aired a program, "Model for the Muslim Woman," in which an Iranian woman explained that she did not consider Fatima, the daughter of the Prophet Muhammad, to be a suitable model for herself. Instead, she preferred a more up-to-date exemplar, the heroine of a Japanese soap opera. Outraged, the ayatollah called the interview "un-Islamic" and wrote the director of Iranian broadcasting, telling him that if the insult was deliberate, the offending parties would "undoubtedly" be condemned to death; if it were to happen again, administrators of the radio would also be "severely punished." A mere three days later, a court sentenced one of the producers to five years in jail, two others to four years each and fifty lashes. The court made clear that this relative leniency was due to an "absence of malicious intent" on their part; otherwise, all of them would have been sentenced to death.[44] The sentence was later rescinded by Iran's chief justice, Musavi Ardebili, thanks in part to the intercession by Khomeini's daughter, Zahra Mustafavi.

A third incident took place a few weeks later after the Rushdie *fatwa*, when Tehran intruded into a Turkish controversy concerning pious female university students who wished to wear a modesty headscarf (called *örtü*) over their hair. After a prolonged dispute, the courts on March 7 prohibited this form of dress. The Khomeini government vehemently disapproved. Iranian newspaper editorials attacked Ankara and small radio transmitters reaching eastern Anatolia rallied protests action against the court's decision. No less than one hundred and fifty Iranian parliamentarians signed a letter condemning Ankara's policy and called for a reconsideration of relations with Turkey, "in accordance with that country's attitude to Islam and Muslims."[45] In response, the president of the Turkish Grand National Assembly said he was "amazed and saddened"[46] at the Iranian action, and the media echoed his protests. But their indignation fell on deaf ears. Indeed, the Iranians threatened to reduce trade with Turkey from $1 billion a year to $400 million, or even less. This threat induced the Turks to withdraw their ambassador from Tehran and the Iranians responded in like fashion. There is no way to interpret this Iranian response as an act calculated for political gain, either domestic or foreign. It reflected instead the fact that Islamic issues did often receive first priority in the Tehran of 1989.

In brief, those (such as George Black) who argue that Khomeini "has used Rushdie as a target of convenience," are wrong. The answer is very clear: "The Ayatollah does not want to use Rushdie; he wants to kill him. We must respect the man's sincerity."[47] But the question remains, why did Muslims generally and Khomeini in particular respond so strongly to *The Satanic Verses*? The answer to this question lies partially in the robust importance of taboo in Muslim life and partially with the fundamentalist Muslim understanding of fiction.

NOTES

[1]The following discussion derives largely from Nu'man 'Abd ar-Razzaq as-Samarra'i, *Ahkam al-Murtadd fi'sh-Shari'a al-Islamiya: Dirasa Muqarina*, 2d edition (Riyadh: Dar al-'Ulum, 1403/1983); Rudolph Peters and Gert J.J. de Vries, "Apostasy in Islam," *Die Welt des Islams* 17 (1976-77): 1-25; and Joel L. Kramer, "Apostates, Rebels and Brigands," in Joel L. Kraemer and Ilai Ayalon, eds., *Religion and Government in the World of Islam* (Tel Aviv: Tel Aviv University, 1984), pp. 34-73. The points presented in this discussion are necessarily very general, for Islamic law has changed over the centuries; it is interpreted by five main law schools and several minor ones; and it has much altered in modern times.

[2]*Keyhan*, March 5, 1989; Islamic Revolution News Agency, February 14, 1989.

[3]*L'Express*, March 17, 1989.

[4]Ameena Meer, "Interview: Salman Rushdie," *Bomb*, Spring 1989, p. 36; *Far Eastern Economic Review*, March 2, 1989.

[5]Muhammad 'Abd as-Salam Faraj, *Al-Farida al-Gha'iba*. Trans. Johannes J.G. Jansen, *The Neglected Duty: The Creed of Sadat's Assassins and Islamic Resurgence in the Middle East* (New York: Macmillan, 1986), pp. 169-75.

[6]*Fatwa* of June 25, 1983 issued by Mufti Sa'd ad-Din al-'Alami. Quoted in Annie Laurent, "Syrie-Liban: Les faux frères jumeaux," *Politique Étrangère* 48 (1983): 598; and Charles Saint-Prot, *Les Mystères syriens: La Politique au Proche-Orient de 1970 à 1984* (Paris: Albin Michel, 1984), p. 215. See also *Der Spiegel*, July 4, 1983 and Radio Jerusalem, June 26, 1983.

[7]*Kayhan International*, March 26, 1989.

[8]"An Interview with Salman Rushdie," *Scripsi*, August 1985, p. 125.

[9]Martin Kramer, "The Moral Logic of Hizballah," Dayan Center Occasional Paper no. 101, 1987.

[10]*Keyhan*, January 8, 1988.

[11]Sepehr Zabih, *Iran Since the Revolution* (Baltimore: Johns Hopkins University Press, 1982), p. 206.

[12]*The Independent*, February 22, 1989.

[13]*Newsweek*, February 27, 1989.

[14]"Ab'ad Harb al-Kitab," *Al-Majalla*, March 1, 1989.

[15]*The New York Times*, February 18, 1989.

[16]*Le Monde*, March 4, 1989.

[17]*Le Nouvel Observateur*, February 23, 1989.

[18]Associazione Nazionale Stampa Associata, February 22, 1989; Deutsche Presse Agentur, February 23, 1989; *Iran Liberation*, February 27, 1989.

[19]*The New York Times*, February 22, 1989.

[20]*The Philadelphia Inquirer*, February 16, 1989.

[21]*The Independent*, February 16, 1989.

[22]*The Washington Post*, February 24, 1989.

[23]Radio Peace and Progress, February 24, 1989.

[24]*The New York Times*, February 16, 1989.

[25]*The Wall Street Journal*, February 22, 1989.

[26]*Al-Qabas*, March 22, 1989.

[27]*Business Week*, March 6, 1989.

[28]Islamic Revolution News Agency, February 16, 1989.

[29]*Cyprus Mail*, February 19, 1989.

[30]*Keyhan*, May 16, 1989.

[31]Tehran Television, June 8, 1989.

[32]*The Observer*, February 26, 1989.

[33]Tehran International Radio, March 23, 1989.

[34]*Kayhan International*, March 26, 1989.

[35]Islamic Revolution News Agency, March 7, 1989.

[36]Emmanuel Sivan, *Radical Islam: Medieval Theology and Modern Politics* (New Haven: Yale University Press, 1985), p. 3.

[37]James Bill, "Iran and the Crisis of '78," *Foreign Affairs*, Winter [1978/79], p. 336.

[38]Michael Ledeen and William Lewis, *Debacle: The American Failure in Iran* (New York: Alfred A. Knopf, 1981), p. 196. Ledeen and Lewis err in seeing Khomeini's model as medieval, but this does not affect the point they are making.

[39]Gary Sick, *All Fall Down: America's Tragic Encounter with Iran* (New York: Random House, 1985), p. 159.

[40]Ernest Krausz, "Religion and Secularization: A Matter of Definitions," *Social Compass* 18 (1971-72): 212. Krausz defines religion as "an institutional aspect of society based on beliefs in a superhuman or supernatural realm" (p. 211).

[41]*Payman*, May 1942, pp. 546-60, quoted in Ervand Abrahamian, "Kasravi: The Integrative Nationalist of Iran," in Elie Kedourie and Sylvia G. Haim, eds., *Towards a Modern Iran: Studies in Thought, Politics and Society* (London: Frank Cass, 1980), p. 113.

[42]Ruhollah Khomeini, *Kashf al-Asrar* (Tehran: n.p., 1979), p. 232.

[43]*Payam Shahid*, 24 (1980), quoted in Amir Taheri, *Holy Terror: Inside the World of Islamic Terrorism* (Washington, D.C.: Adler & Adler, 1987), p. 65.

[44]Islamic Revolution News Agency, January 30, 31, 1989.

[45]Radio Tehran, March 20, 1989.

[46]*Hurriyet*, March 21, 1989.

[47]George Black, "Shame," *The Nation*, March 13, 1989; The Editors, "Two Cheers for Blasphemy," *The New Republic*, March 13, 1989.

6.

WHY FUNDAMENTALIST MUSLIMS PICKED ON RUSHDIE

Fundamentalist Sensitivities

Not only are Muslims very touchy about perceived disparagements of their religion, but they tend to look at fictional works in a singularly literal way. Together, these sensitivies help explain the vehemence of the reaction to *The Satanic Verses*.

Taboo. Fundamentalist Muslims monitor closely the portrayal of their religion in the Western media. Mobs stoned the U.S. Embassy in Pakistan in 1962 on the basis of a rumor that an American-Italian movie company planned to produce a film about the Prophet Muhammad. In 1977, a group of American-born black Muslims occupied three buildings in Washington and took more than a hundred hostages in an effort, among other things, to stop a reverential movie they had not seen, *Muhammad, Messenger of God*. The Saudi government once protested to CBS Television that a dog was named Muhammad on the show *Hawaii Five-0*. More basically, Muslims tend to be shocked by the very notion of making the Prophet Muhammad a character in a novel.

Taboos pertaining to Islam are vibrantly alive in all countries with substantial Muslim populations (with the single exception of

Albania). Lapsed Muslims cannot express their views, much less are non-Muslims allowed to reveal antagonistic feelings about Islam. The response to anything which might deride Islam stems from a set of constraints so strong, it is almost impossible to convey the intensity of feeling to a Westerner.

Even after the offensive nature of Rushdie's novel is explained to them, Europeans and Americans still find the book no more than mildly provocative. Roger Rosenblatt expressed a common mystification when he observed that it is not clear, "to non-believers at least, what exactly is offensive about the book to Moslems."[1] Paul Gray put it even more strongly in a review of the book; despite what is being said about *The Satanic Verses* containing a blasphemous portrait of the Prophet Muhammad and insulting Islam, "the novel does nothing of the sort.... If Muhammad himself was willing to admit that he had been deceived, it is difficult to see why a tangential, fictional version of this long-ago event should cause such contemporary fury."[2] Philippe Sollers asked readers of *Le Monde*: "You, have you read this novel, *Satanic*? Frankly, does it strike you as evil? Even though we have [the Marquis de] Sade available in paperback?"[3] Many readers noted that the offending passages are not only fictional but the deliria of a paranoid schizophrenic.

Attempts by Muslims to convey the depth of their feelings simply confirmed this gulf. A notice placed in the British newspapers by the Birmingham Central Mosque compared Rushdie's blasphemy to "Christ using four letter words; Matthew and Mark indulging in indecencies and molesting children; Moses as a racist and lecherous person." One Muslim suggested that what Rushdie did is like "taking Mary and saying she is a harlot."[4] Another compared it to a book abusing the queen of England. Even Ali A. Mazrui, the sophisticated left-wing professor at the University of Michigan, tried to find a Christian analogy to the Mahound tale; he came up with the Virgin Mary portrayed as a prostitute, Jesus "as the son of one of her sexual clients," the twelve apostles as Jesus' homosexual lovers, and the Last Supper as an orgy.[5]

But all these analogies with Christianity missed the mark
entirely. Europeans and Americans are too accustomed to attacks
on organized religion to respond with outrage, for taboo and
sacrilege are virtually dead in the West. Blasphemy is an old
story, and can no longer shock, for it is too much a part of daily
life. Indeed, vituperation against religion is a major underlying
theme of Western art through the twentieth century. Commenting
on the death threat against Salman Rushdie, the American
novelist John Updike noted that "it is perhaps in the nature of
modern art to be offensive.... In this century if we are not
willing to risk giving offense, we have no claim to the title of
artists."[6]

True, the portrayal of Jesus' sexual longings in Martin Scorsese's *The Last Temptation of Christ* did cause the movie to
provoke a small furor in 1988, but the issue lacked the fury and
the venom of *The Satanic Verses* incident. Christians who
picketed movie theaters did so more out of a sense of moral
indignation and obligation than political outrage; they knew that
Monty Python's *Life of Brian* had covered the same territory
earlier and that future films would cover it again. Further, *The
Last Temptation of Christ* was highly unusual, if not unique, in
the attention it provoked. Most blasphemies enter the market
without fanfare. For example, Joseph Heller's *God Knows*
aroused no special outrage, even though it turned several Biblical
stories into pornographic fare. The title derives from the following passage, spoken in the novel by King David:

> I've led a full, long life, haven't I? You can look it up. Samuel I
> and II. Kings. Chronicles also, but that's a prissy whitewash in
> which the juiciest parts of my life are discarded as unimportant or
> unworthy. Therefore, I hate Chronicles. In Chronicles I am a pious
> bore.... God knows I fucked and fought plenty and had a rousing
> good time doing both.[7]

Heller's recounting of Biblical tales attracted no special notice
other than a few, half-hearted protests.

If any writing has shock value in the West, the subject matter has a more mundane quality. Two American examples come to mind: suggesting that blacks are genetically less intelligent than whites or making fun of the Jewish holocaust. But even these topics get treated without gaining much attention. Studies explaining lower I.Q. scores among blacks as the result of alleged lower capabilities raised an initial controversy, then became part of the academic literature. George Steiner's novel *The Portage to San Cristóbal of A.H.* provides a fictive apology for Adolf Hitler. Several passages in the book seem to be specifically designed to outrage. One of these is Hitler's portrayal of himself as the Jewish messiah.

> Did Herzl create Israel or did I?... Perhaps I *am* the Messiah, the true Messiah, the new Sabbatai whose infamous deeds were allowed by God in order to bring His people home.... Should you not honor me who have made you into men of war, who have made of the long, vacuous daydream of Zion a reality? Should you not be a comfort to my old age?[8]

Such is the Western inability to be shocked—even this sort of writing passed with hardly any notice.

Perhaps the most telling case of all concerns *The Protocols of the Elders of Zion*, a fabrication of the Russian secret police which is not only expressly intended to harm Jews, but one which has repeatedly done so over the past century. The Nazis, for example, derived many of their theories from *The Protocols*. Despite this record, the book is freely available both in the West and in the Muslim countries. Indeed, it has become a major influence among Muslims in recent decades, having been sponsored by several governments: the Egyptian one used to distribute it, those of Saudi Arabia and Iran still do. (Tehran's enthusiastic efforts to spread this libelous document cast heavy doubts on statements by Iranians about their respect for the religious sensibilities of others.) The book continues to circulate, and there are few serious efforts to have it banned. For anyone accustomed to freedom of speech at this level, Rushdie's novel seems child's play.

It sometimes seems that, just as high standards of living lead to a birth dearth, so freedom of speech lessens the power of writing and speech. In the Muslim world, as in the Soviet bloc, where repression is common, books have a power rarely felt in the West. In part this has to do with taboos. In part too, it reflects the rarity, and therefore the venerated quality, of the written word. By contrast, books in the West are more common, more like a commodity which is marketed and promoted like other commercial goods. "One best seller follows the other and all get lost in an ocean of paper."[9] Rushdie himself understood exactly the power of his work.

> Because it's still a predominantly illiterate culture [in India and Pakistan] the respect for the written word is enormous. And therefore the influence of the written word is enormous that it really is not in the West anymore. Writers really do make trouble. When they speak, people listen. People are constantly asking me to prophesy.[10]

The Nature of Fiction. The fundamentalist Muslim reaction to *The Satanic Verses* also highlighted some unusual notions about the nature of fiction. Two points deserve notice.

First, many Muslim critics complained that Rushdie had not told the truth, as though his highly elaborated account was intended exactly to recapitulate Islamic history. Mir Husayn Musavi, the prime minister of Iran, lambasted the book as "neither a critical appraisal nor a piece of historical research."[11] Muhammad Husayn Fadlallah, the Khomeini of Lebanon, complained that Rushdie did not rely on "scientific and logical arguments."[12] Shaykh Ahmad Kaftaru, mufti of the Syrian Arab Republic, applied Soviet-style criteria to *The Satanic Verses*: "The novel is worthy of neither reading nor respect due to its lack of scientific, accurate or objective methods of research."[13] The religious affairs director in the Turkish government, Mustafa Sait

Yazıcıoğlu condemned the book for "unfounded lies" and not being "serious or scientific."[14] The grand imam of Al-Azhar Mosque in Cairo called on Muslims to write a book answering Rushdie and to "refute his lies."[15] Likewise, Fahmy Huwayda, an Egyptian specialist on Iran, attacked the book for its many lies.[16] The Kuwaiti government found Rushdie guilty of veering off from "objectivity and scientific research"[17]—another peculiar accusation against a novel. Even the Libyan ambassador to the United Nations Commission on Human Rights turned literary critic, castigating Rushdie ("the friend of the devil") for writing what is "not at all an objective or scientific opinion."

Muslims living in the United States also missed the point. Sayed M. Syeed, secretary general of the Association of Muslim Social Scientists, railed against the novel by calling it "a total distortion of historical facts."[18] Syed N. Asad drew a distinction without a difference; the offending chapters, he said, "are not at all fictional. They are taken out of the Koran and other religious sources, and fictionalized."[19] These notions even spread to non-Muslims. Lord Shawcross assailed Rushdie for irresponsibility on the grounds that the book was written "not with any intention of contribution to scholarship."[20] Lord Jakobovits, the chief rabbi of Britain, condemned what he called the "falsification of established historical records."[21]

Rushdie answered his critics with his usual grand sense of purpose. "The book is being judged and misjudged by having the historical method applied to what is in fact an imaginative text. . . . To say that a work of fiction is basically a work of fact in disguise [whose aim] is to distort facts is wrong. The real purpose of fiction is not to distort facts but to explore human nature, to explore ideas on which the human race rests itself."[22] But Rushdie's rebuttals were to no avail, for he and his critics read *The Satanic Verses* with totally different criteria.

Second, the critics assumed that Rushdie personally subscribed to every word in his book. This explained their conflation of the author's characters with the author himself. The elusive, indirect quality of Rushdie's writing was reduced to the sentiments expressed by his protagonists. Though not entirely unjustified, for there is often a close correlation between the ideas of an author and the speech of his fictional characters, such literal-mindedness undermines the novelist's craft. To presume that novelists agree with every word in their works wreaks havoc with literature, condemning writers of the past and circumscribing those of the future. (Ironically, Rushdie himself falls into this trap, referring in *The Satanic Verses* to "the racist Shakespeare.") Further, an author can portray madness without being mad, or blasphemy without being blasphemous. Writers of fiction require the space to explore controversies, to experiment with novel thoughts, and therefore to write passages which are not their own thoughts, or with which they thoroughly disagree.

It makes no sense, therefore, to hold Rushdie personally to account for all the views in *The Satanic Verses*. This is what he protested against when he repeatedly complained about his words being taken out of context. Indeed, it is logically impossible, for Rushdie's characters argue and take up opposite viewpoints; how could he be held to account for all sides of a debate?

The source of this literal-minded understanding of the novel by Muslims may lie in the fact that they find the medium a new, and still a somewhat unfamiliar form. The notion of the literary imagination proceeding into the hypothetical, where context shapes no less than words, remains alien to many Muslims, and fundamentalists reject this approach in its entirety. They tend to see the very act of writing fiction as subversive, in part because it conjures an alternative reality into existence, challenging the one created by God. Thus, the reading of a novel in the Muslim Middle East tends to be more a programmatic experience than a literary one. This approach also harks back to the traditional sense that the written word must describe truth; storytelling in the bazaar is one thing, but a published and bound book is quite another. Finally, with censorship of political materials nearly universal in the region, fiction serves as an important mechanism for conveying protests against the established order. Accustomed to interpreting fiction in this light, Muslims read between

Rushdie's lines in ways the author, who enjoys full freedom of speech in Britain, may never have expected.

The Title

Very few of the Muslims who expressed outrage at *The Satanic Verses* had actually read the book. Those who did included a Beirut-based group, the Organization of Revolutionary Justice, which explained that its decision to kill Rushdie followed on having "attentively read *The Satanic Verses* and studied the case of Salman Rushdie."[23] Jalal Ganje'i, religious leader of the Iranian opposition group, Mojahedin-e Khalq, asserted "I have read most parts of *The Satanic Verses*."[24] Lukman Harun, vice-chairman of the Muhammadiyah organization in Indonesia, a fundamentalist group, startled a reporter by asking to borrow his copy of the banned book.[25]

But with these few exceptions, virtually all those who condemned the book—and in some cases lost their lives in this cause—lacked first-hand familiarity with it, or with excerpts of it, even in translation. Muslim critics, high and low, were not shy about admitting this ignorance. Benazir Bhutto explained, "Because I am a Muslim, I have not read it."[26] Parvez Akhtar of Bradford, England, told a reporter, "I haven't read the book and I don't want to."[27] Both of them had access to the book, even if others, due either to censorship or to ignorance of the English language, did not. The striking thing is that those who could read it chose not to.

This fact caused Rushdie paroxysms of frustration. "The thing that is most disturbing is that they are talking about a book that doesn't exist. The book that is worth killing people for and burning flags for is not the book that I wrote. The people who demonstrated in Pakistan and who were killed haven't actually read the book because it isn't on sale there."[28]

This lack of familiarity is one of the remarkable features of the protests against *The Satanic Verses*. It also provides a possible clue as to why this author and this book caused such a furor. Why did Muslims feel they did not have to read the book? Surely, it was not just a matter of distaste for the subject matter or an unwillingness to read hundreds of pages of magical realism. The reason may lie in the fact that Muslim protesters felt they knew enough already, namely that an author named Salman Rushdie living in Great Britain wrote a book called *The Satanic Verses.* Apparently, these three pieces of information alone sufficed to provoke a profound emotional reaction. How so?

The name Salman Rushdie tells a Muslim protester that the author is, or was born, a Muslim; by rights he should protect the reputation of the Prophet Muhammad, not mock it.

That Rushdie lives in England reinforces the first point. A Muslim in the West should stand by his religion with special determination. Behavior that might be tolerated in the heartlands of Islam appears treasonous in West Europe. Further, residence in London evokes a sense of unease among these Muslims; it suggests that Rushdie has in some way joined the Christian world, that his allegiances may have changed. In berating Rushdie, they are to some degree venting a fury at the power, the wealth and the secularism that prevails in the West. Rushdie's having abandoned his ancestral country, language, and way of life—except as material for his fiction—sits badly. Rushdie's living in Great Britain, when combined with the other factors, suggests a betrayal. Even Edward Said, an outspoken admirer of Rushdie and his defender against the ayatollah, allowed that this fact perturbed him: Why, he asked, "must a member of our culture join the legions of Orientalists in Orientalizing Islam so radically and unfairly?"[29]

Finally, the protesters knew the book's title. Without exception, they found it sacrilegious. Rushdie believed they should not:

> Even the novel's title has been termed blasphemous; but the phrase is not mine. It comes from al-Tabari, one of the canonic Islamic sources. Tabari writes...[that] Muhammad then received verses which accepted the three favorite Meccan goddesses as interces-

sionary agents. Meccans were delighted. Later, the Archangel Gabriel told Muhammad that these had been "Satanic verses," falsely inspired by the Devil in disguise and they were removed from the Koran.[30]

Rushdie's explanation of the title requires careful analysis, for it contains the elements of a colossal misunderstanding.

What Rushdie wrote about Tabari is correct—with one exception. The phrase "Satanic verses" itself does not come from Tabari. A look at Tabari's text reveals that he includes the word "Satan" in two phrases: "Satan threw [something] into his formulation, and these verses were revealed;" and "Satan caused to come upon his tongue."[31] The words "the Satanic verses" are not found in Tabari. Admittedly, what Tabari (and several other Muslim historians who cover this event) wrote was very close to "Satanic verses," but it was not identical to that phrase.

Further, Muslims know the two abrogated lines, "These are the exalted birds/And their intercession is desired indeed," not as the Satanic verses incident, but as the *gharaniq* incident. (*Gharaniq* is the word translated here as "birds.") In other words, *the phrase "Satanic verses" is unknown in Arabic* (as well as Persian, Turkish, and the other mother-languages of Muslims). Accordingly, when Muslims hear the phrase "Satanic verses," it does not register. Even those who have studied Muhammad's life in detail and are familiar with the *gharaniq* episode have no idea to what Rushdie is referring.

Where, then, does the phrase come from? From the orientalist tradition, the Western scholars who study Islam. The phrase was formulated in the West, and appears to have first been used in William Muir's pathbreaking 1861 book, *The Life of Mahomet*, where Muir refers in passing to "the two Satanic verses."[32] The 1936 English translation of Tor Andrae's study *Mohammed: The Man and His Faith* includes the term "Satanic lines."[33] But by far the most important use was by W. Montgomery Watt in his authoritative 1953 study, *Muhammad at Mecca*. Watt's ten-page analysis of the *gharaniq* issue is titled, "The Beginnings of Opposition; The 'Satanic Verses.'"* Watt also used this term in his book *Muhammad: Prophet and Statesman*,[34] a popularized abridgement of his two-volume study *Muhammad at Mecca* and *Muhammad at Medina*. Anyone in the West who has studied Islamic history in the last thirty-five years was bound to read Watt's studies of Muhammad, and so to have imbibed the phrase "Satanic verses."

Rushdie took the phrase for his title from Watt (or some other Western scholar of Islam). In so doing, he unwittingly adopted a part of the orientalist tradition, not a politic act for a Muslim, especially a lapsed one. Then, exacerbating his mistake, he told Muslims that he took the phrase from Tabari, that is, from the Islamic heritage. This transfer, obviously, did not sit well with pious Muslims. Syed Ali Ashraf tersely summed up their case against Rushdie: "He sides with the Orientalists."[35]

But that is far from the worst of Rushdie's trespasses. The real problem lies in the phrase "the Satanic verses" itself, for it has explosive implications when connected to the Qur'an. Detached from its orientalist reference, the title seems to imply that Muhammad received the whole of the Qur'an not from God, nor even that he made up its contents by himself, but that he received it from the devil. Translating the title into the languages spoken by Muslims makes this connection all the more explicit. Rushdie's title in Arabic is known as *Al-Ayat ash-Shaytaniya*; in Persian, as *Ayat-e Shetani*; in Turkish, *Şeytan Ayetleri*.† *Shaytan* is a cognate for "satan" and poses no problems. But, unlike "verses," which refers generically to any poetry or scripture, *ayat* refers specifically to "verses of the Qur'an." Back-translated literally into

---

*W. Montgomery Watt, *Muhammad at Mecca* (Oxford: At the Clarendon Press, 1953), pp. 100-109. Professor Watt explained (in a letter to the author, dated May 5, 1989) that his use of quotation marks around "The Satanic Verses" suggested that he "may not have been sure whether it was already an accepted descriptive." He subsequently (letter of August 15, 1989) noted that his use of the phrase may have come from Muir.

†On occasion, other words were used for "verses," such as the Arabic word *ash'ar*, meaning "poetry" (*Uktubir*, July 16, 1989).

English, these titles mean "The Qur'an's Satanic Verses." With just a touch of extrapolation, this can be understood to mean that "The Qur'anic Verses Were Written By Satan." Simplifying, this in turn becomes "The Qur'an Was Written By Satan," or just "The Satanic Qur'an."

Understanding the title as "The Satanic Qur'an" has two implications. First, the title itself becomes hideously blasphemous. Ali A. Mazrui called the title "perhaps the most fundamental blasphemy" in the novel,[36] and his view was widely shared. Second, Muslims assumed that Rushdie argued in his book that the entire Qur'an came from the devil—not just two abrogated verses. One religious leader, Abdelhamid Zbantout, made this understanding explicit: "I am indignant that someone could write that the prophet received the revelation from Satan, and not from Gabriel."[37] Mazrui held that "Rushdie's blasphemy does not lie in his saying that the Qur'an is the work of Muhammad. The blasphemy lies more in Rushdie's suggestion that it is the work of the Devil."[38] A British convert to Islam, Yaqub Zaki, spelled out this misreading even more clearly:

> Rushdie's use of the name of the devil responsible for the fraud is intended to indicate that the whole Koran is fraudulent and Muhammad a mean imposter; not a question of two verses spotted as such but all the 6,236 verses making up the entire book. In other words, the title is a *double entendre*.[39]

These assertions are wrong. The title is not a double entendre. Nowhere in the novel does Rushdie state or imply that the Qur'an came from the devil; he suggests Muhammad as the source of the Qur'an, and even that is unclear. But angry Muslims reading the title as "The Satanic Qur'an" missed these subtleties entirely in the heat of their outrage. Later, no one bothered to verify these false assumptions, so they became received truths endlessly repeated.

Herein lies probably the most direct cause of the furor: Muslims heard the title as "The Satanic Qur'an" and they found it unimaginably offensive. Other books had to be read to uncover the blasphemies; in this one, the outrage announced itself in gold relief letters on the cover. (And for those who looked closely, the Persian miniature on the dust cover, showing "Rustam Killing the White Demon," only confirmed an impression that the book primarily concerned Satan.) Add to this what Muslims heard about the inflammatory contents which dealt with such topics as the Qur'anic revelation and Muhammad's wives, which revived the extinct name of Mahound, and which portrayed God as a balding middle-aged man with dandruff, and the externals alone damned Rushdie so thoroughly it was no wonder no one felt a need to read the book.

A novelist selects a title on the basis of, among other things, its originality, concision, drama, topicality and memorability. Rushdie's choice of *The Satanic Verses* meets all these criteria. What the author did not realize was that, combined with his irreverent treatment of Muhammad and the Qur'an in the text, his title had an incendiary effect. More than anything else, this apparently innocent choice of title explains why so many Muslims responded with fury to what would otherwise have been just another novel. Had the book been titled something like "Shaandaar Café," "The New England," or even "The Angel Gabriel," there would probably have been no uproar.

The title also helps explain the conspiracy theories that grew up around *The Satanic Verses*, for as word of the novel got out, and then became a front-page story, many Muslims knew in their hearts that such a diabolical plot could only come from the West. They devised a whole scheme and filled in the details: Western leaders, consulting with their orientalist experts, had come up with the despicable book for a latter-day Crusader-style effort to sabotage Islam. Who else would know enough to devise so crafty an account of Satan delivering the Qur'an to Muhammad? The more that pious Muslims thought about it, the larger the issue grew, and the more impassioned their response. That the book was a work of fiction became increasingly irrelevant; what mattered was the challenge to the Islamic fundamentals, and the need to mount a defense. Such concerns were at the center of the Muslim response around the globe, including Iran.

NOTES

[1]Roger Rosenblatt, "Zealots With Fear in Their Eyes," *U.S. News & World Report*, February 27, 1989.

[2]Review of *The Satanic Verses*, *Time*, February 13, 1989.

[3]Philippe Sollers, "La littérature est-elle dangereuse?" *Le Monde*, March 3, 1989.

[4]Sayed M. Syeed, secretary general of the Association of Muslim Social Scientists, quoted in *The Philadelphia Inquirer*, February 14, 1989. Also Hasan Abdul-Hakim, a British convert, in *Time*, February 27, 1989.

[5]Ali A. Mazrui, *"The Satanic Verses" or a Satanic Novel? The Moral Dilemas of the Rushdie Affair* (Greenpoint, N.Y.: Committee of Muslim Scholars and Leaders of North America, 1989), p. 13.

[6]*The Wall Street Journal*, August 10, 1989.

[7]Joseph Heller, *God Knows* (New York: Knopf, 1984), p. 4.

[8]George Steiner, *The Portage to San Cristóbal of A.H.* (New York: Simon and Schuster, 1979), pp. 169-70. I am indebted for the Heller and Steiner references to Martin Peretz, "Embroiled Salman," *The New Republic*, March 20, 1989.

[9]Jean-Claude Lamy, "Affaire Rushdie: Les deux scandales," *Jeune Afrique*, March 15, 1989.

[10]"An Interview with Salman Rushdie," *Scripsi*, August 1985, p. 112.

[11]Radio Tehran, February 21, 1989.

[12]Agence France Presse, February 27, 1989.

[13]Syrian Arab News Agency, March 1, 1989.

[14]Radio Ankara, March 14, 1989.

[15]*Al-Ahram*, February 22, 1989.

[16]*Al-Watan*, February 28, 1989.

[17]Kuwaiti News Agency, March 9, 1989.

[18]*The Philadelphia Inquirer*, February 14, 1989.

[19]*The New York Times*, February 26, 1989. Even more perplexingly, Asad added: "Unfortunately, this book was not sufficiently examined by the Muslim reviewers before its publication."

[20]*The Times*, March 3, 1989.

[21]*The Times*, March 4, 1989.

[22]*Far Eastern Economic Review*, March 2, 1989.

[23]Agence France Presse, March 8, 1989.

[24]Radio Peace and Progress, February 24, 1989.

[25]*The Independent*, February 24, 1989.

[26]*Der Spiegel*, March 27, 1989, p. 165.

[27]*The Observer*, February 19, 1989.

[28]*The Guardian*, February 13, 1989.

[29]PEN American Center, *Freedom-to-Write Bulletin*, March 1989, p. 14; also, *The Observer*, February 26, 1989; *The Washington Post*, February 27, 1989. As Said is neither a Muslim nor an Indian, it is not readily apparent what he meant by "our culture."

[30]*The Observer*, January 22, 1989.

[31]At-Tabari, *Jami' al-Bayan fi Tafsir al-Qur'an* (Cairo, 1321/1903), vol. 17, p. 119;

idem, *Ta'rikh ar-Rusul wa'l-Muluk*, ed. M.J. de Goeje et al. (Leiden: E.J. Brill, 1879-1901), vol. 1, p. 1192.

[32]William Muir, *The Life of Mahomet* (London: Smith, Elder, 1861), vol. 2, p. 152.

[33]Tor Andrae, *Mohammed: The Man and His Faith*, trans. by Theophil Menzel (New York: Barnes and Noble, 1936), p. 24.

[34]London: Oxford University Press, 1961, pp. 60-63.

[35]*Impact International*, October 28, 1988.

[36]Mazrui, *"The Satanic Verses" or a Satanic Novel?* p. 6.

[37]*Le Nouvel Observateur*, February 23, 1989.

[38]Mazrui, *"The Satanic Verses" or a Satanic Novel?* p. 9.

[39]Yaqub Zaki, "Rushdie's Real Crime," *The Times*, February 28, 1989.

PART II: PROTESTS AND REPERCUSSIONS

7.

A GREAT CONSPIRACY AGAINST ISLAM

Why should a novel, even an incendiary one, matter so much? The answer lies in the intricate historical vision of fundamentalist Muslims, including Khomeini, and in their deep fears of the West.

Defending Islam

A powerful brew of religious animosity and political mistrust informs fundamentalist attitudes toward the West. They base their view of history on a syllogism: Muslims were once strong, but are now weak; when Muslims were strong, they lived fully by the precepts of their faith; therefore, Muslims are weak because they do not live up to these precepts. Were they to do so, it follows, they would regain the strength of centuries past. Were Muslims to live in strict adherence to the Qur'an and the laws of Islam, they would not only attain the just society, but also realize their inherent strength. The paramount goal of Khomeini and the Iranian leadership then, was and is to get Muslims to live fully in accordance with the sacred law of Islam, the Shari'a.

This is not an easy task, as both fourteen centuries of Islamic history and ten years of the Islamic Republic in Iran have amply shown. And while a non-fundamentalist might point to the

123

inherent difficulty of fulfilling the Shari'a's many precepts as an explanation for Muslim lapses, fundamentalist Muslims do not accept this reason. They look elsewhere for a culprit, and the seductive culture of the West is their favorite suspect by far. In the fundamentalist view, Western sirens for two centuries now have been luring Muslims away from strict adherence to the requirements of their faith. If Muslims are ever to regain the lead they enjoyed in the medieval period, they must engage in a self-conscious battle against Western civilization.

In the fundamentalists' view, the problem is compounded by the fact that the West (including the Soviet Union) benefits from Muslims being weak, for this allows it to plunder Muslim lands and hire Muslims for cheap labor. Therefore it actively pushes its customs and baubles on vulnerable Muslims. In justifying the Iranian response to *The Satanic Verses*, 'Ali Akbar Hashemi Rafsanjani, speaker of the Iranian parliament, explained the deep historical roots of this effort:

> From the day the Western colonialists harbored the intention of colonising the Islamic countries—or to be more precise, to demolish and create havoc in the Islamic world—they sensed that they must deal with something called Islam. They realized that as long as Islam is in force, their path will be a difficult one, or may be virtually closed off.
>
> Whoever is familiar with the history of colonialism and the Islamic world knows that whenever they wanted to get a foothold in a place, the first thing they did in order to clear their paths— whether overtly or covertly—was to undermine the people's genuine Islamic morals.

Confirming this thesis, Rafsanjani quoted an unnamed British foreign secretary telling Parliament, "So long as the Qur'an is revered by Muslims, we will not be able to consolidate a foothold among the Muslims."

Of course, the imperialists could not entirely do away with Islam, so they did the next best thing, which was to emasculate the religion, reducing the faith to empty ceremonies devoid of real content. By 1978, this ceremonial Islam (or "American-style Islam") prevailed at the state level everywhere in the world. But then, Rafsanjani continued, "with the advent of the Islamic Revolution, pure Islam entered the scene, and all they had done became undone."[1] The Islamic Republic of Iran asserted Muslim strength as no state had dared for two centuries, spurring "a wave of Islamization and Islamic awareness."[2] The Iranians threatened to lead all Muslims (and other oppressed peoples) against the hegemony of the great powers, what the Iranians call global arrogance. According to Tehran, the White House and Kremlin had to fight to beat back the danger coming from Iran; not to do so meant forfeiting their favorable positions. "All the West's plots," explained President Khamene'i, "are aimed at stopping Islam and the revolution from becoming a world model."[3]

In response, the Iranians fought back with all they had. The war between Islam and "international blasphemy"[4] took two main forms after 1979: military and cultural. First, according to Interior Minister 'Ali Akbar Mohtashemi,

> the United States and the Soviet Union used their entire military, political, and intelligence resources to fight Islam within Iran. They believed that if they could defeat Islam in Iran with military warfare...they could then easily confront the Muslims and the Islamic world."

Toward this end, the great powers put their lackey President Saddam Husayn of Iraq up to a war, which he obediently carried out. But military aggression failed against the hard rock of Islamic fervor. "After ten years," explains Mohtashemi, "the world gave up the hope of fighting Islam within Iran through military conflict."[5]

Stumped, the foes of Islam had to find a second battlefront. Toward this end, the governments "summoned all their devilish experts and mercenaries to draw up anew a strategy against Islam."[6] Specifically, Western specialists on Islam conducted research programs and held seminars "to plan a comprehensive way to confront Islam." At the conclusion of all these efforts, global arrogance hit on a plan—to conduct warfare (once again) on the level of culture. Rather than use military force, the West's "new war against Islam" sought to subvert the religion. With the conclusion of the Iraq-Iran war, the West began a campaign to subvert pure Islam and reinstate the ceremonial variety. The technique adopted was that of distortion, which would alienate Muslims from their faith and weaken their devotion to its laws.

Some Iranian analysts brought in another factor—the decline of the socialist ideal. Worried less about an aggressive Soviet Union, they said, "Western imperialism has positioned itself against the growing Islamic sentiments in the world."[7]

According to a commentary on Radio Tehran, the effort to undermine pure Islam entails two steps. First, "the aim is to weaken the Islamic faith among Muslims, thereby secularizing Muslim societies; this is then followed by an expansion of [Western] influence and the ultimate plundering of those societies' vital resources."[8] *The Satanic Verses* provided a keystone to the first goal, weakening the faith.

Not for a minute were the Iranian authorities fooled by the story put out that this book had been written by a single author pursuing the whimsies of his own imagination. In the course of their many speeches and interviews on the subject, they detailed the whole series of maneuvers which lay behind *The Satanic Verses*. According to Rafsanjani, Muslims who read this book, "will not see a mad Indian behind it; they will see Britain, Germany, France and the United States."[9] In his view, the intelligence services of these states knew what they were doing when they picked Rushdie to be the ostensible author. They chose

a person who seemingly comes from India and who apparently is separate from the Western world and who has a misleading name [i.e., a Muslim name].... All these advance royalties were given to that person. One can see that they appointed guards for him in advance because they knew what they were doing.... All this tells us of an organized and planned effort. It is not an ordinary work.... I believe there has not previously been such a well-planned act as this.[*]

The act in question required five years and $1.5 million. Rushdie's membership in the Royal Society of Literature proved that he enjoyed government patronage. British intelligence even managed to have *The Satanic Verses* introduced as "the book of the year" in Britain.[10] (This may refer obliquely to the fact that *The Satanic Verses* was shortlisted for the Whitbread and Booker prizes, and that Home Secretary Douglas Hurd sat on the committee judging the 1988 Whitbread Prize, which Rushdie won.)

Mystified by Rushdie's motives for writing scurrilous attacks on his own tradition, fundamentalists resorted to conspiracy theories. Reducing Rushdie from an independent writer to an agent of imperialism and Zionism had a double virtue for fundamentalists: it focused attention on their abiding enemies, and it assured fellow-believers that no Muslim on his own initiative would write so scurrilous a book as *The Satanic Verses*.

How, an outsider might ask, could this novel undo the achievements of the Islamic Revolution? By using distortion and scorn, which have the effect of alienating Muslims from their faith. It hurts to be "ridiculed by world arrogance,"[11] and the pain turns believers against Islam. According to the Iranians, efforts to defame Muhammad and tamper with the doctrines of Islam had been tried before (for example, in Iran during the shah's reign), but the Rushdie book exceeded all others in its audacity and its scope.

The European Community's solidarity with Great Britain confirmed the depth of the Western conspiracy. According to Rafsanjani, the decision to back Britain "is a clear sign which proves claims that the issue of this blasphemous book . . . is a plot

---

[*]Radio Tehran, February 15, 1989. This suspicion is not entirely without foundation, for the $850,000 advance royalties paid to Rushdie were extremely high. The explanation does not lie in state complicity but in the efforts of Rushdie's brash literary agent, Andrew Wylie.

designed by Western imperialism to fight true Islam."[12] "From the way all the Western leaders suddenly entered the scene in haste and fervor," Rafsanjani later added, "we can see that they wanted to have such an incident and they welcomed it."[13] It also showed, according to an analysis by the Central News Unit Research Group in Tehran, that the insult to the Prophet Muhammad was "not an action by an individual or something stemming from taste, but a collective and extensive effort to instigate a cultural confrontation with Islam."[14]

Because Muslims understood the plots brewing against them, they responded "with their rage."[15] Or, in the more colorful wording of Hizbullah, the fundamentalist Muslim party in Lebanon: "Global arrogance was behind a variety of plots to stain Islam's face," but the Muslims found a "tooth-smashing answer to all such imperialist-Zionist conspiracies."[16] Specifically, Muslim protests prevented *The Satanic Verses* from being made into a film. If not for the vigilance shown, President Khamene'i predicted, "in a few years you would have seen the sacred name of the prophet and allies and wives...being broadcast in the ugliest, most offensive, and distasteful manner." Thanks to the steadfastness of Muslim masses and Khomeini's courage, all those who participate in conspiracies against Islam know to "expect the danger of death from Muslims who have accepted the imam's edict."[17]

The Iranian leadership also portrayed *The Satanic Verses* incident as a major event in the reassertion of Islam. A newspaper editorial explained how the Turkish government had been taking quiet but effective steps toward "ridding Turkey of Islam." Fortunately, *The Satanic Verses* administered a salutary shock to the true Muslims of Turkey, awakening them to the dangers in their midst. This then neutralized "the propaganda of the secular regime" and stopped anti-Islamic efforts dead in their tracks.[18]

Some Muslims, perceiving a worldwide rivalry of Islam with Christianity in the race for new converts, held that the Church would rely on any dirty trick in the effort to win more souls. For them, publication of *The Satanic Verses* seemed exactly what was needed to make Islam unattractive. An Iranian newspaper interpreted the novel as an attempt at "spreading a false picture of Islam in order to restrict the spread of Islam."[19]

In the end, *The Satanic Verses* was regarded as only a minor part in the great conspiracy against Islam. The book and its publishers were "only a link in the chain of the new anti-Islamic cultural ploys."[20] The real problem, as Rafsanjani put it, "is not merely the publication of a book or a novel against Islam, but...that a well-calculated and extensive plot has been orchestrated against Islam behind the curtain."[21] He put it more succinctly on another occasion: "This is not about the book and reader, it is over the West trying to dictate to Islam."[22] Khamene'i made the point more generally: "We Muslims should be as wary of the enemy's cultural front as we are of his military front."[23] The lesson is clear; Muslims must be on extreme guard against the seeming benefits of Western civilization. Not coincidentally, this is the message fundamentalists were all along trying to get across.

The United States and Israel

Iranian leaders assumed that British intelligence did not act alone in putting Rushdie up to the job. As ever, "Little Satan" worked hand-in-glove with "Great Satan," the United States. An Iranian government statement called Rushdie "an inferior CIA agent" and referred to the book as a "provocative American deed."[24] According to Radio Tehran, "the role of America's spy network in planning an anti-Islamic atmosphere is so expanded that one cannot remain indifferent toward it."[25] As Interior Minister Mohtashemi put it, "the book's author is in England but the real supporter is the United States."[26] To justify this position, the Iranians seized any straw connecting Rushdie to the United States, such as the fact that he was recently married to an American, novelist Marianne Wiggins.

The irony of identifying Rushdie with the American government was not lost on less excited voices. Rushdie, after all, was a

Muslim of Indian origins living in England and holding a British passport. As the *Pakistan Times* observed in an editorial on the Islamabad riot, "It is hard to see how [the United States government] became the prime object of mob anger . . . when both the author and the first publication of the book belonged elsewhere."[27] Further, Rushdie was widely known as a "man of the left," or even the extreme left, who viscerally opposed the policies of the U.S. government. After all, he had even written a book vaunting Washington's enemies in Central America, and had been celebrated for this outlook in Iran.

How, then, did Rushdie and the United States become intertwined in the minds of fundamentalist Muslims? Because Anti-Westernism has a way of turning into anti-Americanism. The United States represents the political power of the West. Britain may have once been the imperial overlord, but it has been nearly defanged; the military threat is virtually gone and London has long shown itself far more interested in commerce than in matters of principle. Too, American culture, with its global impact, symbolizes the entire West. Whether Rushdie lives in London or New York City is a minor detail to fundamentalist Muslims; the point is that the United States presents the main threat to their vision of the just society. The United States is the leader of the Western world, that lascivious place where it is acceptable, even honorable, to attack the Prophet and the Qur'an.

Some Americans welcomed the symbolism of this role. The editors of *The New Republic* agreed on the propriety of drawing a connection between freedom of speech and the United States.

When the mobs in Islamabad marched against Rushdie's book before the American cultural center, many were baffled by the association. In fact, the association was beautifully appropriate. If you are for the banning and the burning of books, if you deny the right of a writer to write and the right of a publisher to publish, if you believe that an opinion may be refuted by a bullet, you are anti-American. The militant mullahs are right. Philosophically and historically, the United States is their enemy. The defender of *The Satanic Verses* is The Great Satan. For this we may be proud.[28]

Where London and Washington forged ahead, Tel Aviv could not be far behind. No Middle East story is complete without Israel, even when that country has no role at all, as in the Rushdie case. And indeed, Iran's Interior Minister Mohtashemi pointed to the Zionists having a "direct involvement" in the book's appearance,[29] while President Khamene'i noted that it was the Zionist-controlled "radios, newspapers, televisions, and news agencies" which advertised the book and "made it famous."[30] Even the official statement breaking diplomatic ties with the United Kingdom blamed publication of *The Satanic Verses* on "agents of international Zionism."[31] The *Tehran Times* went further, seeing the Zionist lobby behind the whole Common Market confrontation with Iran.

The Syrian government, more fixed on regional politics than Islam, offered an explanation for Zionist involvement. The Syrian minister of *awqaf* (religious foundations), 'Abd al-Majid Tarabulsi, pointed out that the book came out when it did so as to deflect the attention of "world Muslims from the Palestinian uprising."[32]

In Pakistan, religious leaders smelled a "Zionist conspiracy" behind the troubles and rioters carried banners denouncing *The Satanic Verses* as "An American-Jewish Conspiracy."[33] Pro-Iranian religious leaders in Lebanon portrayed the book as a "malicious onslaught by Jewish arrogance."[34] An opposition leader in Bangladesh denounced the book in parliament as part of the Zionist conspiracy. A newspaper in the United Arab Emirates reported that Mossad, the Israeli secret service, had offered Rushdie protection for life.[35] (Rising to the bait, a somewhat disreputable Israeli businessman and politician, Shmuel Flatto-Sharon, offered to host Rushdie indefinitely at his luxurious villa outside Tel Aviv; he also spoke of publishing the book in the banned languages and shipping it surreptitiously to those countries where it was banned.)

Before leaving the subject of fundamentalist Muslim perceptions of the West, two curious points should be noted. First, the conspiratorial mentality prevails so widely among fundamentalist

Muslims that some of them were bound to see the plot as more complex than a simple attack on Islam. Khomeini's fundamentalist enemies, Sunnis especially, who tended to see his *fatwa* doing their cause more harm than good, interpreted the *fatwa* as part of an elaborate deception. In Egypt, for example, some radical groups saw "the whole affair as a plot to discredit Islam, a trap into which the Iranians, in their haste, have fallen."[36]

Second, a parallel attitude emerged among those who supported Khomeini and Rushdie. On the one hand, both sides emphasized that principle guided their own actions. Those who stood with Khomeini accepted his religious motives at face value, just as those who stood with Rushdie saw themselves standing by the code of free speech. On the other hand, each side accused the other of political purposes. Unable to take Khomeini's religion seriously, those who condemned him searched for ordinary political motives behind his extraordinary *fatwa*—an effort to rally support behind his unpopular government, to expand his power abroad, or the like. As for those who condemned Rushdie, they discounted the real motives of Western governments, which had to do with freedom of expression, and insisted on dredging up ulterior motives. Fundamentalist Muslims could not believe that Western leaders backed Rushdie on the basis of principle. In their view, the leaders must have agreed with what Rushdie wrote because they wanted to harm Islam or the Islamic Republic of Iran. The support Rushdie received from Western governments had an anti-Islamic purpose; harping on freedom of expression was nothing more than a disguise for endorsing Rushdie's calumnies. Thus, President Khamene'i remarked that when the European governments

> entered the arena [they] proved that, yes, the issue was a political one—that it was not a purely cultural issue.... The Western policies and countries exposed themselves. They proved that they are opposed to the Islamic Republic with their very existence. They proved that they view Islam as a very serious and actual danger.... It was revealed that what they claimed to be a cultural move was in fact a political move.[37]

In brief, Western incomprehension of the power of religion was mirrored by Muslim incomprehension about the devotion to a principle so abstract as freedom of thought.

The Struggle With Saudi Arabia

Assuming that Khomeini's *fatwa* of February 14 was motivated primarily by religious feelings, this still leaves his second decree, that of February 19 (reaffirming the sentence against Rushdie and his publishers), to be accounted for. The second *fatwa* ran counter to Khomeini's customary practice, which was to make a tough statement (for instance, to prohibit the private import of goods or to harass Iranians returning from residence abroad), then allow his subordinates to explain what he "really" meant. In the process of explaining his emphatic assertion, they would virtually undermine it. As always, Khamene'i and Rafsanjani tried to do this with the February 14 *fatwa*, but this time Khomeini did not let them. Quite the contrary, his second edict toughened the original statement and precluded his lieutenants from softening his decree.

This unusual act demands explanation, for if Khomeini promulgated his first edict in a mood of righteous fury, the second one was formulated in a cooler, more political atmosphere. And politics does enter. Seeing the response to the first edict, Khomeini, a brilliant tactician, must have seen that he had found an issue which brought him several advantages. It had the unique virtue of dividing Muslims from Westerners along the default lines of culture. Nothing else could so starkly highlight the conflicting political and intellectual traditions of entire civilizations. For Khomeini, who saw Western cultural influence as the greatest obstacle to achieving his vision of an Islamic society, this distinction had great utility. Anything which made Muslims realize the unattractive, alien nature of the West served his purpose.

Conversely, the *fatwa* reached out to the ninety percent of Muslims adhering to the Sunni branch of Islam. In the course of the war with Iraq, Khomeini lost the support of most Sunnis, so a gesture in their direction had timely utility. Shi'is are notorious for caring less about the Prophet Muhammad than his son-in-law 'Ali; this partially explains why the Wahhabi sect controlling Saudi religious life deems Shi'is not to be Muslims.[38] By picking a fight on the question of respect for Muhammad, Khomeini made his Shi'i views more acceptable to the eight to nine hundred million Sunni Muslims. *The Satanic Verses* provided a rare issue on which Sunnis and Shi'is could agree, even if Sunnis did not relish the prospect of falling behind Khomeini in defense of the Prophet's honor.

Perhaps most important, the edict provided a weapon in the Iranian competition with Saudi Arabia to represent Islam internationally. For a decade, Tehran and Riyadh had been struggling to make their very different interpretations of Islam prevail. Each had founded a host of international institutions toward this end, propagated its views through dense media networks, and made full use of available instruments of state. The Iranians would then call for the Saudis' overthrow every so often. *The Satanic Verses* became an important battleground in this duel. The Saudi government, it should be remembered, had led the anti-Rushdie campaign for months. Rushdie himself blamed his troubles "essentially, on Saudi money," calling the influence of Iran "marginal."[39] One source estimates that the Saudis had spent £250,000 just in Bradford, England, during the two months before the January 14 book-burning ceremony.[40] The only Iranian response all this while was a December 1988 book review which ripped into *The Satanic Verses*, calling it a "total moral degredation."[41]

But all those months of Saudi leadership were forgotten the moment Ayatollah Khomeini, in his inimitable way, arrogated center stage. The two states then engaged in an open contest to control the issue. They differed over the importance of legal procedure. Riyadh emphasized that the Iranians were pursuing Rushdie in a non-Islamic manner. You cannot start with the sentence, they said; first you must ascertain the facts in an orderly fashion. Nor can you reject a Muslim's repentence in advance. In reply, President Khamene'i disparaged Saudi-style legalism. Jurisconsults who argue for a trial are "deceitful," he said, for they make the religious law "a flag under which they can crush revolutionary Islam."[42]

Each of the two states had its press network ignore the other's efforts. The Iranian media called only on Khomeini partisans for comments and claimed that all Muslims supported Khomeini's decision. "The fact that the imam's decision has not been challenged by any pro-West ruler in the Muslim world shows the immense support it enjoys among Muslim masses."[43] For its part, the Saudi-backed media made no mention of Ayatollah Khomeini's *fatwa*! Thus, the March 1, 1989 issue of *Al-Majalla*, a weekly magazine, which featured the Rushdie case on the cover, not once referred to an Iranian role in the matter. (For that matter, it also did not cite any of those voices which called for freedom of speech.) Its entire coverage was restricted to the comments of religious spokesmen operating within the Saudi Islamic ambit, such as the Islamic Council of Europe, which deemed Rushdie an apostate and, following Riyadh's lead, called for his trial.

Realizing that they were outmaneuvered, and that they had lost the issue to Khomeini, the Saudis subsequently changed tactics and decided to downplay the Rushdie matter, virtually banishing the topic from their media. As Tehran geared up to make *The Satanic Verses* the main topic of the Organization of the Islamic Conference (OIC) meeting in mid-March 1989, the Saudis made every effort to keep the issue off the agenda. While Tehran pressed for the novel to be taken up by the Political Committee, the Saudis sought to relegate it to the OIC's Cultural Committee. The Iranians won this skirmish, but lost the war, for the Conference's final statement devoted just one paragraph to *The Satanic Verses* (it was buried in the nineteenth political topic out of twenty-three), and never mentioned Rushdie by name (thus implicitly refuting Khomeini's edict against him). The Iranian media attempted to portray the defeat they suffered as "a major victory for the Islamic Republic,"[44] and virtually every Iranian newspaper proclaimed this news in banner headlines. Even though the OIC statement paid minimal attention to Rushdie, Iranian media reported the meeting as though his condemnation had been its central event.

The March 29 murders of 'Abdullah al-Ahdal, the Saudi imam of a mosque in Brussels, and the mosque librarian, Salem el-Beher, pointed to another round in the two states' competition. Though the motives for the killings were unclear, they appear to have been carried out by followers of Khomeini who were hoping both to intimidate their Saudi rivals and to strike a blow against Saudi-style Islam in Western Europe.

The *fatwa* against Rushdie and his publishers did have political benefits for Khomeini, but these were far more subtle than most analysts realized. More important yet was a widespread feeling among Muslims of outrage and insult at the text of the book. Indeed, the intensity of Muslim responses to Khomeini's edict shows just how deeply *The Satanic Verses* affair penetrated Muslim life.

NOTES

[1]Radio Tehran, February 24, 1989.
[2]Radio Tehran, March 7, 1989.
[3]Radio Tehran, March 12, 1989.
[4]*Keyhan*, February 15, 1989.
[5]Radio Tehran, February 16, 1989.
[6]Islamic Revolution News Agency, February 15, 1989.
[7]Radio Tehran, March 1, 1989.
[8]Radio Tehran, February 15, 1989.
[9]Radio Tehran, February 24, 1989.
[10]Radio Tehran, February 16, 1989.
[11]Islamic Revolution News Agency, February 15, 1989.
[12]Islamic Revolution News Agency, February 21, 1989.
[13]Radio Tehran, February 24, 1989.
[14]Radio Tehran, February 23, 1989.
[15]Radio Tehran, February 15, 1989.
[16]Islamic Revolution News Agency, February 18, 1989.
[17]Radio Tehran, March 3, 1989.

[18]*Jomhuri-ye Eslami*, March 12, 1989.

[19]*Jomhuri-ye Islami*, February 14, 1989.

[20]Radio Tehran, February 23, 1989.

[21]Islamic Revolution News Agency, February 15, 1989.

[22]Radio Tehran, March 10, 1989.

[23]Radio Tehran, February 17, 1989.

[24]Radio Tehran, February 13, 1989; Islamic Revolution News Agency, February 14, 1989.

[25]Radio Tehran, February 13, 1989.

[26]Islamic Revolution News Agency, February 17, 1989.

[27]*Pakistan Times*, February 13, 1989.

[28]The Editors, "Two Cheers for Blasphemy," *The New Republic*, March 13, 1989.

[29]Radio Tehran, February 16, 1989. This may refer to the fact that Peter Mayer, the executive chairman of Viking, is Jewish.

[30]Radio Tehran, February 17, 1989.

[31]Islamic Revolution News Agency, March 7, 1989.

[32]Islamic Revolution News Agency, March 6, 1989.

[33]*The Philadelphia Inquirer*, February 13, 1989.

[34]Voice of the Oppressed, February 24, 1989.

[35]*Gulf News*, February 26, 1989.

[36]*The Guardian*, March 3, 1989.

[37]Radio Tehran, March 3, 1989.

[38]Muhibb ad-Din al-Khatib, *Al-Khutat al-'Arida li'l-Usus allati Qama 'alayha Din ash-Shi'a al-Imamiya al-Ithna 'Ashariya* (Cairo: Al-Maktaba as-Salafiya, 1380).

[39]*L'Express*, February 24, 1989.

[40]*Foreign Report*, May 11, 1989.

[41]*Kayhan Farangi*, text in *The Independent*, February 21, 1989.

[42]Radio Tehran, March 16, 1989.

[43]Islamic Revolution News Agency, February 21, 1989.

[44]Radio Tehran, March 17, 1989.

8.

MUSLIM RESPONSES TO KHOMEINI

The abiding fear that Westerners seek to sap Muslim strength goes a long way to explain the heartfelt outrage to *The Satanic Verses*. Not for the first time in recent Middle East history, the suspicion of a plot inflamed public opinion, affected policy decisions, and led to violent protests. No one could remain neutral to the edict. Khomeini's support tended to come from the disaffected; in contrast, governments did their best to avoid taking a stand with him or against him (though they clearly had little sympathy for his edict). Many Muslims agreed that Rushdie deserved punishment but not death, and a small number of individuals, intellectuals mostly, braved the dangers of fundamentalist Muslim retribution to speak out against the edict.

Support

The Iranians found little official support for their position, even in other Muslim countries. Only the Libyan government publicly stood by the ayatollah and his edict.* The Kuwaiti

*IRNA, the Iranian press service, claimed other support, such as that of the United Arab Emirates, but it is hard to place much credence in IRNA dispatches without corroborating reports from the other side, for IRNA not uncommonly distorted what others said, and at times put words in their mouths. Iranian officials also resorted to duplicity. After calling the British Foreign

138

government announced that it shared an "identical stance" with Tehran on the matter of *The Satanic Verses*; but it carefully avoided agreeing with Tehran on the condemnation of the book's author.[1] A newspaper in the United Arab Emirates hinted at support for the ayatollah by saying that literary refutation of Rushdie would not suffice. The mufti of Xanthi, Greece, endorsed the edict. The Nigerian Supreme Court for Islamic Affairs declared that Rushdie "deserves the maximum punishment for his grievous offense," while the sultan of Sokoto, Ibrahim Zasuki, held that the death edict "is not the ayatollah's directive. It is Allah's directive."[2] But beyond these rare voices, there was little high-level support for the Iranian position.

At the unofficial level, the Iranians received automatic and unanimous support from their large network of activists around the world, some of whom issued bloodcurdling calls for Rushdie's head. In Pakistan, a former religious affairs minister, Kausar Niazi, not only asserted that Rushdie "has to be murdered, there is no other way...the people are after his blood"; he also suggested that any Pakistani Muslim who came to Rushdie's defense should himself be executed.[3] To the principal of the main Shi'i school in Islamabad, Rushdie "is an infidel and must be beheaded."[4] In Peshawar, a preacher offered 500,000 rupees, or $30,000, to the "young and brave Pakistani who kills the infidel Rushdie."[5] The Shi'i leader of Pakistan called for the government publicly to hang the policemen who had fired on protesters outside the American Cultural Center in Islamabad.

Violent demonstrations continued in the Indian subcontinent for a month after Khomeini's edict. On February 14, Indian police defused a time bomb and fired tear gas at stone-throwing demonstrators in the city of Srinagar, Kashmir, wounding several. The incident also aggravated Muslim emotions toward Christians in Pakistan. Whipped up by speeches attacking Rush-

---

Office three times in early March, to try to arrange for a meeting in Geneva, only to be refused, the Foreign Ministry in Tehran announced that it had turned down British efforts to arrange a meeting in Geneva.

die and his Western protectors, a mob marched on St. Thomas
Church, the only Protestant church in Islamabad, in mid-February 1989. In the two hours before the police bothered to intervene,
the rioters tore down the church's newly constructed walls,
destroyed construction equipment, and set fire to a guard's tent.
An attempt in March to restart the church caused another
demonstration and attack on the site. After this episode, the
police informed church officials that the building's permit had
been rescinded.

On February 17, forty persons were injured during riots in
Srinagar; two of them were children burned by a crude explosive
device. The largest number of deaths in a single incident occurred
on the 24th, when rioting in the Bendi Bazaar section of south
Bombay (Rushdie's home town) turned into a three-hour fracas
between the police and fundamentalist Muslims. The rioters
burned cars, buses, and even a small police station. In answer, the
police killed twelve persons, detained five hundred, and arrested
eight hundred. The Gandhi government also increased police
efforts and banned those it considered provocateurs from traveling freely about the country.

A security guard at the British Council Library in Karachi was
killed by a bomb explosion on the 26th. One person was killed in
Srinagar on the 27th. (It is noteworthy that almost all deaths in
the subcontinent occurred in the three places connected to
Rushdie: Kashmir, Bombay and Karachi.) A British Council
Library in Dhaka was stoned on March 2. The next day, fifteen
thousand people returned to attack the Library, and one hundred
fifty persons were injured by police clubs and tear gas. Thousands of demonstrators ransacked part of the Karachi airport on
March 4 in protest against the Rushdie novel, smashing doors and
looting the VIP lounge—their way of welcoming home from Iran
Sajid 'Ali Naqvi, a pro-Khomeini Shi'i leader. As late as March
21, protests against *The Satanic Verses* caused a half-day nation-
wide strike in Bangladesh in which fifty people were injured in
pitched battles against police guarding British and American
property.

Demonstrations, for the most part non-violent, took place in many other parts of the Muslim world. Khartoum hosted two large protests, on March 3 and 17. In Istanbul and Ankara, protesters chanted the name of their president Kenan Evren, but turned it into "Salman Evren." On April 3, two bombs went off on British proprerty in Ankara, the first violence against Westerners in Turkey for many years. Over two thousand protesters marched in Kuala Terengganu, in the north of Malaysia. Some three hundred persons, some of them Iranians, yelled slogans outside the British and French embassies in the Philippines. In Hong Kong, Muslims petitioned authorities to ban the book. At a demonstration in front of the British Embassy, Muslims in Japan chanted "Death to Rushdie."

The Iranians often directly involved themselves in provoking anti-Rushdie activities. It was only after visiting the Iranian Cultural Center in Freetown, Sierra Leone, for example, that a local group of Muslim functionaries declared their support for Khomeini's stance to combat "the new plot by world oppression against Islam."[6] Iranian representatives brought similarly overt pressure to bear in a number of other small and poor countries.

The Iranians gloried in these demonstrations, calling them a "manifestation of Muslim power throughout the world" and "symptoms of this very majesty."[7] After a large demonstration in London, a Tehran newspaper gleefully recommended that the British "and other arrogant powers" carefully watch the newsreel footage of the event "once again."[8]

The pattern of protests against *The Satanic Verses* raises an interesting question, for these took place in many parts of the Muslim world but hardly at all in the Arabic-speaking countries. The Arabs are usually at the forefront of any controversy involving Islam, but this time, with the exception of a few radical groups, they were silent. Why? It may have had something to do with the overwhelming repressive apparatus of the state that has emerged between Morocco and Iraq, which simply prevented potential protesters from reaching the streets. The only time citizens seem willing to go take matters into their own hands is when their own interests are at stake. A general mood of apathy may also have accounted for the quiet. Since 1967, when Syria, Jordan and Egypt were simultaneously crushed in war by Israel, Arab populations have hardly ever felt passionately about abstract political causes (price rises and other matters of direct personal concern are another matter). This mood had been evident before, notably in mid-1982, when the war in Lebanon and the massacres at Sabra and Shatila (outside Beirut) prompted demonstrations in the West, and even in Israel, but not in the Arab countries. *The Satanic Verses* appeared to confirm a deep disengagement from politics by Arab Muslims.

Hedging

Many leaders sought to avoid the whole Rushdie issue. They did not refer to it in public and instructed their media either to report the controversy without comment, or to ignore it. Even when asked point-blank about the matter, they skipped around it. "I don't care to comment about the action of the Government of Iran myself," was King Husayn of Jordan's reply to such a question.[9] Benazir Bhutto of Pakistan used almost the same words: "I do not want to start a controversy with Iran."[10] "Turkey is not a party to the arguments concerning the book," came the word from Ankara.[11] In Egypt, the media downplayed the international fracas; for its part, the parliament debated *The Last Temptation of Christ* at much greater length than *The Satanic Verses*. Political allies of Tehran also refused public support. President Hafiz al-Asad of Syria begged off when asked about the edict: "I am not an authority on religion."[12] Syria's chief authority on religion, the mufti, did no more than request Rushdie (like the Muslims in Britain) "to admit his mistake, withdraw the book, and prevent its further circulation."[13]

From the vantage point of those wishing to stay clear of trouble, the obvious step was to ban the book and say no more. The Muslim states as a totality chose this path when their foreign ministers met in mid-March 1989 for a meeting of the Organization of the Islamic Conference. Notwithstanding intense Iranian efforts to find support for Khomeini's *fatwa*, the OIC over-whelmingly voted to do no more than call on member governments to ban the book.

Virtually every government with a Muslim majority or plurality did just this, as did a number of governments with substantial Muslim minorities, including those of Papua New Guinea, Thailand, India, Sri Lanka, Kenya, Tanzania, Liberia, Sierra Leone and South Africa. Most remarkably, two Western states with negligible Muslim populations banned the book. In Venezuela, the authorities imposed a fine of 15 months imprisonment for owning the book, and even reading it was made an offense. In Japan, sale of the English-language edition was banned. Fines were imposed. The Revolutionary Government of Zanzibar threatened that anyone found with the offending book would be sentenced to three years in prison, a fine of 20,000 shillings ($2,500), or both. The Malaysian government imposed almost the identical penalty, three years in prison, 20,000 ringgit (about $7,400), or both.

Some governments went further. Iran and several other states banned all books published by Viking, including its very popular Penguin series. Rushdie himself was barred from several countries. Secondary bannings of issues of magazines (such as *Time*, *Newsweek*, *Asiaweek* and *Far Eastern Economic Review*) covering the controversy were fairly common.

These regulations were occasionally taken seriously; when a Christian citizen of the Sudan was spotted at the Khartoum airport returning from London with two copies of *The Satanic Verses*, the books were taken away and he was subjected to unspecified legal measures. In the Comores, a small island country off East Africa, all foreign magazines were impounded out of fear that they might carry extracts of the satanic book. The authorities in Mali went to almost comic lengths to protect their citizens from the book. According to a report on the weekly cabinet meeting, as covered by Radio Bamako,

The president informed the Cabinet of the decision by the party to ban the importation, distribution, and propagation of the book,

The Satanic Verses. The president has charged the ministers of
defense, information, territorial administration, and basic development, as well as the minister of agriculture with carrying out
this decision.[14]

In other countries, application was much more lax. Foreign
magazines with extracts of the book were allowed into Senegal.
In Indonesia, possession of the book was punishable by a month
in prison or a fine. Yet, at the same time, local magazines ran
lengthy synopses of the book.

Iranian leaders understood this fence-sitting for what it was,
and made their displeasure known. They castigated Muslims who
kept silent about Rushdie, accusing them of "treason against
Islam and the Holy Qur'an."[15] The Iranian media scornfully
referred to the Arab leaders' behavior as "eerie" or "stony and
shameful."[16] As usual, 'Ali Akbar Hashemi Rafsanjani minced
no words: "Those who are real cowards talk in a contradictory
way. They say: 'We condemn *The Satanic Verses* but we do not
accept the death edict.'"[17] But Tehran did almost nothing beyond
complain verbally about the weakness of state support.

A great many Shi'i leaders, even ones living in Iran, kept silent
on the Rushdie *fatwa*. Given the severe restrictions on their
freedom of speech, this silence can probably be understood as
expressing disagreement. Virtually all the grand ayatollahs—
Golpayegani, Kho'i, Montazeri, Najafi, Qomi—avoided the
issue, telling interviewers that they had not read the book and
therefore could not comment on it. They also made it clear that
they had no intention of reading the book, either. In at least one
case, that of Hosain 'Ali Montazeri, this silence had important
political ramifications. Just a few weeks after the *fatwa*, Khomeini removed Montazeri from his position as Khomeini's
designated successor, a status he had enjoyed since November
1985. According to some reports,[18] Montazeri's reluctance to
support the *fatwa* was the key factor in his deposition.

Even in Iran, an assertion would turn up in the media or
politicians' speeches that indicated less than wholehearted sup-

port for the edict. Omid Mas'udi wrote in *Keyhan* that the first thing for the West to do would be "to hand over Salman Rushdie to a just Islamic court"[19]—the Saudi position coming from Tehran! In general, however, the watchdogs in Iran did their job well, so that dissenting voices were rarely heard.

Opposition

The Satanic Verses controversy caused great anguish in Turkey, where it raised issues of principle and interest, of government philosophy and popular will, and of identity between East and West. Yet, in the end, the government held true to its secular principles. At first, the controversy appeared to be beneficial for it would obstruct Iranian trade with Europe and bring a windfall of business to Turkey, a prospect which led the prime minister's brother, Yusuf Özal, to call *The Satanic Verses* affair "a blessing on Turkey from God." This cynical delight did not last long, however, and was replaced by a dilemma. For the authorities to allow the book into the country would mean upsetting fundamentalist Muslims in Turkey, alienating Tehran, and losing out on the expected commercial bonanza. To make this point clear, Iranians exerted pressure to have the book banned; the Iranian consul in Erzurum, for example, distributed copies of the Khomeini *fatwa* to religious leaders throughout eastern Anatolia. But to censor the book would have created problems of its own, for the authorities in Ankara continued to adhere to the secular principles laid down by Atatürk in the 1920s, despite considerable pressure; prohibiting *The Satanic Verses* would have further damaged the legitimacy and consistency of those embattled principles. No less important, banning the book would have tarnished the country's Western credentials and reduced Turkey's already slim chances of being accepted into the European Community.

Symbolic of his no-win predicament, Prime Minister Turgut Özal took to uttering such enigmatic statements as, "A crazy man threw a stone in the well, and a thousand intellectuals are doing battle to get it out"[20]—leaving it unclear whether "a crazy man" referred to Rushdie or Khomeini. (Insiders revealed that he was referring to the former.) And while Ankara did sign the OIC communiqué calling for a ban on the book, no legislation to this effect was introduced. In the end, Turkey was the one country with an overwhelmingly Muslim population where the book remained legal, although this policy was carried out quietly, even stealthily, at the official level.

Unofficially, opinions were stated very forcefully. A number of prominent Turks condemned Khomeini. Erdal Inönü, leader of the opposition Social Democrats, announced that "killing some-body for what he has written is simply murder."[21] Writing in the Turkish daily, *Cumhuriyet*, Ali Sirmen called Khomeini "a nearly 90-year-old man who still thirsts for blood," termed his edict a call for "terrorist activities," and waxed nostalgic for the shah.[22] Altan Oymen labeled the edict a "criminal offense" and called the Khomeini regime a "terrorist administration."[23] Professor Mehmet Hatipoğlu of the Theology Faculty at Ankara University characterized the call for Rushdie's death as un-Islamic.[24] Nadim Gürsel, the Turkish novelist, called the edict "a real move backwards"[25] and the Turkish Writers Union came out forcefully against the *fatwa*.

Although the authorities in all other Muslim countries acknowledged the alleged blasphemy of *The Satanic Verses* and banned the book, some of them opposed Khomeini's edict. Not surprisingly, the Iraqi government felt no qualms about attacking it. President Saddam Husayn observed that "murder and incitement to murder is more harmful to Islam and Muslim than Salman Rushdie's tendentious and sinister book."[26] Taha Yasin Ramadan, the first deputy prime minister, announced that "Iraq does not concern itself with such matters, for Iraqis are not guardians over the world such as Iranian leader Khomeini tries to be."[27] The Iraqi Foreign Ministry's undersecretary, Nizar Hamdun, objected to the death sentence on Rushdie and denied that Khomeini had the right to speak on behalf of the entire Muslim world.

Hamdun's counterpart in Kuwait, Sulayman ash-Shahin, suggested that *The Satanic Verses* did not deserve so much attention, noting that the brouhaha might do little more than "serve as publicity for the book and realize profits to the writer and publisher."[28] Asked about the *fatwa*, General Ershad of Bangladesh replied: "How can I endorse this sentence? No one can be punished without a trial. And no civilized state would accept it." The Egyptian foreign minister, 'Ismat 'Abd al-Majid, blamed Khomeini for creating the problem, and held that "Khomeini had no right to sentence Rushdie to death."[29] Zaki Badr, the Egyptian interior minister, was the Muslim leader who expressed what many of his colleagues lacked the courage to say. "Khomeini is a dog, no that is too good for him. He is a pig." With regard to Rushdie, Badr commented: "Of course, the book is wrong, but to kill him—this is not the way."[30]

Predictably, the most consistent condemnation of Khomeini came from the Iranian opposition. Mas'ud Rajavi, leader of the Mojahedin-e Khalq, noted that "the world gets a new glimpse of the medieval and faltering Khomeini regime's abhorrent behavior every day." The Mojahedin was the only Muslim organization to demonstrate in the West against the Khomeini edict, which it did in a number of cities.

Most of the larger Palestinian groups criticized Khomeini. Putting on their best behavior in the era of incipient dialogue with the U.S. government, they had to condemn the public announcement of a murder. Thus, Salah Khalaf of Al-Fatah protested against "using the name of Islam for terrorist ends. Death threats give Muslims a bad image and lead people to side with Salman Rushdie."[31]

Several individual voices from the Arab countries also criticized Khomeini. Perhaps the most remarkable statement came from Abdelwahab Meddeh, a Tunisian writer: "I feel welling up in me a real need to blaspheme, to try out for myself all the negative clichés about the prophet and Islam."[32] Ahmad Baha' ad-Din, Egypt's leading columnist, devoted one article after another in *Al-Ahram* to the concept of free speech. In an act of singular bravery, Naguib Mahfouz, winner of the 1988 Nobel Prize in literature, called Khomeini a "terrorist."[33] Not long after, Mahfouz joined eighty other Arab intellectuals in declaring that "no blasphemy harms Islam and the Muslims so much as the call for murdering a writer."[34] Fundamentalist Muslims had long been irked by Mahfouz's writing (especially by his allegorical tale of 1959, *Sons of Our Quarter*), and they were all the more irritated by his winning the Nobel Prize. *The Satanic Verses* incident reportedly caused some fundamentalists to review their activities and blame themselves: "If only we had behaved in the proper Islamic manner with Naguib Mahfouz, we would not have been assailed by the appearance of Salman Rushdie. Had we killed Naguib Mahfouz, Salman Rushdie would not have appeared."[35] With such sentiments in the air, Mahfouz naturally received a host of death threats. The Egyptian police deemed these serious enough to extend protection to him; they further increased Mahfouz's security when Shaykh 'Umar 'Abd ar-Rahman, an Egyptian religious figure resident in Tehran, condemned him to death for supporting Rushdie.

An impressive number of Muslim intellectuals signed petitions, subsequently published, in support of Rushdie. Most noteworthy, one of these, called "Defense of the Writer and His Right to Life," was written up in the Lebanese daily, *As-Safir*.[36] The Arab Association for Human Rights placed advertisements, signed by a group of notable writers, announcing their complete opposition to Khomeini's edict.

Understandably, Muslims resident in the West felt freest to speak out. The chairman of the Imams and Mosque Council in Britain, Zaki Badawi, offered his own house as asylum to Salman Rushdie. Hesham El Essawy of the Islamic Society for the promotion of Religious Tolerance (and one of the original instigators of the British campaign against Rushdie) characterized the *fatwa* as a "dangerous development." 'Ali Mughram al-Ghamdi, chair of the U. K. Action Committee on Islamic Affairs, asserted the Muslim community's intent "to fully abide by the law" and its rejection of violence of any kind.[37] Hanif Kureishi, the other British Muslim writer who stirred up the anger of his community (for his movie *My Beautiful Launderette*) signed a public letter which expressed his solidarity with Salman Rushdie.

Muslim writers living in France signed a petition declaring, "Against fanaticism and intolerance, we are all Salman Rushdie." The instigator of that petition, the Algerian sociologist Mohammed Harbi, on his own called for Muslims to condemn the edict, for if they did not, Khomeini "would continue in the same path, and freedom of expression is very precious." Rachid Mechidi of the reformist Institut Alif in Drancy, France, called the *fatwa* "pure demagoguery."[38] A Turkish mosque imam in Paris deemed it "useless and dangerous."[39] Tedjini Haddam, rector of the Paris mosque, called on the Muslim community to "respect the secularism of French society."[40] Moncef Marzouki, a Tunisian author, "unreservedly condemned the call to murder" from Tehran.[41] Muslims played a prominent part in the March 2 demonstration in Paris protesting Khomeini and the fundamentalists. Yousif Ashouri, living in West Germany, wrote perhaps the strongest public statement of all: "If Islam is so fragile and sensitive that it cannot withstand fair questioning and discussion by ordinary people, then it is worthless as a religion and does not deserve survival. Rushdie should be praised for his brave stand on such a totalitarian issue."[42]

Muslim students at the University of Iowa staged a reading of *The Satanic Verses* to show that not everyone from Islamic countries supported the ayatollah. "That's madness, that's not Islam," responded Siraj Wajjah, head of a mosque in New York City, to the edict.[43] Reza Afshari, a historian at Pace University (outside New York), wrote that "We all must welcome this first truly iconoclastic work of world-class literature by an author from an Islamic background.... As long as the charge of blasphemy is invoked with such criminal ferocity, there is a need for books like *The Satanic Verses*."[44]

A Palestinian journalist in Israel, Abdullatif Younis, offered Rushdie his unqualified support:

> Many true Moslems—the writer of these lines among them— believe that secularism is the cure for all illnesses in the Moslem world.... A showdown (hopefully bloodless) between secularists and fundamentalists in the Moslem world is inevitable. Indeed, it has already begun. Salman Rushdie gave the signal. His *Satanic Verses* rendered Moslems all over the world a great service.[45]

From Yugoslavia, Sloman Selenic, president of the Yugoslav Writer's Association, announced that Khomeini belongs to the "family of messiahs—historic lunatics—who can make mankind happy only by killing people."[46] In India, a prominent scholar of the Qur'an, Rafiq Zakaria, deemed the *fatwa* "totally illegal."[47]

Support from Muslims had special importance for Rushdie, for it showed he was not alone. Rushdie broached this theme in December 1988: "I know plenty of Muslims who think like this, who sit around cafes and have similar discussions to this. I don't pretend to be the first person to ever have these thoughts."[48] On another occasion, he provided names of allies, including the Somali Noureddine Farah and the Tanzanian Abdul Razak Gurnah. One of Rushdie's few statements from confinement stressed that he had received many letters of support from Muslims (mostly from India and the Soviet Union, a surprising duo). He drew two conclusions: that there was "not an unbridgeable gulf" between traditional Islam and his version of the religion; and that some Muslims recognized that his book was written within the bounds of Islamic tradition.

As these comments suggest, an educated Muslim elite joins Rushdie in doubting the central verities of Islam. Indeed, just as few Catholic intellectuals accept the literal truth of the virgin birth, so are the universities full of Muslims who do not believe that Muhammad received the Qur'an from God. But they dare not express their thoughts on this or other matters pertaining to the essence of Islam. When asked whether he could have written *The Satanic Verses*, Shaker Laibi, a secular Muslim living in Western Europe, replied: "Yes, I could have written it. But I would not have signed it with my own name."[49] His point was confirmed in a remarkable letter from Karachi, Pakistan, and published in *The Observer* at the peak of *The Satanic Verses* controversy.

> Salman Rushdie speaks for me in *The Satanic Verses*, and mine is a voice that has not yet found expression in newspaper columns. It is the voice of those who are born Muslims but wish to recant in adulthood, yet are not permitted to on pain of death.
>
> Someone who does not live in an Islamic society cannot imagine the sanctions, both self-imposed and external, that militate against expressing religious disbelief. "I don't believe in God" is an impossible public utterance even among family and friends.... So we hold our tongues, those of us who doubt....
>
> Then, along comes Rushdie and speaks for us. Tells the world that we exist—that we are not simply a mere fabrication of some Jewish conspiracy. He ends our isolation. He ends it and simultaneously deepens it; frees us only to imprison us anew.[50]

Not being able to express their views, skeptical Muslim intellectuals take refuge in two ways. First, they become violently sacrilegious at the margins, making scurrilous jokes and hostile comments without ever taking on the central dicta of Islam. Such comments are usually tolerated, as long as they are not written down or made public. But not always; punishment can sometimes come swiftly, and without warning. In the poignant phrase of Amir Taheri, "All of us, Muslim writers and poets, have graveyards full of friends."[51]

Second, intellectuals abandon their homelands for the West, that place where freedom of expression is found. As a result, a disproportionate number of the finest and most creative thinkers on Islam now live in West Europe and North America. As Khalid Durán notes, "Independent Muslim thinkers, as opposed to walking encyclopedias, can make progress only when they live apart from the world of Islam."[52] This trend has become all the more emphatic since the rise of fundamentalist Islam in the mid-1970s, leading Fadia A. Faqir, a Jordanian novelist living in England, to query: "Is exile the only answer to the resurgence of Islam?"[53] Rushdie, who wrote an anti-Islamic book and lived in the West, made use of both these refuges.

Still, the voices of dissent were very much the exception. Most public figures who disagreed with the ayatollah stayed quiet, seemingly accepting Khomeini's *fatwa*. In private conversations they expressed no little horror at what Khomeini had done, but the fear of retribution at the hands of fundamentalist Muslims kept them from speaking out. The example of Naguib Mahfouz served as a deterrent.

Rushdie more than once expressed a wish that his writings might inspire Muslims to reflect on their religion, to reconsider its verities, and to recognize its shortcomings; the two subplots in *The Satanic Verses* were written with this in mind. But, far from realizing this goal, his novel had the exact opposite effect. It enraged millions of Muslims, and thereby drove them into reflexively repeating the old pieties. Whatever the book might have achieved, it failed in the most spectacular way imaginable to stimulate Muslim thinking.

NOTES

[1]Islamic Revolution News Agency, March 20, 1989.
[2]British Broadcasting Corporation, February 27, 1989; *The New York Times*, March 5, 1989.
[3]*The Philadelphia Inquirer, The New York Times*, February 16, 1989.
[4]Agence France Presse, February 15, 1989.
[5]Agence France Presse, February 17, 1989.
[6]Radio Tehran, February 16, 1989.
[7]*Resalat*, March 5, 1989.
[8]*Kayhan International*, June 19, 1989.
[9]Cable News Network, February 25, 1989.
[10]*Indian Express*, March 21, 1989.
[11]Anatolia, February 27, 1989.

[12]Radio Damascus, March 27, 1989. Asad adopted the Saudi line, saying that Rushdie, were he a Syrian national, would have been put on trial.

[13]Syrian Arab News Agency, March 1, 1989.

[14]Radio Bamako, March 8, 1989. (FBIS is not sure about the word "agriculture.") It is curious that the party should publicly give the government orders.

[15]Islamic Revolution News Agency, February 15, 1989.

[16]Islamic Revolution News Agency, February 26, 1989; *Tehran Times*, February 23, 1989.

[17]Radio Tehran, March 10, 1989.

[18]*Uktubir*, July 16, 1989.

[19]*Keyhan*, May 16, 1989.

[20]*Der Spiegel*, March 6, 1989.

[21]*The Economist*, March 18, 1989.

[22]*Cumhuriyet*, February 22, 1989; March 24, 1989.

[23]*Cumhuriyet*, February 26, 1989, *Milliyet*, March 22, 1989.

[24]Anatolia, February 22, 1989.

[25]*Jeune Afrique*, March 15, 1989.

[26]*Ash-Sharq al-Awsat*, March 8, 1989.

[27]*Al-Watan*, March 4, 1989.

[28]Kuwait News Agency, February 16, 1989. Despite this stance, the amir of Kuwait later called the book part of an "international plot" (Islamic Revolution News Agency, March 11, 1989) and had it banned.

[29]Middle East News Agency, March 10, 1989.

[30]*The Observer*, March 19, 1989.

[31]Agence France Presse, March 10, 1989.

[32]*Jeune Afrique*, March 15, 1989.

[33]*Der Spiegel*, February 27, 1989.

[34]*Le Monde*, March 8, 1989.

[35]Yusuf al-'Aqid, "Al-Wudu' bi-Dima' Najib Mahfuz," *Al-'Arab*, July 3, 1989. Shortly after the *fatwa*, rumors spread that a conference would be held late in 1989 in Mecca to condemn both Mahfouz and Rushdie.

[36]"Difa' 'an al-Katib wa-Haqqu fi'l-Hayat," *As-Safir*, March 24, 1989.

[37]Quoted in Lisa Appignanesi and Sara Maitland, eds., *The Rushdie File* (London: Fourth Estate, 1989), pp. 100-01, 113.

[38]All three quotes are from *Le Nouvel Observateur*, February 23, 1989.

[39]*Le Nouvel Observateur*, March 23, 1989.

[40]*The Independent*, July 20, 1989.

[41]*Le Monde*, February 25, 1989.

[42]*Newsweek* (European Edition), March 13, 1989.

[43]*The New York Times*, February 21, 1989.

[44]Reza Afshari, "The Poet and the Prophet: The Iconoclasm of *The Satanic Verses*," unpublished manuscript, August 1989, pp. 7-8.

[45]*Jerusalem Post*, March 8, 1989.

[46]Tanjug, April 20, 1989.

[47]*Far Eastern Economic Review*, March 23, 1989.

[48]Ameena Meer, "Interview: Salman Rushdie," *Bomb*, Spring 1989, p. 36.

[49]*Hebdo*, March 9, 1989.

[50]*The Observer*, March 12, 1989.

[51]Amir Taheri, "Pandora's Box Forced Open," *Index on Censorship*, May 1989, p. 9.

[52]Khalid Durán, "Prekäre Lage muslimischer Intellektueller," *Neue Zürcher Zeitung*, March 9, 1989.

[53]*The Times Literary Supplement*, January 6, 1989.

9.

WESTERN RESPONSES TO KHOMEINI

Western responses to the Khomeini edict of February 14, 1989 came in three waves. The first week that followed was characterized by retreat and confusion. Publishers delayed or canceled editions of *The Satanic Verses*, politicians temporized, writers avoided the media, and even Rushdie apologized. Then, when it became clear that concessions would win nothing in return from Khomeini, public opinion hardened and leaders adopted a more defiant stand, lasting from about February 20 to 28. With the start of March, a second round of retreats began, as writers, politicians and religious figures turned against Rushdie. The issue dropped nearly out of sight in mid-March.

Governments

Democratic governments responded in surprisingly timorous fashion. After riots in Islamabad, the American embassy there released a statement which expressed "deep regret" at the loss of life, then went on: "the embassy wishes to emphasize that the U.S. government in no way supports or associates itself with any activity that is any sense offensive or insulting to Islam or any other religion."[1] James A. Baker III, the newly-installed secretary of state, could muster no more condemnation than to call the death threat "regrettable."[2] President George Bush's only public comment on the matter was as meek as it was inelegant: "However offensive that book may be, inciting murder and offering rewards for its perpetration are deeply offensive to the norms of civilized behavior." By dubbing both *The Satanic Verses* and the death edict as "offensive," Bush implied that he saw the two as equally repugnant. Further, his declaration that the U.S. government would hold Tehran responsible for attacks "against American interests,"[3] seemed to suggest that death threats against Viking and fears in bookstores across the country were not a matter of American national interest.

To make matters worse, other than the Islamabad embassy statement, the U.S. government at no time made a formal statement or adopted a position on *The Satanic Verses* episode; the few remarks touching on the issue came in response to questions from the news media. The behavior of American officials suggested that, no less than their Middle Eastern counterparts, they dearly wanted the issue to go away. Susan Sontag, president of American PEN (Poets, Essayists and Novelists), was on the mark in her testimony to a subcommittee of the Senate Foreign Relations Committee: "At times, the promise or presence of federal law enforcement officials has been vital to the meaningful exercise of a Constitutional right—to vote, or register in school or march on a public street. This time, when First Amendment freedoms are at risk, the message has been: you're on your own."[4]

The normally vociferous members of Congress temporarily lost their voices when it came to the struggle between ayatollah and novelist, an issue they found both mystifying and without potential gain. At first just a solitary Republican (Senator Slade Gordon) and three Democrats (Senator Patrick Leahy, Representatives Gary Ackerman and Tom Lantos) denounced the threats. Subsequently, the Senate unanimously passed a resolution which declared its commitment "to protect the right of any person to write, publish, sell, buy, and read books without fear of intimidation and violence" and condemned Khomeini's threat as "state-sponsored terrorism."

Both British Prime Minister Margaret Thatcher and Neil Kinnock, leader of the opposition, kept silent about the ayatollah's threat for a full week. Nor were any of the fundamentalist Muslims in Britain who threatened Rushdie's life charged with an offense, though incitement to murder is punishable in Great Britain. In justifying its inaction, the Crown Prosecution Service explained that the decision not to prosecute was based in part on an assessment of the public interest. On June 19, the High Court in London agreed to a judicial review of the Muslim Action Group's petition to try Salman Rushdie and Viking under the British blasphemy laws, only to reject the request one month later.

The Canadian government temporarily banned imports of *The Satanic Verses*; worse, the prime minister finessed the freedom-of-speech issue by relegating the decision to Revenue Canada, a tax agency. The Prohibited Importations Branch scrutinized the book but found that it did not fall within the legal definition of hate literature. Bonn called the incident a "strain on German-Iranian relations."[5] The Swiss Foreign Affairs Department called in the Iranian ambassador and expressed its "regret" over the incitement to murder Rushdie.[6] But it was the Japanese government that came out with the limpest formulation of all: "encouraging murder," it intoned, "is not something to be praised."[7] Indeed, alone among the non-communist industrial states, Japan made sure that the Rushdie affair in no way affected its diplomatic relations with Iran.

In at least two cases, Western governments pressured publishers not to go ahead with plans to translate and release *The Satanic Verses*. Christian Bourgois, a member of the Presses de la Cité group and French publisher of *The Satanic Verses*, explained that his quick decision not to go ahead with the book was based on the personal advice of the interior minister, Pierre Joxe. Muslims in Israel who vowed to block publication of the novel were joined in this effort by ultra-orthodox Jewish members of parliament. Their combined efforts led the Ministry of Religious Affairs to request that the Keter publishing house drop its plans for a Hebrew translation.

Several governments—including the British, French and Soviet—sought a way out of the diplomatic impasse by noting that Khomeini's edict was issued not by the Iranian government but by the "spiritual leader" of the Islamic Revolution. This was false, for two reasons. Representatives of the Iranian government pointed out to anyone who would listen that Khomeini's authority was spelled out in Article 110 of the Islamic Republic's constitution, and that it included such powers as command of the armed force and the right to dismiss the president. Further, the entire machinery of the Iranian government, including its legal specialists, rushed to align itself with Khomeini's action. Forty judges of the State Supreme Court issued a statement endorsing the *fatwa* and demanding the writer's speedy punishment. Curiously, as late as March 1, the Soviet news agency TASS maintained the position that "the Iranian Government has not condemned Rushdie to death," even though the government had indeed condemned him, repeatedly and loudly.

To be sure, not every leader responded weakly. President François Mitterrand of France confirmed his reputation as the intellectual's politician when he labeled the threat against Rushdie and his publishers an "absolute evil."[8] Laurant Fabius, president of the French National Assembly, called Khomeini an "assassin."[9] In the Common Market, the West German government came out most forcefully against the ayatollah. It was the first to recall its head of mission from Iran, on February 17 and Foreign Minister Hans-Dietrich Genscher called the European Community resolution of February 20 "also a signal to assure the preservation of civilization and human values."[10] Moreover, at the EC meeting on February 20, the Germans and French called for an additional step besides withdrawing the heads of mission from Tehran; they wanted to restrict Iranian diplomats to a sixty kilometer radius around the capital cities. The British, however, rejected this proposal.

Attempts to propitiate Tehran failed, for instead of toning down Tehran's policies, these encouraged the Iranian authorities to ask for more and more. The prime minister and the foreign secretary of Britain humiliated themselves by officially attacking a novel, something unheard of in British public life. Rather than gain good will in Tehran, their weakness stimulated yet more demands, ones they could not possibly fulfill. *The Satanic Verses* controversy confirmed once again that appeasement does not pay, especially when dealing with a militant, dogmatic state such as Iran's.

But a long and painful series of events since 1978—including the fall of the shah, the U.S. embassy takeover, and the Iran/*contra* fiasco—suggest that Western politicians are unable to learn and remember a simple fact of life about revolutionary Iran: kowtowing not only does no good, it usually leads to counterproductive results. Further, appeasement has a cost that goes beyond the merely practical. When Iranians stand steadfastly by their policies and Westerners waver, the effect is to signal the world that the West, for all its wealth and ostensible power, lacks resolve. Waffling also encourages fundamentalist Muslims to press harder the next time.

Intellectuals and Journalists

Here was a topic tailor-made for writers, intellectuals, columnists, editorialists and academics: the issue concerned freedom of speech and state persecution of a novelist. How did they respond?

Inevitably, a few hopped on the Khomeini bandwagon. Most notably, Georges Sabbagh, director of the Near East Studies Center at UCLA, told an interviewer that Khomeini was "completely within his rights" to call for Rushdie's death. Asked if Muslims should feel they have a right to kill Rushdie, he answered, "Why not?"[11]

Overwhelmingly, however, American intellectuals vehemently opposed both censorship and the threat on Rushdie's life. But, partly out of shock, partly out of fear, they took the issue up slowly. Karen Kennerly, executive director of the PEN American Center, put the best face on the writers' quiet: "They were stunned and didn't know what would be good for Rushdie."[12] Susan Sontag was more candid: "The press is giving a very full and generous account of this, but I don't see the writers yet speaking out. I think, in fact, people are scared. It's as simple as that."[13]

Writers did eventually speak out on Rushdie's behalf, eloquently and very strongly, but their manner revealed a strong motive of self-interest. This became painfully clear at the special joint meeting of PEN, Article 19, and the Authors Guild which took place in New York on February 22, 1989. The theme of remarks made by E.L. Doctorow, Frances Fitzgerald, Gay Talese and others was that writers are not just important (Susan Sontag: "our integrity as a nation is as endangered by an attack on a writer as on an oil tanker"), but uniquely so. Writers also had a tendency to diminish Rushdie's predicament by reducing it to routine size. Ralph Ellison best captured this theme with his oft-quoted aphorism, "A death sentence is a rather harsh review."[14]

Solid as it was, the writers' support for Rushdie left a bad taste. In both Europe and the United States, those who had for so many years pooh-poohed the very notion of terrorism suddenly discovered it when one of their own was the target. Twenty years of IRA and PLO atrocities made almost no impression on them so long as the targets were policemen and airline passengers; when terrorists directed their fire elsewhere, writers pleaded for an understanding of their revolutionary rage. Only when the victim was a friend and a fellow-writer did they wake up, momentarily anyway, and begin talking about an assault on civilized life. Christopher Hitchens epitomized this about-face when he declared in February 1989 that "we risk a great deal by ceding even an inch of ground to the book-burners and murderers." But two and a half years earlier, he had written an article for *Harper's* deprecating terrorist as a "junk word," casting doubt on the reality of the danger, and suggesting that the terrorist bogey had been invented by conservatives as a way to disguise racist politics.[15]

Further, the writers seemed incapable of resisting the opportunity to indulge in vainglorious statements. Norman Mailer's hyperbolic solidarity with Salman Rushdie was perhaps the most memorable effort to exploit the events of February to embellish one's own standing.

> It is our duty to form ranks behind him, and our duty to state to the world that if he is ever assassinated, it will become our obligation to stand in his place. If he is ever killed for a folly, we must be killed for the same folly.... For if one writer can be killed on a hit contract, and all concerned get away with it, then we may be better off being hit each of us, one by one, in future contracts, until our chiefs in the Western world may be finally aroused by the shocking spectacle of our willingness, even though we are selfish creative artists, to be nonetheless martyred in a cause.

In Midge Decter's words, some of America's most celebrated literary lions "preened and strutted in their efforts to share in the cachet of someone else's peril."[16] Even the writers' usual constitutency disliked this oratory. Andy Ross, owner of a Berkeley, California, bookstore that was bombed, mocked the PEN writers as "literary prima donnas" and openly resented their high-handedness. Mailer irritated him especially, "spouting off right and left every time you turned on the TV. I mean, there he was probably sitting in a fancy penthouse somewhere, telling those of us who were actually out there on the front lines about how it's our moral responsibility to sell the book and if we don't, we are a bunch of cowards."[17]

Too, a number of writers took covert pleasure from the threat against Rushdie, seeing in this an affirmation of the importance of literature—and therefore of their own work. Carlos Fuentes made this point more explicitly than most: "The Ayatollahs, nevertheless, have done a great service to literature, if not to

Islam. They have debased and caricatured their own faith. But they have shifted the wandering attention of the world to the power of words, literature and the imagination."[18]

The Royal Academy of Letters in Sweden, the eighteen-member body that judges the Nobel Prize for Literature, issued a spineless statement denouncing efforts to impede freedom of expression, but did not refer to Khomeini by name. Then, in a move without precedent, three members of the Academy, two novelists (Kerstin Ekman and Lars Gyllensten) and a poet (Werner Aspenström) renounced that body's failure to condemn threats from Iran, declared their unwillingness to be further associated with it, and resigned from the organization. The Academy chose to list its dissidents as "non-attending members" rather than try to fill the embarrassing vacances.

Editorialists for the most part condemned Khomeini without reservation, though a number stopped short of supporting Rushdie. In one notably weak commentary, for example, *The Independent* of London called Khomeini's edict "a source of the most acute embarrassment" to British Muslims who had earlier protested against *The Satanic Verses*.[19]

The most avid support for Rushdie tended to come from the left, which is not surprising. Noting Rushdie's call to "the intellectual community in this country and abroad to stand up for freedom of the imagination, which is an issue much larger than my book or indeed my life," *The New Republic* proposed that "one day the Muslim world may remember that sentence gratefully, may look back upon its late 20th-century Anglo-Indian Voltaire."[20] Edward Said praised Rushdie as the "distinguished writer and intellectual who has spoken out for immigrants', black and Palestinian rights, against imperialism and racism."[21] Alexander Cockburn admonished Rushdie for apologizing to Khomeini, because his regret would not propitiate Khomeini—"and was manifestly untrue anyway. Rushdie wrote a consciously blasphemous work, so the 'sincere followers' were precisely the people he desired to piss off."[22] The West German Bundestag (parliament) as a whole called Khomeini's exhortation to murder "a declaration of war" against international law,[23] but only the Green Party voted in favor of terminating all economic agreements with Iran. In Sweden, it was the Greens who tried to put through a condemnation of the death threat.

Reservations came mainly from the right. Patrick Buchanan, the columnist, differentiated between freedom of speech and quality of speech. "While protecting Mr. Rushdie's right and Mr. Rushdie himself—from his enemies and ours—we should shove his blasphemous little novel out into the cold." In opposing what he called the "Western literary herd," he attacked their motives: "Artistic freedom and the First Amendment are modern versions of the medieval cathedral where felons fled for sanctuary.... The First Amendment has succeeded phony patriotism as the last refuge of the scoundrel." Buchanan came up with one of the best lines in the entire affair. Noting Rushdie's affection for Daniel Ortega and his hatred of Margaret Thatcher, he proposed a way to resolve the incident: "Since he is so high on Danny the Red and so down on Mrs. Thatcher, maybe Sal will want to fly down to Nicaragua and seek sanctuary there."[24]

Religious Leaders

Christian and Jewish leaders consistently showed considerable sympathy for the Muslim position—though not the murder threat, to be sure. Catholics seemed to feel especially ambivalent. In an article conveying the views of Pope John Paul II or some other high ranking figure, *L'Osservatore Romano*, the Vatican's semi-official mouthpiece, criticized Rushdie more specifically and at greater length than the ayatollah. Cardinal John J. O'Connor of New York encouraged Catholics "not to dignify the publication of this work," which was generally understood to mean they should not read the book.[25] Cardinal Albert Decourtray of Lyons, president of the French bishop's conference, called *The Satanic Verses* an "insult to religion."[26]

Jean-Marie Lustiger, the cardinal of Paris, adopted perhaps the most pro-Khomeini position of any religious figure in the West, telling a television audience that Western governments have no right to meddle in religious or cultural issues of no concern to them. Their only legitimate worry was "international law and personal law; that is, can one condemn someone to death without a trial?"[27] Lustiger seemed to adopt the Saudi viewpoint—that a regular courtroom procedure would render the edict acceptable. By protesting both *The Satanic Verses* and the Khomeini *fatwa*, Lustiger (and Muslim middle-of-the-roaders) seemed to strike a balance. But close examination showed this to be more apparent than real. Based on moral grounds, their opposition to the novel very much outweighed their merely juridical objection to the edict.

Protestant leaders echoed these views. The archbishop of Canterbury, Robert Runcie, suggested that the British laws of blasphemy be extended to cover other religions as well. Jimmy Carter, the born-again Christian (and noted practitioner in the realm of U.S.-Iran relations), wrote about the need to be "sensitive to the concern and anger" of Muslims and called the severance of diplomatic relations with Iran an "overreaction."[28] A tacit agreement seemed to be evolving among the guardians of religious truth: I condemn attacks on Muhammad, you return the favor for Jesus.

Jewish leaders too joined the bandwagon. Immanuel Jakobovits, chief rabbi of the United Hebrew Congregations of the Commonwealth, wrote that "the book should not have been published" and appealed for legislation to proscribe such "excesses in the freedom of expression."[29] The chief Ashkenazi rabbi of Israel, Avraham Shapira, called for a ban on the book in his country on the grounds that attacks on religion may be "contagious": "One day, this religion is attacked, and the next day it will be that one."[30] This viewpoint was even found in the United States. Yosef Friedman, an orthodox rabbi, was one of the demonstrators outside the Iranian Mission to the United Nations on February 22 calling for the novel's being banned. He told a reporter, "We of course do not advocate killing the author. But the book should be banned. It is offensive to all religions, it's meant to undermine all religious belief. We approve of its removal from stores."[31] It seemed that, confronted by blasphemers and other free thinkers, the pious of the world tried to close ranks and form a most unlikely spiritual brotherhood.

No leading religious figure or organization stood by Rushdie in his hour of need. Virtually the only exception was Paul Valadier, the editor of a French Jesuit magazine, who, outraged by the Khomeini edict, wrote an article on "Religion and Violence." In it, he declared that "religions contribute to maintain tensions and to revive violence between men."[32] As a result of writing this piece, he lost his position as editor. It was small wonder that other religious leaders sympathetic to Rushdie kept their mouths shut.

By staking out the most extreme position, Khomeini created an opening for other religious leaders to look reasonable, so that they could make demands that would in normal circumstances be considered improper, or even beyond the pale. The assertiveness of religious figures led some observers to see the issue confronting Western countries less in terms of freedom of expression, and more as one of encroachments on the secular state. Were the rights hammered out at so much cost in the seventeenth century really to be reduced by a foreign extremist? Not likely, but the issue had to be addressed. As *The Economist* put it, "Rabbis, priests and mullahs are, it seems, uniting to restrain free speech, lest any member of their collective flock should have his feelings hurt.... The Rushdie affair is showing not just that some Muslims do not understand the merits of free speech. It shows that many Western clerics do not either."[33]

Many Western writers felt obliged to point out, for the first time in many decades, that the religiously faithful have no right to silence the blasphemous, nor do they have any moral superiority over atheists. Why should those religiously oriented enjoy special immunity from insults? Why should their anger matter more than that of Viking Penguin officials or bookstore owners with smashed windows?

How did this peculiar issue come to be debated again? It resulted from a subtle, yet profound change in the understanding of blasphemy. As Michael Walzer pointed out, blasphemy was traditionally understood as a crime against God.

> But today we are concerned for our pain and, sometimes, for other people's. Blasphemy has become an offense against the faithful— in much the same way as pornograpy is an offense against the innocent and the virtuous. Given this meaning, blasphemy is an ecumenical crime, and so it is not surprising (though, in fact, I was surprised) that Christians and Jews should join Muslims in calling Salman Rushdie's *The Satanic Verses* a blasphemous book.[34]

The notion of blasphemy being directed against people rather than God exactly suits a secular age. And it goes far to explain the informal alliance of clerics against Rushdie.

If Christian and Jewish spokesmen were widely criticized for this attitude in the West, their sympathy was heard and gratefully acknowledged in Tehran. A television commentary noted that "realistic Christian and Jewish circles have understood the conditions and objectives of these colonialist efforts to negate divine values and to insult the divine prophets."[35] Interior Minister 'Ali Akbar Mohtashemi went even further, pointing to "the insulting anti-Christian films which have recently been released by some Western countries," and concluding that there exists "an insidious colonialist movement working against the sanctities of all divine religions and prophets."[36]

Far from respecting the Christian West for allowing Jesus to be mocked, Muslims bemoaned this permissiveness. They did so partly because Islam recognizes Jesus as a prophet, and therefore pays him respect; and partly out of a sense of propriety for sacred figures. As Habibollah Bi'azar Shirazi, Iran's ambassador to Greece, explained, "Reverence for people's beliefs should be the cornerstone of international relations."[37] On learning that *The Last Temptation of Christ* would be shown at the Eighth Istanbul Film Festival, Iranian media linked this to *The Satanic Verses* affair, calling it part of the plot "hatched by world arrogance and international Zionism."[38] This led to an extraordinary scene in

Istanbul, where fundamentalist Muslims and fundamentalist Christians joined forces to stand outside a theater to protest a screening of *The Last Temptation of Christ*.

Publishers, Bookstores and Libraries

Publishers found themselves in a special position, for they alone, along with Rushdie himself, were threatened by Khomeini's decree. Viking Penguin, the British and American publisher of *The Satanic Verses*, was subjected to incessant harassment. Its London premises resembled an armed camp, with around-the-clock police protection, metal detectors, and escorts required for visitors. In New York, the police department designated the Viking offices a "sensitive location" and dogs sniffed packages coming by mail. Viking was believed to have spent about $3 million on security measures during the first half of 1989. Nonetheless, Viking flinched only once—in February, when it recalled and pulped a paperback edition of *The Satanic Verses*. (This action became public knowledge when a thousand copies of the paper edition slipped through the recall and went on sale in Geneva.) The company leaders' quiet determination to go about their work and not to accede to any form of pressure made them among the few heroes in this saga.

Other publishers, however, faltered. In the days after the ayatollah's *fatwa*, almost every house with rights to the book had second thoughts. Not unreasonably, they all felt intimidated; and as book houses have historically had no reason to be security-conscious, a great deal of scurrying took place in mid-February. Presses de la Cité in Paris, for example, had an around-the-clock police guard and metal bars on its windows. In addition, the firm removed the brass nameplate from the outside wall of its building and its top figures took unlisted telephone numbers.

Some publishers, such as the Greek one, postponed publication indefinitely—in effect, canceling the book. In Holland, Veen announced that it would consult with the government and Muslim organizations. Shamed by the public outcry, however, most publishers decided to overcome their hesitations and go ahead with *The Satanic Verses*. Mondadori in Italy decided to distribute the first printing of twenty thousand copies already in stock. Translations subsequently appeared in Spain, Norway, Brazil and Holland.

In some countries, publishers talked about grouping together to spread more widely the risk of putting out *The Satanic Verses*. The French edition contained the following explanation at the front of the book: "The novel *The Satanic Verses* is published by Christian Bourgois with the 'support of the Ministry of Culture and Communications of the French Republic' and the friendly support of [a listing of twenty-one major houses]."[39] (The offices of one of those copublishers, Fayard, was subsequently bombed in an act probably connected to *The Satanic Verses*.) In Spain, Seix Barcal was joined by eighteen companies in a special venture. In Germany, Kepenhauer & Witsch was joined initially by twenty-four companies, then by seventy more. But the most unusual joint venture was surely in Brazil, where no commercial house was prepared to serve as the novel's lead publisher. In stepped Fernando Moraes, the communist secretary of culture for São Paulo, who arranged for a joint publication in which the state of São Paulo was the publisher of record.

Pusillanimity on the part of mainstream houses created an opportunity for bootleg publishers. In some countries (including Israel), they merely reprinted the English version of *The Satanic Verses*; interestingly, Viking made no legal efforts to block these editions. In France, the outcome was more dramatic; the legitimate publisher of *The Satanic Verses* dithered so long that Jean-Edern Hallier, a satiric writer, came out with a pirate edition. Although his first version was confiscated at a plant in southern France and a court assessed Hallier one million French francs ($156,000) in damages, the illegal edition did eventually appear. What made the book so unusual was the fact that Hallier, in an effort to keep costs down, did not bind and cut the folio pages of the book. As a result, it was distributed (often gratis) in a newspaper-size format. Scorning the legitimate French publishers as "worthless, terrorized soup salesmen," Hallier justified his illegal publication as obeying an unwritten law "pertaining to human dignity."[40]

As though wishing to live up to Hallier's scorn, when Christian Bourgois did finally publish *Les Versets sataniques*, he did so in a surreptitious way, without promoting the book, sending it to the usual list of stores, or allowing (as is usual) for bookstores to return unsold copies. Further, the release took place in mid-July, on the eve of the country's summer break. Even the translator was afraid, hiding behind the well-known pseudonym Alcofribas Nasier (the anagram used by François Rabelais for some of his publications).

Booksellers were not threatened from Tehran, but their glass windows were on the front line of violence. Local Muslims issued warnings and threats of their own. In France, for example, Abul Farid Gabteni, president of the Voice of Islam, threatened bookstores that "if the book is shown in store windows, this will produce uncontrollable reactions."[41] In the United States, the FBI was notified of seventy-eight threats to bookstores in early March 1989, clearly only a small proportion of the total number. Waldenbooks alone received forty anonymous threats; B. Dalton got thirty in less than three hours.

In Great Britain, intimidation meant that hardly a single bookstore sold Rushdie's novel openly. In the United States, it was not at all available in about one-third of the bookstores, and many others which carried the book kept it under the counter. *The Satanic Verses* had the inadvertent effect of showing the difference between independent stores and the franchises, much to the credit of the former. After extensive discussions and reflection, owners of independent bookstores nearly always decided to go ahead and sell (if not openly display) the book. This decision won them much favorable comment, most notably from William Safire, who urged book buyers to "patronize your local independent bookseller," and not the chains.[42] The owner of Cody's Books, one of the two Berkeley, California, stores that was bombed, characterized the choice to carry *The Satanic Verses* as "perhaps the most difficult decision of my life;"[43] many other owners, unprepared logistically or psychologically for the fundamentalist Muslims' threat, shared in this agony.

In contrast, the great chains—Waldenbooks, B. Dalton, and Barnes & Noble in the United States, Coles in Canada, W. H. Smith in Britain, Vroom en Dreesman in Holland—quickly pulled the book, though widespread criticism (including a protest march in New York City) in some cases caused them to reconsider. When B. Dalton polled its managers and employees, it found that an impressive ninety percent favored selling the novel;[44] this backing made it fairly easy for the company to reverse course and carry the novel. Even so, the decision whether to sell *The Satanic Verses* was left to the individual store manager.

To promote proper security in stores, the American Booksellers Association set up a twenty-four-hour emergency security hot line (funded by B. Dalton), while its weekly publication, *Newswire*, offered specific tips. The Canadian Booksellers Association urged that the police be notified when *The Satanic Verses* arrived—and that the deadly book not be placed in windows. Some bookstores devised their own forms of protection. The store at Dulles International Airport outside Washington, D.C., posted a prominent sign, "We do not stock *The Satanic Verses*." Booksmith, a store on Fifth Avenue in New York City, devoted a wall to the non-fiction best-sellers numbered 1-10 and the fiction best-sellers numbered 2-11.

Booksellers suffered nearly all the violence in the West. In Italy, followers of the ayatollah set fire to a bookstore in Padua owned by Mondadori, the Italian publisher of *The Satanic Verses*, and smashed the windows of four bookstores displaying the book. Fires were set at two stores in Oslo soon after the Norwegian translation appeared. These warnings were sometimes serious: two stores in Berkeley, California, were firebombed, as was *The Riverdale Press*, a weekly newspaper in the Bronx. Although no one was hurt in any of these incidents, an undetonated pipe bomb was found on the floor of the poetry section in Cody's Books in Berkeley. When the police detonated this bomb, they found it was powerful enough to have destroyed the entire business and killed everyone in it. Other stores carrying the book had to contend with demonstrators outside their door with signs bearing "Assassinate the Writer" and other intimidating messages.

But it was in Great Britain that violence against bookstores occurred most often and persisted the longest. In London, zealots bombed two large Charing Cross Road bookstores (Collets and Dillons) on April 9. In May, explosions went off in the town of High Wycombe and in London, on King's Road. In early September, Liberty's, a large London department store, was bombed in connection with the Penguin Bookshop inside the store (which, ironically, did not carry *The Satanic Verses*). Days later, a bomb went off at the Penguin store in York, while unexploded devices were found at Penguin stores in Guildford, Nottingham, and Peterborough.

Reviewing these events, Maureen J. O'Brien, a journalist specializing in the book trade, concluded that "the business of bookselling in [the United States] and other countries will never again be quite the same."[45] Ayatollah Khomeini brought an age of innocence to an abrupt end; and many in the bookstore trade feared that others would follow his example.

Libraries adopted a variety of policies. Some, such as the British Library, the Bodleian, and the National Library of Scotland, placed the book on the restricted shelves (along with pornography and rare books), so the book could only be read under careful supervision. The obvious intent was to prevent readers from mutilating the volume. At other libraries, the concern was the reverse—that *The Satanic Verses* not harm readers. Thus, some libraries placated the Muslim protesters by placing warning stickers on the book.

The Soviet Bloc and Third World

Moscow emerged from the confrontation with high marks. It did not try, in the old style, to exploit the benefits from a crisis between the West and a non-aligned state. The easy, natural thing would have been to pander to Tehran and fundamentalist Muslims by blaming the West for the whole controversy. There were elements of this opportunism, as when Radio Baku described the EC decision to withdraw ambassadors from Tehran as "unprincipled and biased,"[46] but this sort of remark was fairly rare.

Instead, the Kremlin acted in an unusually responsible manner. On the diplomatic level, it offered to play "a positive role" in ending the dispute, an intent that was noteworthy in itself. Although no one in the West took this offer very seriously, few diplomats were so rude as to point out publicly that Soviet ideology in roughly equal measure opposes both freedom of speech and respect for religion.

More impressive were the analyses offered in the Soviet media. The Arabic programming of Radio Peace and Progress held both sides accountable:

> The problem lies...in the current policies of some Western countries that have not rid themselves of arrogance and discrimination against Iran, which has suffered in the past from the noose of Western economic hegemony, as well as direct aggression. However, Iran's reaction has been conjectural and negative toward all manifestations of insult.

The analysis went on: "We hope that the leaders of Iran, as well as the leaders of the West, will take all the necessary steps to remove the political crisis brought about by publication of *The Satanic Verses.*"[47] The same radio station put matters even more constructively in its Persian language broadcast: the call from Tehran for Rushdie's execution

> is a source of great regret because it has eliminated the hopes...in the Soviet Union that the political crisis in relation to the said novel would die down.... Resorting to terror and threats in this way will have no other outcome for Iran but the exacerbation of international crises with dangerous consequences for Iran itself.[48]

Another analysis on the same station blamed Iran more bluntly: "Tehran's extremist reaction to *The Satanic Verses* has led to the current diplomatic war between Iran and the West."[49] This from that old source of unadulterated disinformation, Radio Peace and Progress? Radio Moscow was equally constructive in its broadcasts to Iran, ruing the "negative effects" for Iran and the West from *The Satanic Verses* controversy. The commentary went on to call for an end to the tensions through talks and the creation of an atmosphere of trust.[50]

Soviet media intended for domestic consumption took a similar approach. *Pravda* referred to demonstrators supporting Khomeini as "Muslim fanatics."[51] *Argumenty i Facty* likened the Iranian bounty on Rushdie to "pouring oil on flames."[52] Speaking on Soviet television, Aleksandr Bovin characterized Khomeini's fanaticism as "strong and dangerous," adding: "to condemn the author to death is barbaric and smacks of the Middle Ages. It is an affront to every civilized being."[53] For *Literaturnaya Gazeta*, the sight of children carrying placards reading "Kill Rushdie" was "particularly dreadful."[54] *Izvestiya* reported receiving "letters and telegrams from Soviet citizens" calling the Khomeini edict "counter to the norms of international law and the principles of humanity."[55] Vsevolod Ivanovich Solva, deputy chief of the Foreign Ministry information office, put an official (if inarticulate) imprimatur on these assertions: "no one has the right to excommunicate disapproval of authors from life, or indeed any person at all."[56]

The official Soviet position was equally constructive on the question of ending the diplomatic crisis between Iran and the EC. Indeed, the Foreign Ministry welcomed the European decision of March 20 to return heads of mission to Tehran, a spokesman calling this "a positive step to help settle the situation."[57] Soviet commentators were acutely conscious of the responsible position their government was taking on *The Satanic Verses* affair. D. Makarov proudly explained to Soviet readers:

Soviet diplomacy is acting fully in accord with the concept of the new political thinking while resisting the temptation to put on the propaganda eye-glasses of any one of the parties involved, and it is conducting delicate work to settle this far-from-simple conflict.[58]

Just so; the Soviet position in this matter was one of the most solid examples of new thinking to date.

On the matter of publishing the book in the U.S.S.R., Soviet authorities adopted a cagey stand: while there were "no immediate plans to publish the book," according to Mikhail Nenashev, chairman of the Soviet State Committee for Publishing, "the authorities would have no objection if a private company published the book."[59]

Soviet writers tended to stay on the sidelines as observers. The only demonstration, a half-hour protest outside the Iranian embassy led by the editor of *Glasnost*, Sergei Grigoryants, included just fifteen protesters. The newly-organized Soviet chapter of PEN condemned both blasphemy and the death threat. A commentary in *Literaturnaya Gazeta* noted with some embarrassment that only two Soviet writers, Anatoly Rybakov and Tatyana Tolstaya, had signed the widely-published "World Statement" in support of Salman Rushdie.

The response to Rushdie in Eastern Europe was mixed. While the Bulgarian and Polish governments simply banned the book, a semi-legal Polish journal serialized the book in translation. In Yugoslavia, the Communist party's daily newspaper, *Borba*, began to serialize *The Satanic Verses* but stopped under the pressure of telephone threats, presumably from local Muslims. Despite the threats, a book publisher planned to bring the book out. In East Germany, both the GDR Writers Association and the PEN Center condemned Khomeini in the strongest terms.

In the Third World, few individuals or institutions stood up to the ayatollah. As much as possible, they wanted neither to endorse his death sentence nor confront him, but to remain out of harm's way. Peking, for example, was conspicuously silent on the whole matter. Exceptions to this pattern were rare. Among governments, the most notable stance was that of the Philippines; notwithstanding nearly two decades of active Muslim rebellion in the country's south, Manila indicated it could not ban the book, on the grounds of constitutional guarantees of free speech. In India, K.N. Singh, general secretary of the Congress-I party, rejected the edict on the grounds that the Congress party, followers of Mahatma Gandhi and Pandit Nehru, "always depre-cated violence and terrorism of all kinds."[60] But such voices were as rare as they were courageous.

Perhaps not surprisingly, the only public figures in the Third World to stand consistently by Rushdie were his fellow writers. Wole Soyinka, the Nigerian writer and Nobel Prize winner, published a remarkable document. Khomeini, he began, is

> easily diagnosed as a sick and dangerous man who has long forgotten the fundamental tenets of Islam.... Iran must be ostracised as long as it boasts a common criminal at its pinnacle of power.... And the Ayatollah must be punished for his arrogance, for his hubris and the implicit blasphemy in his arrogation of a Supreme Will....
>
> It is not Salman Rushdie's work which should be banned from India, but Ayatollah Khomeini's person, voice, thoughts, sayings, etc., etc. Indeed I would go further and declare that everything which is Iran should be banned as long as Ayatollah Khomeini remains accepted as a leader in Iran, everything except the voices of Iran's political and cultural dissidents and the protests of her repressed womanhood.[61]

Shortly after this statement, Soyinka had to contend with three hundred Muslims rioting outside the British consulate in Kaduna, Nigeria, carrying placards with such messages as "Wole Soyinka must die."[62] Muslim student leaders at Bayero University in Kano called for "urgent measures" to deal with Soyinka.[63] Chinua Achebe, also of Nigeria, called on Rushdie not to despair, and "to keep fighting for the freedom of the human spirit." Anita Desai of India counseled courage and Octavio Paz of Mexico advised firmness. Mario Vargas Llosa of Peru declared "total solidarity."[64]

International organizations wanted nothing to do with *The Satanic Verses* issue, for it polarized emotions and challenged the comfortable assumptions of a single order which underlie such institutions. UNESCO Director-General Frederico Mayor made a weak statement calling for both religious respect and freedom of expression. Efforts by non-governmental organizations to condemn Khomeini at the United Nations Commission on Human Rights got nowhere. When the representative of the World Union for Progressive Judaism at the Commission raised the topic on February 17, arguing that "silence now will make us all accomplices of terror and tyranny,"[65] Muslim states made it clear they would oppose such efforts. In the face of this obduracy, not a single Western government attempted to push through a resolution on Khomeini. By similar token, Iranian efforts also fell flat. For example, the foreign ministers of the non-aligned movement in May turned down Tehran's proposed amendment against "blasphemy against any revealed religion."[66]

While most Westerners abhorred the ayatollah's edict and supported Rushdie's right to insult whomever he wanted, important pockets of softness and appeasement were evident. The relatively weak response to *The Satanic Verses* issue raised many questions about censorship, its costs and benefits, and the likelihood of a chilling effect to be felt in the West for years to come.

NOTES

[1]*The Philadelphia Inquirer*, February 14, 1989.
[2]*The New York Times*, February 17, 1989.
[3]*The Philadelphia Inquirer*, February 22, 1989.
[4]PEN American Center, *Freedom-to-Write Bulletin*, March 1989, p. 4.
[5]Deutsche Presse Agentur, February 17, 1989.

[6]Kuwaiti News Agency, February 21, 1989.

[7]*The Washington Post*, February 23, 1989.

[8]*Le Monde*, February 23, 1989.

[9]*Le Monde*, March 2, 1989.

[10]*The New York Times*, February 21, 1989.

[11]*Time*, February 27, 1989.

[12]*The New York Times*, February 18, 1989.

[13]*The Washington Times*, February 20, 1989.

[14]*The New York Times Book Review*, March 12, 1989.

[15]Christopher Hitchens, "Wanton Acts of Usage," *Harper's*, September 1986, pp. 69.

[16]Midge Decter, "The Rushdiad," *Commentary*, June 1989, pp. 22-23. In some cases, they seemed to add to the peril of others. Thus, the effect of writers demonstrating outside a B. Dalton store in Boston was to prompt a telephone threat threatening the store's management not to give in to their demands. As a result, the store had to be evacuated.

[17]*Publishers Weekly*, September 29, 1989.

[18]*The Guardian*, February 24, 1989.

[19]*The Independent*, February 15, 1989.

[20]The Editors, "Two Cheers for Blasphemy," *The New Republic*, March 13, 1989.

[21]PEN American Center, *Freedom-to-Write Bulletin*, March 1989, p. 13; reprinted in *The Observer*, February 26, 1989, *The Washington Post*, February 27, 1989. The compliment is not surprising. Earlier, Rushdie had used the adjective "brilliant" to describe Said's 1978 book, *Orientalism*.

[22]*The Nation*, March 20, 1989.

[23]Deutsche Presse Agentur, February 23, 1989.

[24]Patrick Buchanan, "Religious Insults and Satanic Verses," *The Washington Times*, February 20, 1989.

[25]*The New York Times*, February 20, 1989.

[26]*Der Spiegel*, February 27, 1989.

[27]March 27, 1989, quoted in Bernard Oudin, *La Foi que tue*, 2d ed., (Paris: Éditions Robert Laffont, 1989), p. 16.

[28]Jimmy Carter, "Rushdie's Book Is an Insult," *The New York Times*, March 5, 1989.

[29]*The Times*, March 4, 1989

[30]*Le Monde*, March 8, 1989.

[31]*Publishers Weekly*, March 10, 1989.

[32]Paul Valadier, "Religions et violence," *Etudes*, April 1989, p. 522.

[33]*The Economist*, March 11, 1989.

[34]Michael Walzer, "The Sins of Salman," *The New Republic*, April 10, 1989.

[35]Tehran Television, March 3, 1989.

[36]Radio Tehran, March 12, 1989.

[37]*Tehran Times*, March 18, 1989.

[38]*Jomhuriye-ye Islami*, April 3, 1989.

[39]Salman Rushdie, *Les Versets sataniques*, trans. Alcofribas Nasier (Paris: Christian Bourgois, 1989).

[40]Jean-Edern Hallier, "L'Imprimerie nationale de la liberté, c'est nous," in Salman Rushdie, *Les Versets sataniques*, trans. János Molnár de Párno (Paris: L'Idiot international, 1989), p. 2.

[41]*Le Monde*, July 21, 1989.

[42]*The New York Times*, February 20, 1989.

[43]*The Washington Times*, April 14, 1989.

[44]*Publishers Weekly*, March 10, 1989.

[45]*Publishers Weekly*, September 29, 1989.

[46]Islamic Revolution News Agency, February 22, 1989.

[47]Radio Peace and Progress, February 22, 1989.

[48]Ibid.

[49]Radio Peace and Progress, February 24, 1989.

[50]Radio Moscow, March 2, 1989.

[51]*Pravda*, February 26, 1989.

[52]*Argumenty i Facty*, March 4, 1989.

[53]Moscow Television, March 19, 1989.

[54]*Literaturnaya Gazeta*, March 8, 1989.

[55]*Izvestiya*, March 10, 1989.

[56]Radio Moscow, March 19, 1989.

[57]TASS, March 22, 1989.

[58]*Argumenty i Facty*, March 4, 1989.

[59]Agence France Presse, February 24, 1989.

[60]Radio Delhi, February 25, 1989.

[61]*The African Guardian*, February 23, 1989.

[62]*Ar-Ray al-'Amm*, February 28, 1989; *The New York Times*, March 5, 1989.

[63]British Broadcasting Corporation, February 27, 1989.

[64]"Words for Salman Rushdie," *The New York Times Book Review*, March 12, 1989.

[65]Reuter, February 17, 1989.

[66]*The Independent*, May 20, 1989.

10.

IRAN'S SHADOW IN THE WEST

The Satanic Verses affair exposed a reluctance among Western governments, writers and booksellers to fight very hard. It seems scarcely believable, but the West, which had so much greater resources than Iran, especially an Iran recovering from almost a decade of war, ran scared of Tehran. How was it that the American, British, French and German governments could be intimidated by a state possessing little more than clearly defined goals and strength of will? The reasons are worth exploring in some detail, for they have important implications.

In part, the Western reluctance may have to do with an inability to recognize fundamentalist Islam as hostile; in part, it may have to do with an undue feeling of confidence and bonhommie fostered by the apparent decline of the totalitarian left. Too, there seemed to be a sense that acquiescence was much easier than struggling. But two factors were most critical in the Western reaction to the Rushdie affair: the influence of local fundamentalist Muslims and the fear of Iranian retaliation—either by launching terrorist activities, harming Western hostages held in Lebanon and Iran, or restricting commerce. Tehran acted with the determination of an extremist, the tactics of a rug merchant, and the flexibility of a guerrilla. In brief, it had exactly those qualities most effective for confronting the West.

Local Muslim Pressure

Fundamentalist Muslims resident in the West furthered the ayatollah's cause in a number of ways, both non-violent and violent. To begin with, they echoed Khomeini's arguments against Rushdie from within by making their voices heard through the media, in the classroom, and in private discussions. Some of their efforts, such as the advertisement placed by the Birmingham Central Mosque and carried in British newspapers on March 3, asking why "the entire British Nation should pay for one man's greed," prompted widespread discussion.

While these efforts achieved no major successes, they did have an important effect on the tenor of the discussion about Rushdie in Europe and America. Even in diluted form, the Muslims' representation of Khomeini's viewpoint prevented an easy consensus from being reached. Pro-Khomeini activities insured that both sides would be represented in the West. A debate, often spirited, took place in nearly every country professing freedom of expression. This had various effects, one of which was to circumscribe governmental responses. Another, and perhaps a more profound one, was to create a sense of moral relativism. Many Europeans, and even more Americans, who initially saw the issue as one of good versus evil came eventually to see it as a clash of civilizations, each with its proper priorities and sanctities. By their presence, the fundamentalist Muslims turned an issue of right and wrong into something far more nuanced.

Fundamentalist Muslims did not just talk but made full use of their electoral weight. This was especially the case in Britain, where most Muslim residents were citizens and where they shared a common origin in the Indian sub-continent. Nothing symbolized Muslim voting power more than the fact that an elected politician, Barry Seal, the Labour Member of the European Parliament for Yorkshire West, spoke at the famous book-burning rally in Bradford. Not coincidentally, Max Madden, the member of parliament (MP) representing the many Muslims of Bradford West, was at the forefront of appeasing the ayatollah. He filed one bill to extend the British blasphemy laws to cover Islam, another to call on Rushdie to have his publishers withdraw the book, and yet another (co-sponsored with two Labour MPs also representing sizeable Muslim constituencies) to urge a ban on further production of the book. The other two MPs from Bradford did not join in Madden's efforts and paid for it later, in Muslim denunciations and calls for their resignation. Some months later, Madden warned that not taking up the Muslim cause could cost the Labour Party as many as ten parliamentary seats in the next election.

Khomeini's supporters also took to the streets. Fifteen hundred fundamentalist Muslims, mostly of Pakistani origins, demonstrated at the Place de la République in Paris, screaming "À mort Rushdie" ("Death to Rushdie") into the cameras. In the Hague, 5,000 Muslims gathered in front of the Ministry of Justice, burned imitation copies of *The Satanic Verses* along with pictures of the author, and called for Rushdie's death. Nearly 2,000 Muslims protested noisily in Manchester on February 24 and 10,000 in New York City the next day, protesting outside the closed offices of Viking. Also on the 25th, 1,000 Muslims marched in Oslo; the next day, 2,000 marched in Copenhagen. The protests in Scandinavia were the first of such size in a decade or more. Back in England, 3,000 Muslims protested the Rushdie book in Halifax on March 3. On the 4th, demonstrations took place in Sheffield and Derby, complete with book burnings and chants for Rushdie's death. On the 6th, another 3,000 Muslims marched in Derby and burned copies of *The Satanic Verses*. And so on.

Remarkably, a massive rally of some 15,000 to 20,000 Muslims met in Parliament Square in London on May 27, just a few days before Ayatollah Khomeini's death. Calling for the novel's banning and the extension of blasphemy laws to Islam, the protesters burned Rushdie in effigy, as well as the customary copies of his book. The fact that, months after the controversy had erupted, Muslim associations could still bring such numbers out pointed to the depths of passions aroused by *The Satanic Verses*, and the new-found organizing ability of British Muslims. In addition, Tehran reportedly contributed about $1 million to the march, an indication of its interest in the keeping *The Satanic Verses* issue alive. Indeed, the Iranians had hoped to mount the largest-ever demonstration in Britain. Bursting with pride, the Islamic Revolution News Agency reported a crowd of one hundred thousand and announced that Hyde Park that day was turned into "a vast open-air mosque."[1] The protest was marred, however, by a volley of sticks between Iraqi and Iranian factions, leading to intervention by the authorities, injury to eighteen policemen, the arrest of one hundred fifteen demonstators, and charges against seventy-five persons.

Then there was the atmosphere of intimidation. A wide assortment of targets were anonymously threatened with violence, leading to additional police guards being posted here and there around the globe. Politicians requiring extra security included: in Canada, the minister of revenue and the foreign minister; in Britain, the prime minister, foreign secretary and home secretary; and in France, the president of the National Assembly. Artists were publicly threatened in France, Nigeria, and Egypt. The British television interviewer Peter Sissons asked an Iranian diplomat, "Do you understand that we don't regard it as civilized to kill people for their opinions?" Muslim zealots found this an "insulting" question and threatened Sissons' life, so he too had a police guard attached.[2] A public reading from *The Satanic Verses* in Austria had to be cancelled due to telephoned bomb threats—one of which was traced back to the Iranian embassy in Vienna. Followers of Khomeini also issued dozens of threats to publishing houses and book stores throughout the West.

Threats with names attached were even more effective than anonymous ones. These fostered an atmosphere of intimidation the likes of which the West had not witnessed for decades. In Britain, several Muslim leaders endorsed Khomeini's decision, and some even swore to carry out the death sentence. The Union of Islamic Students' Associations in Europe issued a statement offering its services to Khomeini. Others were yet more outspoken, uttering statements that left the rest of the population aghast. "I think we should kill Salman Rushdie's whole family," Faruq Mughal screamed as he emerged from a West London mosque. "His body should be chopped into little pieces and sent to all Islamic countries as a warning to those who insult our religion." A London property developer told reporters, "If I see him, I will kill him straight away. Take my name and address. One day I will kill him."[3] Iqbal Sacranic of the U.K. Action Committee on Islamic Affairs announced that "death, perhaps, is a bit too easy for him...his mind must be tormented for the rest of his life unless he asks for forgiveness to Almighty Allah."[4] Back in Bradford, the secretary of the Mosque Council, Sayed Abdul Quddus, said that Rushdie "deserves hanging."[5] Parvez Akhtar, a financial adviser in Bradford, told a reporter that "if Salman Rushdie came here, he would be torn to pieces. He is a dead man."[6] Newspaper reports filled with such statements made it appear that Khomeini's edict enjoyed support among Muslims of Britain, regardless of age, sex, social status and religiosity.

Most striking, several prominent European converts to Islam endorsed the death edict, much enhancing its respectability. These included the French intellectual Vincent Mansour (né Vincent Monteil) and the Swiss journalist Ahmed Huber. Cat Stevens, the former rock singer who converted to Islam in 1977 and changed his name to Yusuf al-Islam, told Muslim students in Surrey, "He must be killed. The Qur'an makes it clear—if someone defames the prophet, then he must die."[7] Islam reiterated this view on television two months later, saying that if Rushdie turned up on his doorstep asking for help, "I'd try to phone the Ayatollah Khomeini and tell him exactly where this man is."[8] (Yusuf al-Islam's pious anger may have been due in part to the caricature of him as Bilal X in *The Satanic Verses*, where he is portrayed as the favored lieutenant of Khomeini whose "well-nourished, highly trained" voice served as "a weapon of the West turned against its makers.")

Muslims in the United States usually took a more nuanced approach, threatening Rushdie without wishing to take responsibility for doing so. Typical was the comment by Zaheer Uddin, secretary general of the Islamic Circle of North America: "I would highly recommend Mr. Rushdie not to come here. In our agenda, violence is out. But with five million Muslims in the United States, we cannot guarantee his safety."[9] Or Salim Chowdhury, a leader of the Iowa City Muslim community, who announced that "people here are very angry, and they would be very happy to see someone kill him."[10]

Finally, fundamentalist Muslims did undertake violence in the West. Except for the killing in Brussels of two mosque officials, their actions were relatively minor—bookstores damaged in England, Norway, Italy and the United States—but these initiatives had an impact far out of proportion to their actual damage, representing as they did a wave of potential violence which, it was feared, could occur any place, any time. As though to buttress this fear, the Iranians sent signals in support of active steps. Thus, a Tehran newspaper encouraged Muslims in Britain "to seek ways outside the law to guard their rights."[11] Confirming this danger, experts estimated that the ayatollah had some thousand followers in Britain who would be prepared to risk all to get at Rushdie. And this raised the possibility of an even more acute form of intimidation, that of terrorism sponsored by the Iranian government.

State-sponsored Terrorism

Prior to the Rushdie incident, the Khomeini government had repeatedly threatened and assaulted its enemies abroad, and those in West Europe with special frequency. Their victims numbered dissident Iranians, other Middle Easterners, Europeans and Americans.

Exiled Iranians living in the West were hounded and sometimes struck. In Great Britain, Iranian hit squads first made themselves known in December 1981, when three members of Hizbullah were killed while assembling a car bomb. Subsequent targets included Bizan Fazeli, dead from a bomb explosion in his pro-monarchist father's video store in August 1986; Amir Parviz, injured in July

1987 by a bomb placed in his car; and 'Ali Tavakoli and his son Nader, shot in their apartment after insulting the ayatollah in October 1987 at a gathering of Iranian monarchists at the Speakers' Corner in Hyde Park. In Paris, prominent Iranians killed by Tehran's agents included the shah's nephew (1980) and a former Iranian general and his brother (1984). Rushdie, it bears noting, was not the first person to have an Iranian *fatwa* directed against him. Shahpour Bakhtiar, the prime minister of Iran in the brief interregnum between the shah's exit (on January 16, 1979) and Khomeini's assertion of power (on February 11, 1979), lived with a price on his head for a decade. He was attacked one time, in Paris in July 1980, in an operation which killed a French policeman and a French neighbor. Bakhtiar has lived ever since under heavy guard.

Agents also terrorized citizens of Middle East states deemed enemies of the Islamic Revolution. An Israeli military post in south Lebanon was blown up in 1983, leaving sixty dead. The ambassador from the United Arab Emirates was killed in Paris in 1984. Attempts to force the Kuwaiti government to release convicted Iranian terrorist agents led to many attacks in 1984-86, including an assassination attempt against the country's ruler. Operations in 1988 included the assassination of Saudi diplomats in Turkey, Pakistan and Thailand, and the bombing of a Saudi airline office in Nigeria. In all, according to the conservative calculations of the Department of State, the Iranian government was involved in forty-four terrorist operations in 1987, thirty-three in 1988.

Many of the operations were directed against Americans, starting with the seizure of the U.S. Embassy in Tehran. Among the most important attacks were the suicide car bombings against the U.S. Embassies in Beirut (twice) and Kuwait, and the destruction of the Marine barracks in Beirut. Other noteworthy assaults included the year-long abduction of one president of the American University of Beirut, David Dodge, and the assassination of another, Malcolm Kerr. When a Kuwait Air flight was hijacked to Tehran in 1984, the only passengers killed were two Americans. In 1985, the hijacking of a TWA flight to Beirut left one American dead. An Iranian role in the 1988 bombing of a Pan Am plane over Lockerbie, Scotland, appears almost certain.

The Iranian network reached even to the United States. Three events stand out. In July 1980, 'Ali Akbar Tabataba'i, an outspoken Iranian opponent of the regime, was killed in his house outside Washington, D.C., by a former security guard at the Iranian-interests section. In December 1983, the FBI prevented a potentially major incident in a Seattle concert hall hosting a pro-shah theatrical group; Tehran's agents had planned to bar the doors of the hall, splash gasoline on the building, and set it on fire. Finally, in March 1989, a bomb went off in the family car of the captain of the U.S.S. *Vincennes*, the ship which eight months earlier had brought down an Iran Air plane.

Over the years, Iranian assets in the U.S. increased to the point that Tehran was probably able to attack targets at will. "The Iranian network in the U.S.," noted L. Carter Cornick, "is the most dangerous and troublesome of all the terror groups in the U.S."[12] Oliver Revell of the FBI informed Congress that several dozen members of Iran's Revolutionary Guards Corps had entered the United States by posing as students, and that American law lacked a mechanism by which to expel them. He also told reporters that between a half and a third of the eight hundred thousand Iranians in the United States received funds directly from the Iranian government.

The ayatollah's men became famous for fanaticism, craziness and a willingness to die, and these qualities deeply shook Westerners. However poor and beleaguered, the Iranian government was the regime which undoubtedly inspired the most fear beyond its own borders. In comparison, the Soviet, Chinese, even the Cuban regimes appeared old and tame. A poll in mid-1989 showed that French citizens found Iran to be the state most threatening to France.* Tehran's terrible reputation served very

Le Monde, July 4, 1989. When asked "Which of the following countries appear to you today to be the most threatening to France," 25 percent answered Iran, 21 percent the U.S.S.R., and 14 percent the Arab countries in general. In total, 57 percent of the French believed the Muslim states to be most threatening to France.

well whenever its policies led to a clash with the West. If, as
Maggie Gee, the British novelist, described it, *The Satanic Verses*
incident was "a traffic accident between religious passion and
political expediency,"[13] then Iranian momentum made up for
Western bulk. It confirmed, once more, that will and ideology
count for much more than material recources.

Hostages

Between early 1982 and mid-1988, ninety-six foreign hostages
of twenty-one national origins were abducted in Lebanon.
Twenty-five of them were Americans, sixteen were Frenchmen,
and twelve Britons. With the exception of six Iranians, all the
hostages appear to have been seized by groups allied with Iran.[14]
Although the numbers of these hostages was small, the guilty
memory of their suffering had a wide impact on governments
throughout the West. An extreme reluctance to jeopardize their
lives often led to near-paralysis in policy toward Iran. This factor
explains why, for many months, British leaders refused to raise
with their Iranian counterparts the topic of the 1988 massacres of
Mojahedin-e Khalq in Iran. At a later date, William Waldegrave,
minister of state at the Foreign Office, explicitly admitted as
much: "I regarded my duty to this House as being to put help for
the hostages and our citizens at the top of my agenda."[15] Skilled
Iranian manipulation of the hostages' lives made these at times a
major electoral issue in both the United States and France; and, of
course, it lay behind the massive complications and misconcep-
tions in the Iran/*contra* adventure, which put an end to the
American tilt toward Iraq during the Gulf War.

Hostages played a direct role in *The Satanic Verses* affair as
well. The British and American governments initially tempered
their responses to Khomeini's edict in the specific hope of
keeping channels open to Tehran—which was important mostly
for the sake of rescuing the captives held in Lebanon. The actions
of others too were influenced by the hostages. The archbishop of
Canterbury made repeated attempts to mollify fundamentalist
Muslims, including support for the proposal to extend the British

law of blasphemy to cover Islam, support for efforts to muzzle a BBC television discussion of *The Satanic Verses* incident, and a scathing denunciation of Israeli policies in Lebanon. These can only be understood in light of the fact that by early 1989 his personal envoy, Terry Waite, had been forcibly held in Lebanon for over two years, almost certainly by groups connected to Iran.

The Iranian government played on British fears more directly too. Tehran had held Roger Cooper, a British businessman, in jail since December 1985 and threatened periodically to try him as a spy. The fate of this man weighed very heavily on politicians in London. On one occasion, the speaker of the House of Commons refused a debate on *The Satanic Verses* matter, telling the members that anything "intemperate" spoken on the floor might endanger Cooper's life.[16] But, as usual, appeasement failed; despite this squashing of free speech in its very birthplace, Cooper shortly after received a heavy sentence for spying.

Commercial Interests

For West Europeans and Japanese especially (and North Americans are far from immune to this attitude), foreign policy boils down to winning contracts and making sales. For the Iranians, it is a tool by which to achieve something larger and more important. West Europeans and Japanese are extremely reluctant to let anything get in the way of trade with Iran. Their record over the past decade shows that however heinous the Iranian government's actions, the top trading states want nothing to interfere with commerce. So keen are they, it sometimes appears that the only foreign policy of America's principal allies is the encouragement of exports. In *The Satanic Verses* affair, this trait often obstructed efforts at decisive action.

This was the case even in Great Britain. A Conservative MP, Sir Eldon Griffiths, argued that Her Majesty's Government should ignore the threat to Rushdie and place an ambassador in Tehran, adding that the presence of an on-site ambassador would expedite British efforts to export to Iran. Teddy Taylor, another Tory MP, took two simultaneous steps. First, he told reporters that the break in relations with Iran was a "devastating blow to British trade."[17] Second, he led a delegation of Muslims to the Home Office to lobby for an extension of the blasphemy laws to cover Islam. The timing of these efforts strongly suggested a link in his mind between the two issues. It was even more damaging when, after just two months, MPs began to get restless about the cost of publicly protecting Rushdie from his would-be assassins. A Conservative member, Philip Goodhart, suggested that Rushdie be transferred to a missile testing-area on the Hebrides Islands, where no extra funds would be required for his security. That elected representatives would contemplate the sacrifice of so sacred a principle as freedom of speech to save a trifling amount of money only confirmed the Iranian judgment about the corrupt West. What would it not surrender in pursuit of material advantage?

These voices notwithstanding, the Thatcher government did hold to its position on Rushdie. This in itself contrasted with its pliant attitude in 1980 over a television film, *The Death of a Princess*. When the Saudi government protested the movie, authorities in London apologized fulsomely to Riyadh, then did all within their power to prevent the film from being shown. In that case, a Pakistani newspaper correctly noted years later, freedom of expression "had to be compromised by the government's economic compulsions."[18] No doubt Britain's more favorable economic relationship with Iran went far to account for its greater boldness in 1989 than in 1980.

Most Western politicians still had the pride to want to disguise their avariciousness, but not so Prime Minister David Lange of New Zealand. He saw no reason to sacrifice the livelihood of New Zealand's farmers "because of a threat made to a bookwriter in London."[19] By thus declaring the absolute priority of preserving trade links with Iran, Lange articulated what so many other leaders were thinking but were ashamed to acknowledge. In admitting this, he cleared the air and did everyone a favor.

Rarely has an importing country like Iran enjoyed such leverage over its suppliers, and the Iranians recognized their advantage. An editorial from Tehran explained European Community behavior between February and April 1989 by pointing out that when Europeans

> saw that their economic interests in Muslim countries could be damaged, they began to correct their position on the issue of the insulting book. Every official started to condemn the book in one way or another. When they realized that Iran's reaction, its breaking of diplomatic relations with London, could also include them, they quickly sent back their ambassadors to Tehran to prevent further Iranian reaction.[20]

Though a bit simplistic, this account portrayed the situation far more accurately than the steady stream of sophisticated apologetics from Europe about the need for "dialogue" with Iran and the futility of trying to isolate the Khomeini regime. Iranians understood the European zeal for commercial gain, they despised it, and they hoped to exploit it.

In a noteworthy exception to the craven attitude so often espoused by business interests in Europe, West Germany's leading financial daily, *Handelsblatt*, called for a halt to air traffic with Iran and a ban on its oil exports.[21] This stand was all the more impressive given the fact that West Germany, with exports of $1.6 billion in 1988, was Iran's biggest foreign supplier. Every so often, the Iranians brought up this fact and threatened to take their business elsewhere ("Tehran can easily replace West Germany with Eastern Europe"),[22] but to little avail. No less remarkable, the voice of the Swiss establishment, the *Neue Zürcher Zeitung*, called for Iran to be treated as a pariah.

Revolutionary Ideology

Finally, the ambitions of the revolutionary Iranian state intimidated Westerners. There is no contest when one side is prepared to trim and the other to be martyred. A power equation depends on will more than on wealth, and Iranian will was startling in its audaciousness.

Iranian radio boasted that "creating an opportunity for Muslims to comply freely with Islamic principles and act in accordance with the provisions of Islam is for more important than economic relations,"[23] and that was a fair description. In ways, Iranian statements paralleled what came out of France in 1789 and Russia in 1917. Iranian aggressiveness could be heard in the claim that Muslims are rapidly expanding in numbers (Rafsanjani: "One billion will become 2 billion tomorrow and 3 billion the day after tomorrow"); in the cultural triumphalism (Rafsanjani: "You are afraid of our cultural presence in your [Western] countries");[24] and in the overweening sense of power (Islam "is the sole determinant of man's future course).[25] Together, all this meant that "the West views the future with dread and apprehension."[26]

At the same time, it would be a mistake to accept these assertions at face value. Fundamentalist Muslims mixed an exaggerated sense of potential (thus, the boasting) with an equally exaggerated sense of vulnerabilty about the present (thus, the conspiratorial mindset). When Prime Minister Mir Husayn Musavi declared that the Western countries "need to win Iran's favor rather than the other way around,"[27] he sought to convince himself and his Iranian listeners as much as he hoped to bully the West. The same applied when the first deputy foreign minister counseled the Europeans to lay off Iran—"I sincerely advise you to accept a ceasefire in this ideological battle zone, for certain defeat awaits you."[28] In a classic instance of immature self-assessment, *The Satanic Verses* controversy exposed a blend of fears and fantasies for outsiders to witness.

In addition to *The Satanic Verses*, the Iranian government adopted other aggressive stances in early 1989. Two examples stand out. In one of the most remarkable documents of recent years, Ayatollah Khomeini in January sent his first major message to a foreign head of state, a personal letter to Mikhail Gorbachev. In it, Khomeini noted the failure of Marxism ("henceforth communism should be found in the museums of world political history") and Gorbachev's disillusionment with this ideology ("in future interviews you may express your complete faith in it; however, you know yourself that in reality this is not so"). With his usual economy of words, Khomeini wrote of his hope of convincing Gorbachev not to look to the obvious place, the West, for spiritual renewal, but to the south.

> I strongly urge that in breaking down the walls of Marxist fantasies you do not fall into the prison of the West and the Great Satan.... I call upon you seriously to study and conduct research into Islam.... I openly announce that the Islamic Republic of Iran, as the greatest and most powerful base of the Islamic world, can easily help fill up the ideological vacuum of your system.[29]

Interestingly, the Soviets made no efforts at a counterattack. Gorbachev was described as flushing twice as he listened to the letter's assertion of Islamic superiority, but he politely heard it out for two hours. In late February, Foreign Minister Edvard Shevardnadze informed Khomeini that "All the members of the Soviet Presidium have studied the contents of Your Eminence's message. No doubt we agree on a number of major points, but there are certain points on which we disagree."[30] One cannot get much meeker than "there are certain points on which we disagree"! As ever, Iranian commentators recognized weakness. Instead of contesting Khomeini on ideological grounds, they noted that Gorbachev "tactfully chose to point to notions that are mutually agreeable and as such can provide a better footing for Tehran-Moscow ties. This he did notwithstanding the fact that in his message to him Imam Khomeyni has criticised Marxism."[31]

Then in March, as Tehran interfered in the Turkish controversy concerning the right of female students to wear headscarves, Manuchehr Motaki, the Iranian ambassador to Ankara, warned that "Turkey must respect the requirements of our Islamic Revolution."[32] The brazen aggressiveness of this remark takes the breath away; applied consistently, it justifies Iranian interference in anyone's affairs at any time—a headscarf here, a novelist there, and who knows what next?

Yet Iranian bellicosity too shall pass. Two centuries of experience with revolutionary regimes suggests that visionary leaders die off, world-shaking ambitions invariably fail, and disillusion replaces faith. The passing of the ayatollah in all likelihood marks the transition of the Iranian state to a calmer, more inward-looking and status-quo orientation. His death presages changes in Iranian policy resembling those that took place after Mao Tse-Tung's passing from the scene in 1976. In China, when the oldest, most powerful and most radical leader died, the permanent revolution came to an end. A similar transformation is already underway in Iran, for no one can inherit Khomeini's authority and no one dares to impose a vision so far-reaching as his. Indeed, there is no potential leader in Iran (with the possible of exception of 'Ali Akbar Mohtashemi, former minister of the interior) who even remotely aspires to so bold an undertaking. In this sense, Khomeini was isolated from all of his supporters. It seems almost certain that the lurch in Iran's politics that began in 1979 is coming to an end. As it does, the citizens of that country can look forward to resuming a more normal life.

NOTES

[1] *Islamic Revolution News Agency*, May 30, 1989.
[2] *The New York Times*, March 5, 1989.
[3] *Newsweek*, February 27, 1989.
[4] *The Guardian*, February 15, 1989.
[5] *The Independent*, February 16, 1989.
[6] *The Observer*, February 19, 1989.
[7] *The Philadelphia Inquirer*, February 24, 1989.
[8] *The New York Times*, May 23, 1989.
[9] *Long Island Newsday*, February 16, 1989.
[10] *Publishers Weekly*, March 3, 1989.
[11] *Tehran Times*, July 8, 1989.
[12] *U.S. News & World Report*, March 6, 1989.
[13] Quoted in Lisa Appignanesi and Sara Maitland, eds., *The Rushdie File* (London: Fourth Estate, 1989), p. 199.
[14] Maskit Burgin, "Foreign Hostages in Lebanon," in Ariel Merari and Anat Kurz, *International Terrorism in 1987* (Boulder, Colo.: Westview Press, 1988), p. 70.
[15] *The Times*, January 12, 1989.

[16]Stuart Weir, "The Sound of Silence," *The New Statesman*, February 24, 1989.

[17]Press Association, February 28, 1989.

[18]*The Muslim*, February 25, 1989.

[19]Agence France Presse, February 28, 1989.

[20]*Kayhan Havai*, April 18, 1989.

[21]*Handelsblatt*, February 22, 1989.

[22]*Tehran Times*, May 13, 1989.

[23]Tehran International Radio, March 23, 1989.

[24]Radio Tehran, February 24, 1989.

[25]Editorial, *Resalat*, March 5, 1989.

[26]Commentary, Radio Tehran, March 1, 1989.

[27]Islamic Revolution News Agency, February 21, 1989.

[28]Islamic Revolution News Agency, February 21, 1989.

[29]Radio Tehran, January 8, 1989.

[30]Radio Tehran, February 26, 1989.

[31]*Tehran Times*, February 27, 1989.

[32]*Hurriyet*, March 28, 1989. For more details on the controversy, see above, p. 103.

11.

CENSORSHIP AND ITS COSTS

The Iranian campaign against Salman Rushdie and his publishers focused attention on freedom of speech. Would the clash compromise this fundamental right in the West? How would censorship of *The Satanic Verses* affect Rushdie's future career, and what would it mean for the impact of his novel? Also, important questions arose, especially in India, about whether the imposition of censorship saved lives.

A Chilling Effect

A report from New York publishing circles in February 1989 indicated a general feeling that "Ayatollah Khomeini has probably succeeded in preventing publication in this country of books critical of Muslims and Islam."[1] Some observers assumed that this chilling effect would remain long in place, and that it would apply to everything from pop music to the discussion of sensitive texts. On the very day of the ayatollah's death, Susan Sontag, addressing the American Booksellers Association predicted "a globalization of fear and vulnerability."[2] Another writer, Raymond Federman, proclaimed that "Khomeini has proclaimed the new era of fear for literature."[3]

While these warnings overstated the problem, they did not do so by too much. In the first place, the Rushdie incident itself remained a uniquely delicate topic for publishers. In London,

195

William Collins Sons commissioned "The Rushdie Dossier," a collection of documents put together by Lisa Appignanesi and Sara Maitland. Then, just three weeks later, the publishing house got cold feet and canceled the book. Collins first justified its decision on the grounds of not exacerbating problems for Viking. When Viking made clear it had no objections, Collins found a new reason—that bookstores would boycott the work, making it commercially not viable. And when this argument convinced no one, Collins tried out a third justification—that the book was not "objective." At this point, the Fourth Estate, a small press, took over. It retitled the work *The Rushdie File* and published it in July, though the Fourth Estate too had difficulties when eight print shops refused to handle the manuscript. The Fourth Estate was rewarded for its bravery: *The Rushdie File* prompted no threats and the first printing of seven thousand volumes nearly sold out in three weeks.

Some publishers admitted their reluctance to accept a manuscript critical of the Qur'an or Khomeini. "Would I absolutely rule it out?" asked James H. Silberman, president and editor-in-chief of Summit Books. "No. Would I jump to publish it? I don't know." Off the record, another New York editor was more candid: "It would cause people second thoughts. It might even cause them first thoughts because you'd have to wonder if you were going to bring down bombs on the heads of the people who work for you."[4]

A play about Rushdie's predicament by Howard Brenton and Tariq Ali, *A Mullah's Night Out*, had to be retitled *Iranian Nights* under pressure from its cast. Even so, two of the three actors quit before rehearsals began.

Self-censorship, though unmeasurable, was widespread. Bookers for American television shows such as the "MacNeil/ Lehrer NewsHour" and "Nightline" complained that prominent authors refused to discuss the Rushdie issue in the days immediately following Khomeini's threat. Nor were the famous alone in their fear of reprisals. When the campus bookstore at Wayne State University in Detroit refused to stock *The Satanic Verses*, faculty members drew up a petition calling for a boycott of the store. A good number of professors would not sign, however, fearing the fundamentalist response. In Vienna, the Austrian Students Association held its reading from *The Satanic Verses* in a tent when professors refused to allow the event to take place on university grounds. In West Berlin, the Akademie der Künste refused to allow a reading on its premises, citing security reasons. Even students ran scared. In a class on law and diplomacy at the Johns Hopkins School of Advanced International Studies, the undergraduates all agreed that Khomeini's edict constituted state terrorism. But when the instructor, Allan Gerson, asked them to sign a statement to this effect, one third of the students shied away from registering their names, choosing instead to mark the paper only with an "X."

More broadly, a number of works critical of Iran or Islam were withdrawn or altered. Véronique Sanson, a French singer, announced that threats against her life forced her to retract her song "Allah," a protest against intolerance and religious fanaticism. By this time, anyway, many record stores had already pulled the song and the French Interior Ministry had assigned her a police guard. The Los Angeles International Film Festival refused to screen *Veiled Threat*, a low-budget movie critical of Khomeini. Subsequently, the film lost its distribution in England, France and Italy. To make matters worse, both the British Board of Film Classification and the Foreign Office advised against the movie's release "in the current political climate."[5] The BBC cut from one of its productions a scene in which a despairing girl threw the Qur'an to the floor.

At times, the chill extended to even the most attenuated form of religious sensitivities. Perhaps the most preposterous example of Sontag's "new era of fear for literature" concerned Swamp Thing, the six-hundred-pound green hero of an American adult comic-book series. Swamp Thing, who is bestowed with the ability to travel back in time, had met such figures as King Arthur and Adolf Hitler. But DC Comics decided in June 1989 that the story of his meeting Jesus was too hot, and suppressed it. As a result, there simply was no issue number 88 of *Swamp Thing*; and the comic's writer, Rick Veitch, quit his job in protest.

Inspired both by the Iranian assault on Rushdie and student activism in Peking, thousands of Chinese students of Muslim origins took to the streets on May 12 and the days that followed to protest the publication of a book called *Sex Habits*. They objected to the book's scurrilous treatment of Islam (in the book, pilgrims go to Mecca to mate with female camels, and the minaret and dome of mosques represent the male and female sex organs) and met no resistance by government officials, in part because President Khamene'i of Iran was visiting China at that moment. The book was immediately recalled, all copies were destroyed, and its writers and editors legally prosecuted. Had it not been for *The Satanic Verses* incident, it is hard to imagine that Peking would have acquiesced in this manner.

In Muslim countries too, the Rushdie affair led to new restrictions on freedom of expression. To avoid a repetition of the February and March riots, authorities from West Africa to Southeast Asia watched the media with new vigilance. They were also pressured by fundamentalist Muslims, who, emboldened by Khomeini's remarkable precedent, sought to censor whatever displeased them and to press their case against all forms of Western influence. The scope for freedom of expression narrowed dramatically in many Muslim countries. In the words of Khalid Durán, Rushdie's book became "a weapon turned against free thinking among Muslims."[6]

In Egypt, the prominent feminist writer Nawal as-Sa'dawi abandoned a novel-in-progress, titled "The Book of Satan." In it, Satan was to answer the accusations against him in the Bible and Qur'an. Not unreasonably, Sa'dawi decided that 1989 was not an auspicious moment for such a book. To make matters worse, even after her back-tracking, Sa'dawi received so many death threats, the police had to provide her with around-the-clock protection.

The new atmosphere was perhaps most obvious in Pakistan. Shortly after the Rushdie incident, Interior Minister Atzez Ahsan banned two books dealing with Muhammad. A pop music show on television, *Music 89*, and especially the show's female star, the singer Nazia Hassan, became the center of a major controversy. Although an exceedingly demure program to begin with (Hassan always covered her hair and showed only her face and hands), fundamentalists abhored its Western character; further, they saw the show as a slippery slope to worse things. By constantly harassing Hassan and the television authorities, they forced so many small alterations in the program, it was eventually gutted. As a weary Hassan explained, "Everything in Pakistan, even the way you sing a song, is highly politicised now."[7]

This change in climate caused more than a few Muslim writers and artists to resent Rushdie for bringing fundamentalist Muslim scrutiny to bear on their activities. Dahmane Abderahmane, a young French Muslim, explained: "We condemn Rushdie because he was the man who permitted Khomeini to regain his breath."[8]

What will be the long-term impact of the controversy in the Muslim countries? Some have predicted that independent spirits would think hard before doing anything that might expose them to Salman Rushdie's plight. Critiques of the Qur'an or daring analyses of Muhammad's life will not be likely again for a long time.

Others saw the controversy as having precisely the opposite effect. Amir Taheri, an Iranian newspaper editor in exile, saw Rushdie "as the man who opened up a Pandora's box that many Muslim intellectuals had tried to keep shut for more than one and a half centuries."[9] Sasson Somekh, a specialist on Arabic literature, held that the ayatollah had inadvertently joined with the novelist to create a new genre—anti-Islamic fiction. Sasson suggested that Khomeini

> unwittingly transformed the book into a part of Islamic literature.... Although the novel has been banned throughout the Muslim world, its very "annexation" by the Imam will probably guarantee it a powerful presence in Islamic conscience now and for many years to come.[10]

According to this argument, *The Satanic Verses* would have been part of English literature, and irrelevant to Islam, had Khomeini not attacked Rushdie. The edict turned Rushdie into a Muslim author and possibly established something new, a tradition of explicitly anti-Islamic literature written by Muslims. The mold having been established, others may well take their manuscripts out of the drawer and follow in Rushdie's steps.

These apparently contradictory assessments can be reconciled by positing an initial chill, to be followed by experimentation and the pushing back of boundaries. Censorship was first strong and Rushdie's book made life all the more difficult for free thinkers and iconoclasts. It was clearly a time to put manuscripts away and hide them carefully. Yet their prospects are brighter in the longer term, for no matter how powerful Khomeini and the fundamentalist Muslims may have been in 1989, their undertaking was doomed. Modernity cannot be held off through retreat to a mythical past. Such efforts, even the most determined, cannot prevail and will not last. As the great fundamentalist experiment falters, Rushdie will get his revenge. The books that will then reach print may well make the anti-Islamic qualities of *The Satanic Verses* look innocuous in comparison.

The Impact on Rushdie and His Book

Censorship turned *The Satanic Verses* into a roaring international best seller. It had not been so at first; the large British book chain, W.H. Smith, was selling a mere hundred copies a week of the book in mid-January 1989, and had plans soon to take it off the shelves. But after the Bradford book burning in mid-January, the book shot to the top of the lists in the United Kingdom. In the United States, copies were unavailable for several weeks but as soon as Viking restocked the book (from March 9 onward), it soared up the fiction list, initially selling an unprecedented five times more copies than the number two book, *Star* by Danielle Steel. According to Len Riggio, the president of B. Dalton, his ban on selling the book was ineffectual because *The Satanic*

Verses "was selling so fast that even as we tried to stop it, it was flying off the shelves."[11] A New York City bookstore manager described the situation similarly: "It's flying, flying, flying off the shelves."[12]

The numbers clearly showed the ayatollah's achievement. In the United Kingdom, the book was still number six on the best seller list a full year after publication. In the United States, an initial printing of 50,000 was followed by a second printing of 400,000. By May, more than 750,000 copies of the book had been purchased in the United States and the book was the number one best seller for nine straight weeks. By August, it had been on the charts for half a year. Some bookstores sold over a thousand copies of the book and handlettered signs appeared in many stores announcing "*Satanic Verses*—Sold Out!" In Italy, the book sold 350,000 copies within five months, making it a phenomenal best seller. The same pattern repeated itself in most countries where the novel was available.

Sales of the book were fueled in part by curiosity: what had Rushdie written to cause such a scandal? In part, too, the controversy focused attention on the undeniable talents of the author, winning him a wider audience. Carefully placed on a coffee table, the novel served as a peerless conversation piece. There was also a political factor; many individuals, affronted by the death edict, wished to make a personal statement, and the most effective way to do so was to purchase a copy of the book. And some wanted to own a piece of history—which explains why the value of signed editions of Rushdie's work skyrocketed in Britain, multiplying by over four times in less than a week. It also helps explain why so few purchasers of the novel had read more than a token number of pages. (The other reason may be the book's difficulty.)

In the Muslim world and wherever the book had been banned, *The Satanic Verses* became highly valued contraband. One of the few copies in Kuwait was read simultaneously by several people, who took turns with it. In Turkey, according to President Kenan Evren, *The Satanic Verses* sold for $200 a copy.[13] A few books reached Senegal from the United States; these were photocopied many times over. Despite the book's large size and English language, readers demanded the whole book, and nothing less. In Israel, copies were available only from a post office box, and sold fast at twice their normal retail price. According to *An-Nur*, a Cairene newspaper, Arabic translations of *The Satanic Verses* went on sale in Egypt in July and were sold secretly by select bookstores for E£20.[14] In India, clandestine copies were available under the counter and circulated widely among certain circles in Bombay, Rushdie's hometown. It was considered particularly chic to drop allusions proving first-hand familiarity with the book. But, of course, Iran was the country where the book was most prized. At great risk to all involved, bookstores there smuggled a few copies into the country, and these were passed from hand to hand in the strictest secrecy among intimate friends.

In addition to guaranteeing Rushdie a worldwide audience and making *The Satanic Verses* "the most famous book of the century,"[15] Khomeini assured the novel a unique and enduring place in the history of literature. It became the preeminent symbol of both censorship and freedom of speech, of cultural misunderstanding and shared values. There may never be another work of fiction with such a career.

As for Salman Rushdie himself, the future is unclear. In the first few weeks of their captivity, he and his wife tried as much as possible to retain their old style of life, showing up here and there at parties. But the strain proved too great, and they eventually gave up the effort. In late April, two months after the edict, for example, Rushdie was driven by armored car to Oxford University for a private dinner, then had to be whisked away through a side entrance because of the nearby presence of Muslim students. To make matters worse, the police advised against telephone calls, while every piece of mail underwent the closest scrutiny. Marianne Wiggins, Rushdie's wife, indicated in July that each of them was protected by at least one armed bodyguard at all times and that they had moved fifty-six times since February—or roughly once every three days.

According to their friends, Rushdie and Wiggins were on the verge of breaking up when Khomeini's *fatwa* descended on them. Worldwide attention on the couple virtually compelled them to stay together. But not for long: an already shaky relationship was aggravated by the fear of assassination, the tension of being at the center of an international controversy, and the irritations of spending all hours of the day together in seclusion. The strain built for five months, until late July, at which time the couple finally separated. For Wiggins, this meant coming out of seclusion and resuming a normal life. Given the exigencies of Rushdie's security, the separation had to be a complete one; even she no longer knew her husband's location.

On going into hiding, Rushdie fell nearly silent. He let it be known that worldwide attention and seclusion oppressed him, but that he was bearing up (in the words of a friend, Tariq Ali) "in relatively good spirits." A week into seclusion, Rushdie described his mood as one of succumbing to a "curious lethargy, the soporific torpor that overcomes [me] while [I am] under attack."[16] A poem titled "6 March 1989" (and apparently written on that day) indicated that while Rushdie acutely felt the effects of the campaign against him, he had decided "not to shut up," but "to sing on, in spite of attacks."[17]

Despite Rushdie's decision "not to shut up," to continue to speak his mind, he made no effort to battle his opponents. Symptomatic of this, he took up writing the children's book long ago promised to his son. Neil Kinnock, leader of the Labour Party, met Rushdie in the spring and was later quoted as saying, "I know Rushdie and I know that his position is 'the less noise the better.'"[18] Rather than encourage broadsides, Rushdie asked his supporters to tone down their criticism of Iran, perhaps hoping that this would cause the whole controversy to die down and the threat on his life to be lifted.

This appeared like a sensible course of action, for Iranian state policy shifted dramatically shortly after June 3, 1989, the day Khomeini died. To be sure, the death edict was reaffirmed in late June by both Speaker of the Parliament Rafsanjani and Chief

Justice 'Abd al-Karim Musavi Ardebili. But Iranian politicians also made it clear that the matter would not be allowed to get in the way of relations with the outside world. The British media quoted a pro-Iranian figure, Kalim Siddiqui, saying that while the death threat would not formally be withdrawn, Tehran "is prepared to let the matter drop."[19] Several months later, Foreign Minister 'Ali Akbar Velayati made this intention formal when he suggested that West European governments "don't need to connect the question of Salman Rushdie to political relations between Iran and those countries."[20]

Still, the policy of the Islamic Republic is only part of the story, and perhaps the less important. It bears emphasis that Iranian leaders, political as well as religious, cannot cancel the *fatwa*. Only Khomeini could have repealed it, and he adamantly refused to do so, then died. Even were the successors one day to repudiate Khomeini's "sentence," it would nonetheless remain alive. For many fundamentalist Muslims, Khomeini's prestige was such that no mere epigones or bureaucrats could negate his pronouncement. The death threat remains as an irrevocable legacy of Khomeini's, and it is now beyond the control of both Rushdie and Tehran. (In similar fashion, dedicated Maoists in China and Nasirists in Egypt have championed their deceased leaders' ideology against deviationists in Peking and Cairo.)

The ayatollah's passing may even have increased the danger to Rushdie, and for two reasons. With Khomeini's passing, the edict became permanent; no mortal now has the power to invalidate it. (Foreign Office Minister Lord Glenarthur had it all wrong when he raised the possibility that the edict might have lapsed.) Also, some of Khomeini's more fervent followers may well see the execution of Rushdie as the way to pay final homage to their departed master.

Accordingly, Rushdie will almost certainly not be able to resume normal life; the threat against him is permanent. The seriousness of that threat became even more clear on August 4, when a bomb exploded in a small London hotel, the Beverly, killing its handler. The explosion sparked a fire which heavily damaged two floors of the five-story building and gutted the roof. The man killed, who signed in simply as "Mazeh," was in his twenties, of Moroccan origin, and travelling on a French passport. The police took seriously the claim from the Organization of the Mujahidin of Islam in Lebanon that Mazeh was preparing for an attack on Rushdie.

The permanence of the threat has provoked much speculation about Rushdie's chances for living out his natural term. In all likelihood, he will do so. He could take up an obscure identity in a new location, but this is unlikely, for he depends on intellectual stimulation from others. Further, the huge sales of *The Satanic Verses*—plus the guaranteed market for his future writings— means that he has the funds to protect himself, should the guards provided by the British government be taken away. (He earned about $2 million within the first year of the book's publication.) The real effect of the threats to his life lies elsewhere; it means that he will ever after live in fear and under heavy guard. Though unpleasant, living with guards is by no means impossible, as mafia dons, Henry Kissinger, the deposed shah of Iran, and Shahpour Bakhtiar have all discovered.

Those who are potentially most vulnerable to Khomeini's assassins are Rushdie's publishers. Under Khomeini's sentence, they are no less culpable than the author, yet they are many and they do not benefit from around-the-clock police protection. It is conceivable that, frustrated by their inability to get Rushdie, some fundamentalist hit squads will strike out at this second-best target. This means that every copy editor and secretary who ever worked at Viking Penguin, Mondadori, Éditions de la Cité or the other publishers of *The Satanic Verses* is potentially under the fundamentalists' gun. For this reason too, Rushdie's editors are the unsung heroes of the unhappy incident.

The controversy he began did not make Rushdie a popular figure. Even those who sided with him against the ayatollah blamed him for stirring up a hornet's nest. Perhaps the greatest anger came from lapsed and secular Muslims, who felt imperiled by the fundamentalists' new activism that Rushdie had brought on. British taxpayers begrudged paying the bill for his protection and being exposed to Iranian violence on his behalf. Executives across Europe blamed him for the loss of business. Politicians around the world resented the seemingly unnecessary trouble he caused them. Publishers and librarians quietly cursed him for making them so vulnerable to physical attack and popular criticism. Bookstore owners, constantly fearing for their property and their lives, longed for *The Satanic Verses* to get off the best seller list so they could stop carrying it. "We won't have any rest until that satanic book disappears from the market."[21] Only a handful of voices approved of him and urged him to continue in his ways. Bharati Mukherjee, for example, requested that Rushdie's next novel be "so scaldingly blasphemous that even liberals will cringe."[22] But this was a fringe viewpoint.

Censorship Spawns Ignorance

Censorship prevented an informed Muslim debate from taking place on *The Satanic Verses*. With only the rarest of exceptions, Muslims did not read the book itself, and therefore could not reach independent conclusions about the nature of the charges. At best, they looked at excerpts of sensational passages. At worst, they relied for information on the furious accusations of mobs and politicians.

Acting in ignorance, it was not surprising that Muslim critics regularly got the facts of the matter wrong. Most common, of course, were accusations that, according to Rushdie, the devil wrote the whole Qur'an. Other critics held that he insulted all the caliphs. Mohammed Siddique, a mosque official in Bradford, England, claimed that the book contains "hardly a single page which does not insult"[23]—an absurd claim given that the great majority of the novel deals sympathetically with the travails of Muslims living in Britain. The Iranian news agency held that "Rushdie's book did not insult Iran or Iranian leaders."[24] In fact, the novel includes an eleven-page sketch on Khomeini's stay in a suburb of Paris, replete with mocking passages such as one describing how the Imam had "grown monstrous, lying in the palace forecourt with his mouth yawning open at the gates; as the people march through the gates he swallows them whole." If this is not an insult, Khomeini was far more tolerant than one might suppose.

But the brothel episode became the most baroquely tangled. In the novel, twelve prostitutes take on the names and then the personalities of Muhammad's twelve wives. They do so for marketing reasons, to attract more business, and the idea works. That is all. There is no other connection between the brothel and Muhammad or his wives. This is not what one would gather listening to the critics, however. Most often, Rushdie was accused of portraying the wives of Muhammad as prostitutes. Even Western journalists repeated this canard.[25] An advertisement prominently placed in the British newspapers by the Birmingham Central Mosque went one step further, declaring that "Rushdie has portrayed the prophet of Islam as a brothel keeper." Mar Dawud Assad, president of the U.S. Council of Masajid (mosques), wrote that "Rushdie accuses the prophets, particularly Muhammad, of being like prostitutes."[26] Abolhassan Bani–Sadr, the former president of Iran, reported that Rushdie portrayed the prophet as a homosexual. According to one young French Muslim, Rushdie wrote that "all who pray are sons of whores."[27] A scholarly analysis piled one erroneous detail on another: "The Prophet's wives are portrayed as women of the street, his home as a public brothel and his companions as bandits."[28] In Riyadh, Saudi Arabia, word had it that Rushdie himself owned and operated a brothel in London in which the girls used the names of the Prophet's wives.

Transparent ignorance of this sort put Muslims at a severe disadvantage in arguing the case against *The Satanic Verses*. Accordingly, a columnist in Jordan, Iyad Ibrahim al-Qattan, protested the ban on the grounds that it caused Muslims to be unprepared to contend with hostile foreign propaganda. "I, along with every educated Arab and Muslim, strongly demand that copies of the book, *The Satanic Verses*, be distributed to us all.

We also demand that it be left to us to respond to it."[29] Though not often expressed in public, this viewpoint was widely shared by educated Muslims, many of whom resented being treated like children. The only informed discussion of *The Satanic Verses* among Muslims would take place in the West.

In an effort to answer critics like Qattan, an Iranian ayatollah, Mohammed Emami Kashani, reverted with surprising candor to the traditional Muslim distinction between the elite and the masses. While reading *The Satanic Verses* would "be a sin for the general public," he called on "leaders and experts of Islamic countries to study it to understand the imam's *fatwa*." Specifically, he urged "all leaders, officials, and parliamentarians of Islamic countries to read this book."[30] Superficially appealing as it may have been, this approach was not implemented because it entailed too many difficulties. Who is a leader, who is an expert? How does one assure that they are not tainted by the book? And how would this permission be squared with calls from Iran that every copy of *The Satanic Verses* be destroyed?

The unavailability of the book created a peculiar by-problem for some fundamentalist Muslims: it meant they could not lay their hands on it for purposes of ritual burning! Instead, they had to make do with whatever they could. Thus, in a March 3 demonstration in Istanbul, protesters were reduced to setting aflame a British flag and a picture of Salman Rushdie. Fundamentalists even faced a problem in Britain, for the book had been so thoroughly banned from some towns (such as Derby), they had to send an emissary to London to buy a copy for burning.

Mistaken information was not confined to the text. Other errors making the rounds in the Middle East had it that that Rushdie was a Baha'i or had converted to Christianity, that *The Satanic Verses* had been retracted in Great Britain, and that the British government had banned all public discussion of Islam. Rafsanjani, speaker of the Iranian parliament, announced that "This man's wife recently wrote a book against the prophet Jesus, which caused an uproar there, and the Christians staged an uprising."[31] Rafsanjani may have been thinking of Martin Scorsese's film,

The Last Temptation of Christ, which did cause an uproar, or Marianne Wiggins' book, *John Dollar*, which contained anti-Christian elements but prompted no controversy; in any case, he too got the facts wrong. Highly restricted press coverage was to blame for much of this ignorance.

Did Censorship Save Lives?

The debate about censorship was especially contentious in India, a democratic country with a tradition of free speech, and also the place where Rushdie-related violence led to the death of fourteen people and the injury of scores more. Some analysts, pointing to that violence, argued that censorship had failed. They noted a striking correlation: India was the country where *The Satanic Verses* was both first banned and where rioting had caused the most fatalities. Interestingly, Pakistan was where the book was banned second and where the second largest number of deaths, seven, occurred. Analysts drew the obvious conclusion, that censorship had completely failed. Indeed, it may even have proved counterproductive.

On the other side, proponents of censorship argued that the violence of February and March 1989 demonstrated what terrible disasters were averted. As India is a country where dragging a pig through a mosque or slaughtering a cow near a Hindu temple can precipitate Hindu-Muslim communal riots, the book could have caused a national calamity. Even *The Last Temptation of Christ* was considered offensive to Muslims and was banned. According to Salman Khurshid, an advisor to Prime Minister Rajiv Gandhi, "a delay in imposing the ban could have resulted in the worst riots since independence [from Britain in 1947]."[32] Had the book been permitted in India, Hindu publishers would probably have extracted the most offending passages for reprinting, Muslim protests would have proliferated, and the result would surely have been carnage. Proponents of censorship pointed to a recent story in *The Deccan Herald* which depicted the Prophet Muhammad as an idiot, sparking a riot that left fifty persons dead. Against this perspective, the fourteen fatalities in India caused by *The Satanic Verses* looked minor.

So persuasive was this argument, it even won the endorsement of the writers affected. Wole Soyinka explained that he "understood" New Delhi's decision, even if he did not condone it.[33] More remarkably, Naguib Mahfouz had earlier acceded to the banning of one of his own works in Egypt, on the grounds that it might provoke civil disturbances.

These contrasting views implied two fundamentally different interpretations of India's communal problems and their causes. Those favoring freedom of speech subscribed to the classic doctrines of democracy; educate and inform the masses and they will respond with responsibility—indeed, together they will reach a sounder judgment even than the best educated and most far-sighted autocrats. In keeping with this outlook, free speech advocates blamed politicians for keeping communal problems alive. According to Vir Sanghvi, editor of *Sunday*, "Whatever *The Satanic Verses* said about the Prophet, there would have been no danger of its inciting any violence had the issue not been blown up by a bunch of irresponsible politicians, especially politicians who were unlikely to have read that book."[34] Others, including Rushdie, pointed out that censorship encourages sensitivity and squeemishness, while freedom of speech fosters thick skin.

Those opposed to unconstrained freedom of speech blamed not the leaders but the masses. They considered it vital for the public good to keep potentially inflammatory materials out of circulation. Like Ayatollah Kashani, they would allow leaders and experts to peruse materials not available to the public at large. Whereas advocates of freedom of expression subscribed to a democratic outlook, advocates of censorship promoted an elitist point of view. The same distinction holds outside India as well. Americans are the most democratic of peoples and so tolerate the greatest freedom of speech. North Korea has both the least democratic government and the least freedom of speech.

In response to the accusation of anti-democratic inclinations, proponents of censorship have argued that freedom of expression is fine in the United States, but not so in a society like India, which is not prepared for it. Further, they have distinguished between blasphemy and attacks on the social fabric. They have accepted the resolution hammered out during the Enlightenment that all views should be expressed, particularly those touching on religion, but they insisted on curtailing free expression to avoid outbreaks of violence. Free speech advocates would answer that India will never mature if its rulers mistrust the populace and prevent it from hearing conflicting ideas. In this way, the Rushdie affair recapitulated the classic debate over the merits of free speech.

The Satanic Verses raised similar issues in several other countries where the book was banned, especially Nigeria and the Sudan.

In Iran, however, a debate took place on another level altogether. Indeed, the incident revealed how very little fundamentalist Muslims understood about the concept of free speech. Speaker Rafsanjani asked Westerners, "If an Iranian writer wrote a book in your country, without any lies...about the events in your lives, your wives, daughters, and mothers, and tells people about them, then what is your reaction?" He then answered his own question: of course, the book would be suppressed.[35] On another occasion, he wanted to know if the Western states "approved of the book or not." But it was not just the fundamentalists who were baffled by the concept. In Jordan, for example, a newspaper editorialist stated as a known fact that every country "has a sufficient body of domestic laws that prohibits any publications or utterances that tend to ridicule or defame religion."[36] Obviously, these men knew little about West Europe and even less about the United States.

The Rushdie affair underlined the fact that both secularism and freedom of expression remain essentially Western phenomena. The power of religious leaders revealed the weak hold of secularism, even in countries where it was enshrined as a legal doctrine. In most countries, it turned out, sacred texts are not a topic to be subjected to imaginative treatment, much less any sort of satire. As for freedom of speech, with only a handful of exceptions (most notably, Turkey and the Philippines), even the slightest opposition to *The Satanic Verses* led to the book's being prohibited. Where the authorities dared not invoke religious sanctions, they found other reasons, such as race relations or even political ideology; the Indonesian government banned the book on the grounds that it contradicted the state's secularist ideology!

NOTES

[1]Edwin McDowell, "Rushdie: A Question of Fear," *The New York Times*, February 27, 1989.

[2]*National Review*, July 14, 1989.

[3]Raymond Federman, "The Ayatollah Khomeini and the Future of Literature," *American Book Review*, July-August 1989.

[4]*Newsweek* (European Edition), July 31, 1989.

[5]*The New York Times*, April 8, 1989.

[6]Khalid Durán, "Woher kommen die Verse denn nun wirklich?" *Frankfurter Allgemeine Zeitung*, February 27, 1989.

[7]*Far Eastern Economic Review*, May 4, 1989.

[8]*Le Nouvel Observateur*, March 23, 1989.

[9]Amir Taheri, "Pandora's Box Forced Open," *Index on Censorship*, May 1989, p. 7.

[10]Sasson Somekh, "Rushdie Novel Not an Anti-Religious Work," *Trenton Times*, March 19, 1989.

[11]*Publishers Weekly*, March 10, 1989.

[12]*Long Island Newsday*, February 16, 1989.

[13]Radio Ankara, February 26, 1989.

[14]*An-Nur*, July 12, 1989. The newspaper may have confused the Arabic book about *The Satanic Verses* controversy with the novel itself.

[15]Stephen Vizinczey, "The New Appeasers Who Bow to Mecca," *Sunday Telegraph*, March 19, 1989.

[16]Salman Rushdie, "Beginning of a Novelist's Thralldom," *The Observer*, February 26, 1989.

[17]*Granta*, Autumn 1989.

[18]*The Independent*, July 21, 1989.

[19]*The Times*, June 8, 1989.

[20]*U.S. News & World Report*, October 9, 1989.

[21]*Der Spiegel*, April 3, 1989.

[22]*The New York Times Book Review*, March 12, 1989.

[23]*Bradford Telegraph & Argus*, December 6, 1988. Text in Lisa Appignanesi and Sara Maitland, eds., *The Rushdie File* (London: Fourth Estate, 1989), p. 66.

[24]Islamic Revolution News Agency, February 21, 1989.

[25]For example, Jim Hoagland, "Behind the Islamic Book-Burning" *The Washington Post*, February 16, 1989. Barbara Crossette, "Fantasy or Blasphemy? A Book Is a Burning Issue," *The New York Times*, October 13, 1988 presented the issue of the Prophet's wives as a matter of debate between Rushdie and his critics. *The Jewish Chronicle* of February 24, 1989 explained that the novel portrayed Muhammad as going to a prostitute.

[26]*Trenton Times*, February 21, 1989.

[27]*Le Nouvel Observateur*, March 23, 1989.

[28]M. Rafiqul Islam, "The Rushdie Affair: A Conflict of Rights," unpublished manuscript, April 1989, p. 3.

[29]*Sawt ash-Sha'b*, February 28, 1989.

[30]Islamic Revolution News Agency, March 17, 1989.

[31]Radio Tehran, February 24, 1989.

[32]Reuter, March 1, 1989.

[33]*The African Guardian*, February 23, 1989.

[34]*Newsweek* (European Edition), March 13, 1989.

[35]Radio Tehran, February 24, 1989.

[36]*Jordan Times*, March 5, 1989.

12.

MUSLIMS LIVING IN THE WEST

While the Rushdie affair touched Muslims in all parts of the world, it was those living in the West who experienced the controversy in the most direct and disruptive way. The issue had far more importance for Pakistanis living in Britain, Algerians in France, and Turks in West Germany than to their counterparts at home. Too, it was the actions of local Muslims which most affected Westerners; a peaceful march in the Place de la République had much more impact on French opinion than a Bombay riot leaving twelve dead. In these and other ways, the events of early 1989 marked the emergence of Muslims living in West Europe as a political force.

The activism of Muslims during the Rushdie incident raised a host of new questions for Europeans: would the Muslims in their midst remain in ghettos of their own making, integrate themselves into Western life, or try to impose their political power and way of life on the majority population? Also, would they accept living in a secular order, or would they try to change it into something more familiar to them?

Euro-Islam on the March

The Rushdie affair awakened Muslims both to their own strength in the West and to the very mixed response they aroused among Europeans.

In itself, the presence of Muslims in the West is nothing new. For a full century, dissident and free-spirited thinkers escaping tyranny or censorship have moved to Europe and America. From Muhammad 'Abduh and al-Afghani a century ago to Idries Shah, Adonis, and Rushdie in recent years, the West has long attracted some of the most prominent Muslim writers. Academics too have taken advantage of its refuge; when Fazlur Rahman, a leading specialist on Islam, had to flee his Pakistani homeland in 1968 due to his modernist thinking, he found a home at the University of Chicago.[1]

For all their importance, this elite group of expatriates has always been small in number. Very different are the communities of Muslims which have grown up in the past thirty years, most of whose members live at the bottom of the social ladder—Turkish factory workers in Germany, Algerian street cleaners in France, and Indian store clerks in Great Britain. Many smaller communities have also come into existence, such as the 10,000 Yemenis in the United States working mostly in the agricultural fields of California and the mills of New York State. Others are students who came for schooling and then stayed on, especially Iranians in the United States. In addition, conversions from Christianity have been multiplying, especially among Black Americans, hundreds of thousands of whom are now Muslims.

Muslims total anywhere between 1 and 6 million in the United States.[2] In West Europe, they number about 11 million. Over 3 million Muslims live in France, about 2 million in West Germany, 1 million in the United Kingdom, and almost a million in Italy. Half a million Muslims live in Belgium. Spain, home of the Inquisition, now hosts 200,000 Muslims. In Birmingham, the second largest city of Great Britain, Muslims make up ten percent of the population; in Bradford (where protests against *The Satanic Verses* picked up steam), they constitute fourteen percent of the population. They make up one-quarter of the population in Brussels, Saint-Denis (a suburb of Paris), and Dearborn, Michigan. London is thought to be home to a million Muslims and West Berlin to some 300,000. Muslims outnumber Jews and have become the second largest religious community in most West European countries. In France, Muslims outnumber all non-Catholics combined, including both Protestants and Jews.

Further, the Muslim birthrate far exceeds that of native Europeans and Americans, so that one-fifth of all children born in France have a father from North Africa and Muhammad is one of the most common given names in the United Kingdom. Estimates suggest that the Muslim population of West Europe might reach 20 million by the year 2000.[3]

In a more public and more emotional way than ever before, the Rushdie affair raised questions about the Muslims living in the West. On the political level, Muslim ambitions in Europe were symbolized during the Rushdie crisis when French and German newsweeklies reported parallel statements. A French woman of North African origins told a reporter, "Tomorrow I will be mayor, the day after president of the republic." A German politician sought to scare his co-nationals by announcing, "In the year 2000 we will have a federal chancellor of Turkish origins."[4] President or chancellor may be fanciful, but a Muslim, Mohammed Ajeeb, has already served as lord mayor of Bradford, England, and many Muslims are rising through the mainstream institutions of British life.

The Rushdie affair moved forward this process by uniting Muslims and propelling them to a new level of activism. In France, it led to the organization of the Coordination Committee of Muslims in France. In Britain, organizations such as the Work Committee for Muslim Affairs and the British Muslim Action Front came into existence specifically to combat Rushdie and his book; others, such as the Young Muslim Organisation, acquired new importance. The Islamic Party of Britain, a political organization, was launched in September 1989 with the intent initially to forward the fundamentalist agenda and eventually to field candidates. Throughout Western Europe, Muslims emerged from the dispute better organized and more purposeful than ever before.

One sign of this new voice was the march (ostensibly against Rushdie) by some three and a half thousand Muslims on June 17 in Bradford; sparked by the ayatollah's death, it degenerated into a rampage, leading to the arrest of fifty-four Muslim youths. At one point, the city's central police station was beseiged by angry demonstrators. The Bradford Council of Mosques regretted the violence but blamed the British government and Viking books for the outbreak.

But Muslim ambition goes beyond mere socio-economic improvement and distribution of spoils; it aims to affect the tenor of West European life. In Bradford, for example, Muslims succeeded in getting the British government to establish single-sex schools which serve *halal* (the Islamic equivalent of kosher) foods and teach the Islamic religion. Oral pronouncements of divorce along Islamic lines are valid in British courts. By a special act of parliament, the Belgian government in 1974 recognized portions of the Islamic law. The future may hold other adjustments, from the most minor (Muslim women permitted to cover their hair in French identity card photographs) to the most important (legal prohibition of blasphemy against Islam). Taken singly, these may seem to be small adjustments—together, they suggest an entirely new element affecting the fabric of life in West Europe.

In Britain, for example, fundamentalist Muslims took advantage of the Rushdie controversy to threaten pubs and disco-théques. The significance of this act becomes apparent when one recalls that such establishments are the perennial objects of fundamentalist wrath in the Middle East. Fundamentalist Muslims living in the West had earlier accepted public drinking and dancing as part of European life, but the Rushdie affair showed that they could exert pressure out of proportion to their numbers. As a result, their attitudes may have begun to harden.

This change is confirmed by plans, explicitly laid out, to remake Europe in the image of Islam. Echoing Tehran's threat that British Muslims may be forced "to seek ways outside the law to guard their rights,"[5] Kalim Siddiqui, director of London's pro-Iranian Muslim Institute, warned that Muslims "are rapidly coming to the conclusion that they will have to fight to defend Islam in Britain."[6] On another occasion, he called for Muslims to "take on the police and the judiciary" in efforts against Rushdie, then he added a stunning declaration of intent:

> The presence of two million angry Muslims in a secular society represents a major source of potential social conflict. We are in long-term conflict with our environment, including the British Government. A sustained, well-thought out and controlled campaign, that might include symbolic breaking of the law, may well be required if the Muslim community in Britain is to secure its proper place in British society.[7]

Siddiqui's counterpart in Paris, the director of the Institute of Islamic Culture made a similar declaration: "We can now say, given the importance of the Arab population and the influence of Islam, that France is part of the *umma* [Muslim community] and in a few years Paris will be the capital of Islam, just as Baghdad and Cairo were in other eras." A rally of Muslims in Toronto heard one of their leaders declare: "We want to impose Islamic law. We don't care about the other laws of the world."[8] Taking this line of thought further yet, Harunur Rashid Tipu, the editor of a Bengali-language newspaper in England, explained that the leaders of the Young Muslim Organisation, seek ultimately "to build an Islamic society here." And in the editor's view, "With the speed with which they are building up their character, there is a high chance of their success."[9]

An outside observer is not likely to agree with this assessment. Nonetheless, the very fact that Muslims even conceive of establishing an Islamic society in Europe speaks of a dramatic change in expectations. A century ago, it was the Europeans who built great cathedrals in such Middle East cities as Cairo and Istanbul. These buildings represented the power, the optimism and the high birth rate of Europeans. Nor was it a matter of spreading faith alone; in addition to their Christianity, the British and French espoused liberal notions of secularism and free speech, which they were prepared forcibly to impose on reluctant Muslim societies.

How different today! In recent years, Muslims have been building the cathedrals—grand mosques in such cities as Brussels, Copenhagen, Lisbon, London, New York, Rome and Vienna. (At the same time, in a piquant symbol of change, the Episcopal cathedral in Cairo was torn down to make way for a highway expansion.) After almost five centuries of Islam being prohibited in Spain, a mosque went up at Marbella, outside Cordoba. Western Europe and North America now host a full complement of Islamic institutions: Qur'anic schools, publishing houses, voluntary organizations, interest-free banks, political lobby groups and the like. In Britain, there is even an Islamic Organisation for Media Monitoring

Like the Europeans a century earlier, Muslims sought to bring more than just their religion; with it came the whole penumbra of culture, including anti-secular ideas about religion and politics. Women's clothing symbolized the shift in momentum: a century back, under European influence, Muslim women began taking off their veils. With the Islamic revival of the 1970s, they began covering themselves again. Significantly, this time they wore not veils but scarves, a Western article of clothing—pointing to the inadvertant Western influence on even the most radical funda-mentalist Muslims.[10] Even Muslim women resident in the West joined the movement toward Islamic-style clothing.

Several Middle Eastern states provided enthusiastic support for the efforts of Muslims in Europe to Islamize their surrounding societies. They paid for the cathedral mosques, pressured the governments and encouraged cooperation between local organi-zations. The Saudi government spent the most money on estab-lishing institutions, while the Iranians found the most dedicated followers. Assessing its work at the time of the Rushdie affair, Tehran expressed glee that the West could do nothing to stop Muslims from altering the very nature of European life. Chris-tians and Jews, they said, "now can only stand as stunned spectators and not even attempt to control this onslaught."[11] More than a few in the West worried that the Iranians were right.

Will Muslims Integrate?

Still, it would be wrong to leave the impression that Muslims remain a foreign element in the West, living apart from and despising the civilization around them. A good number of Muslims do partake of Western ideals and principles, and involve themselves in a profound way in endeavors ranging from the space sciences to Hollywood. And it is hard to imagine that the passage of time will not evolve and transform the culture of Muslims living in the West.

With regard to the Rushdie controversy, an opinion survey of Muslims living in France pointed to an interesting pattern. Nine percent agreed with Khomeini that Rushdie should be killed, 47 percent wanted no more than a ban on his book, 25 percent accepted his right to publish, and 19 percent expressed no opinion. On the question of Iran, 9 percent expressed solidarity with the Islamic Revolution, 17 percent felt sympathy, 26 percent were indifferent, 32 percent were hostile, and 16 percent had no opinion.[12] In combination, these figures suggest that just under one-tenth of the Muslims in France can be considered fundamentalists—or about the same proportion as they constitute in their countries of origin. In other words, moving to the West does not seem to increase or reduce the number of fundamentalist Muslims. Or, more accurately: while living in the West causes some Muslims to drift away from their faith, a roughly equal number redouble their commitment to it.

This pattern repeatedly leads to a situation whereby the Muslim leadership holds views quite at variance with those of the bulk of its constituents, a tendency encouraged by the funds flowing from Iran, Saudi Arabia and Libya. Those Westernized Muslims who would serve as a counterweight to extremist tendencies involve themselves instead in mainstream European activities, and so abandon the Islamic arena to their more fervent coreligionists. The Rushdie affair exacerbated this tendency and helped consolidate the fundamentalist domination of organized Muslim life in Europe.

In the long run, living in the West will probably involve a process of Protestantization, whereby faith and feeling increasingly substitute for the rigors of living in accordance with the law. Jews living in Europe underwent a parallel process a century earlier, and even Catholics have undergone a similar transformation. As this change occurs, Islam will take on a different role for many faithful. Instead of its traditional hold on nearly all aspects of life, it will become an ethnic flavoring. Good intentions will become more important than close adherence to the prohibition against alcohol. Holidays will continue to be celebrated, though fewer individuals will be getting up to pray before dawn. Marriages will take place at later ages and children will be fewer in number. Cousin marriages will die out and girl babies will be as much prized as boys.

These changes are already underway. In France, women of North African origin between the ages of 24-29 have a fertility rate lower than the French national average, whereas that of their counterparts in North Africa is considerably higher. Too, 90 percent of Muslims born in France to Arabic-speaking parents do not know the language well enough to read and write it. The hundred or so mosques in France are normally empty, and fill up only on Fridays and holidays. Some Muslims even recognize the similarity of their transformation to the changes in Judaism. Thus, Abdel Aïssou, editorial director at Radio-Beur in France, explained, "I feel Muslim like others feel they are Jews, even while they are atheists."[13]

Also, while rarely discussed, intermarriage will probably have critical importance in determining the future of Muslim communities in the West. Should Muslims marry only other Muslims, it is likely that integration in the wider society will be exceedingly slow. But if Christians and Muslims intermarry in significant numbers the chances are quite good that Muslims in the West will accommodate more to their environment. And what is the rate of intermarriages? Not high—no more than a few thousand a year. But when compared to the almost complete absence of such linkages in centuries past (including the hundred and thirty years of French rule in Algeria), these are large numbers, and they appear likely to increase with time. Further, it should be kept in mind that while Islamic law permits Muslim men to marry Christian women, it prohibits the reverse (Muslim women are forbidden to marry Christian men). Yet, as Muslim men marry out, there are fewer of them left to marry Muslim women, and this makes it virtually inevitable that the women will follow their example. Indeed, the statistics suggest that this taboo is already breaking down. All these trends point to more integration of Muslims living in the West.

Muslim women are important in another way too, for the adoption of a Western way of life is a more radical act for them than for Muslim men. Men were free to move about as they pleased back in Casablanca or Cairo, to wear Western-style clothing, and to take part in public life. The move to Europe changed male activities less than it changed their context and style. For women, life in the West multiplies opportunities so much that it alters the very premises of daily existence. Accordingly, Western ways often prove to be that much more powerful for females. This makes it likely that the integration of Muslims in Europe will be disproportionately forwarded by women.

The evolution of Islam in the West, in turn, may have profound effects on the body of believers in the Middle East and other regions. Living in the most advanced countries, Muslims in West Europe and the United States must contend with a host of issues earlier and more thoroughly than their coreligionists in other regions. Just as the Jewish synthesis was developed in nineteenth-century Europe, then spread to other regions, so its European Muslim equivalent might have profound importance for the future direction of Islamic faith. Indeed, the utterly Western writings of someone like Salman Rushdie are a key aspect of this transformation—and that is one reason why he stirred up so much passion among Muslims opposed to Protestantization. Further, the freedom of expression found in the West permits the great issues of Islam to be discussed intellectually, without the restrictions imposed by soldiers and mullahs throughout the Muslim world.

As Jane Kramer, Paris correspondent for *The New Yorker*, has noted, intellectuals in Algeria wanting to know what goes on in their own country have to read the French newspapers. "There is nothing at home for them to read—no Algerian analyses made in any depth by Algerian experts living in Algeria—to confirm their malaise or give it a community or a context. They have to depend on the Algerian intellectuals here in France for that context."[14] Algerians are not alone in this regard; West Europe has also become central for the cultural life of Libyans, Iraqis, Iranians and others. Symptomatic of this, the first book to appear in Arabic on *The Satanic Verses* was not published in Cairo or Beirut; rather, *Between the Pen and the Sword*[15] appeared in London, where it sold very well (possibly because the Saudi government had decided to buy out the entire print run). Then, as if to rub in the point about the Middle East's lack of free speech, four Arab countries promptly banned the book. The unique ability of Muslims in the West to engage in an unhampered debate makes them particularly critical to the future of their people.

Western Disquiet

The Rushdie affair caused some Europeans to express alarm that Muslims would not assimilate Western ways and values. With delicacy, Ian Davidson warned Muslims in the *Financial Times* that "they may be entitled to their own distinct cultural and religious identity; but only within the limitations permitted by the law."[16] Similarly, in late February, Home Secretary Douglas Hurd traveled to Birmingham to address worshippers at the city's central mosque on the responsibilities of living in Great Britain. In addition to lecturing Muslims on the principles of free speech and the responsibilities of citizenship, he asked them to make greater efforts to integrate their children to fit into society. His talk provoked widely differing reactions. Roy Hattersley, the deputy leader of the Labour Party, told an audience at the same mosque on April 2 that the home secretary's remarks were "absurd, as well as offensive," for they implicitly questioned the Muslims' place in British society.[17] In contrast, an editorial in *The Independent* held that the pious hopes expressed by Hurd were dead. There had been an expectation, the newspaper noted, that "all manifestations of cultural diversity would be benign. It is becoming disturbingly apparent that this is not the case."[18]

This difference of opinion pervaded the public discussion by non-Muslims. Disagreements were especially sharp in Britain's Labour Party. On the one hand, the faction led by Roy Hattersley and Max Madden favored accommodation of the Muslims' wishes, seeing this in the light of Labour's traditional support for a weak, poor group in search of redress. On the other hand, Neil Kinnock's wing of the party opposed the Muslim demands, holding instead to the equally hallowed principles of secularism and freedom of speech. Each faction harked back to an emotional core of the party's message—either help to those at the bottom of society or the freedom to thumb one's nose at authority.

Commentators vented unwonted vitriol. Hugo Young, the noted liberal, invited Iranians to return to their homeland if they found British tolerance not to their taste. Anthony Burgess addressed the Muslims: "We want no hands cut off here. For that matter, we want no ritual slaughter of livestock, though we have to put up with it.... If they [the Muslims] do not like secular society, they must fly to the arms of the Ayatollah or some other self-righteous guardian of strick Islamic morality."[19] A British newspaper, *The Star*, offered to pay the price of one-way tickets for Muslim "fanatics" wishing to return home. Another tabloid, *The News of the World*, stridently warned Muslims living in England to behave themselves. *Sunday Sport* suggested that "those who say their deep religious convictions prevent them from obeying the law of this land should quit Britain immediately and go to live in a country where the conflict does not exist."[20]

Rushdie correctly noted that the battle over his book fed the Western stereotype of "the backward, cruel, rigid Muslim, burning books and threatening to kill the blasphemer."[21] The figure of the Ayatollah Khomeini encouraged such a prejudice, for he appeared, in Anthony Hartly's description, "in the guise of a familiar ghost from the past—one of those villainous Muslim clerics, a Fakir of Ipi or a mad Mullah, who used to be portrayed, larger than life, in popular histories of the British Empire. Nor did his appearance do anything to change that image."[22]

The book burning in Bradford led some Britons to denounce Muslims as fascists. Thus, an editorial in *The Independent* accused the Muslims of "following the example of the Inquisition and Hitler's National Socialists."[23] The gutter press trotted out old stereotypes of Muslims being intolerant and narrow-minded. "Dirty Muslim" became, for the first time in memory, a term of abuse and a range of ethnic jokes became acceptable again. Back in Bradford, graffiti warning Muslims to "leave Rushdie alone—or else" was scrawled on the Islamic center, and an Anglo blue-collar worker was quoted as predicting that "if Rushdie is murdered, the bubble could burst."[24] More ominous, a leaflet distributed there raised the specter of civil war between Christians and Muslims in Great Britain.

No less than seven times within a twenty-four hour period French national television showed footage of Muslims cursing Rushdie at the Place de la République in Paris. The event provoked Jacques Chirac, the mayor of Paris, to express his "outrage": "if they are French citizens, they should be prosecuted, if foreigners, they should be expelled."[25] The Parisian authorities did go so far as to ban anti-Rushdie marches. Prime Minister Michel Rocard warned that further calls to murder would be subject to legal action. More broadly, the demonstration in Paris set back efforts to integrate Muslims into French life and caused many to wonder whether this ideal could ever be achieved. Henri Tinco, a journalist for *Le Monde*, mused that "an Islam that does not respect the laws of its host country has no chance of integrating into a Western society."[26]

The incident offered a chance to let off steam without being called a racist. One resident of Paris described the situation pungently: "for the price of a subway ticket, you find yourself in

Marrakesh."[27] *Paris Match* showed a picture of Muslims carrying pictures of the ayatollah and asked in a caption: "Tehran? No, Paris!" If André Pautard was almost apologetic, writing that "an old, Christian country is reticent about seeing minarets etched on the landscape, right next to the church spires,"[28] the leader of the French movement to oust immigrants, Jean-Marie Le Pen, was not. He used the Rushdie affair to tell the French public that "Islam is a religion of intolerance" and that "what Khomeini has just done with revolting cynicism is exactly what I fear for France and for Europe, that is to say an invasion of Europe by a Muslim immigration."[29]

But it was not just the right that exploited the intensity of feeling against Khomeini; on the left too, organizations having nothing to do with him did what they could to piggy-back on his unpopularity. Thus, People for the American Way, a liberal lobby group, bought full page newspaper advertisements urging readers to "do something to protect" their freedoms—i.e., send money to People for the American Way.

Even though the fundamentalist Muslim bravado of the first days after the edict quickly died down, replaced by somewhat less enthusiastic calls for adherence to British laws, the damage to communal relations had been done. The atmosphere was ripe to debate basic issues. Some took the occasion to express fears for the future of European life. From this point of view, no less worrisome than the actions of the fundamentalist Muslims was the fact that they were allowed to get away with rhetorical murder. British newspapers decried the fact that Muslims could publicly threaten Salman Rushdie's life and not be prosecuted under charges of incitement to murder. Peregrine Worsthorne, a prominent columnist, expressed the dismay that was widespread:

Islamic fundamentalism is rapidly growing into a much bigger threat of violence and intolerance than anything emanating from, say, the [extreme right] National Front; and a threat, moreover, infinitely more difficult to contain since it is virtually impossible to monitor, let alone stamp out, the bloodthirsty anti-Jewish and anti-Christian language being preached from the pulpits of many British mosques.... Britain has landed itself with a primitive religious problem that we had every reason to suppose had been solved in the Middle Ages.[30]

Perhaps the most pessimistic reading came from Bat Ye'or, a specialist on Islam who lives in Switzerland. She saw major consequences following from the influx of Muslims to Europe.

The rules of *Dar al-Islam* [lands under Muslim rule] are slowly spreading to Europe and modifying its democractic and secular principles.... European governments will be more on the defense, pretending that they are governing free societies when in fact they will be bowing to the threats of foreign powers.... Nothing must be allowed to disturb the European goals of accumulating more luxuries, more riches—even if, in the long term, this materialistic lust will lead to self-destruction. By its own doing, Europe is creating in its midst a powerful Muslim base which could easily become a subtle tool for manipulation of its policy by foreign powers.

Of course, beginning with Enoch Powell in England in the late 1960s, politicians in several European countries had sought to stem this tide, but without much success; immigrant labor was too much in demand. Le Pen's National Front and the Republicans in West Germany were the most obvious symptoms of nativist distress. While their efforts had long been stalled, the flexing of Muslim muscles against Rushdie may have provided them with new support. Less than a month after the major anti-Rushdie demonstrations, Le Pen's party did unexpectedly well in French municipal elections, thanks in part to the backlash against Muslim activism. Membership in the neo-Fascist Republican Party of Germany grew by over 50 percent in the two months following the Rushdie affair. Indeed, the Republicans, who had just won a breakthrough vote in West Berlin, were suddenly seen within striking distance of gaining enough votes to deny a parliamentary majority to the ruling conservative coalition in

Bonn in the 1990 elections. On the centennial of Hitler's birth, two months after the Khomeini *fatwa*, many Turkish workers felt so intimidated, they remained indoors all day. Perhaps because neo-Nazis could not find live Turks to assault on that date, they chose instead to desecrate a Turkish cemetery in West Berlin.

Muslim behavior during the Rushdie affair precipitated a number of hostile reactions in Europe. On one level, it stimulated street violence—such acts as a bomb thrown against the mosque in Regent's park, the symbolic burning of Qur'ans, and riots. On another level, widespread Muslim endorsement for the Iranian edict prompted Britons to rethink the wisdom of permitting government funds to go to private religious schools. Providing such support, the *Times Educational Supplement* noted, "makes it clearly necessary to know what a Muslim school which is seeking aided status [i.e., state money] intends to teach children on these matters." State funds, it went on, "pre-supposes a sufficiently broad base of shared values to make this acceptable. Are the shared values sufficiently sturdy to support the notion of Muslim aided schools? Not unless the Ayatollah is effectively repudiated."[31] Two months later, the Association of Metropolitan Authorities' education committee unanimously passed a resolution against state funds going to Muslim schools. In the words of one member of the committee, the vote was understood as one against "introducing a form of apartheid to our schools."[32]

Among Muslims, the Rushdie incident highlighted and perhaps deepened feelings of insecurity. Suspicions were now seemingly confirmed that Westerners harbored residual Crusader impulses. Some commentators, such as the editors of a Jordanian newspaper, made this fear explicit: "The whole affair of that diabolical book has reactivated age-old religious and intellectual intolerances towards the Muslims that are reminiscent of the dark days of the Crusaders."[33] Kassim Ghazzawi of Jordan commented that the news media in the West had "a field day in ascribing to Islam and Muslims all negative stereotypes that I thought had ended with the Crusades."[34] A Pakistani Muslim, S.A. Malik, concluded that "the spirit of the Crusades truly lives on!"* Significantly, even Muslims who rejected the Iranian authorities' vision of a massive plot suspected the motives of Westerners who backed Rushdie. According to Yusif al-'Aqid, columnist for *Al-'Arab, a* London-based Arabic newspaper, "Europe stood with Salman Rushdie not because of freedom of thought but because it was a golden opportunity to revile Islam and the Arabs, and so to sustain the constant and deeply rooted position that began with the first of the Crusades."[35]

Some Muslims found another, even more frightening analogy; not the Crusades but the Jewish Holocaust. Kalim Siddiqui, director of London's Muslim Institute, suggested that the British government should recall the book and incinerate all the copies: "Hitler-style gas chambers for Muslims will be rather more messy," he commented.[36] Shabbir Akhtar, a member of the Bradford Council of Mosques, seconded this apocalyptic view: "The next time there are gas chambers in Europe, there is no doubt concerning who'll be inside them."[37]

At the same time, Muslims found it obliquely pleasing that Europeans took them so seriously. Again, Shabbir Akhtar: "Islam is the only ideology [Christian Europeans deem] worth opposing. In that conviction there is an implied flattery that does not go unnoticed or unrelished by the Muslim faithful."[38] This theme of Islam's importance was also echoed by Iranian propagandists.

Ironically, Rushdie had hoped to highlight precisely this confrontation between Muslims and Westerners in *The Satanic Verses*, and to battle against it. "I tried to write against stereotypes. The zealot protests serve to confirm, in the Western mind,

---

Newsweek (European Edition), March 13, 1989. While the Crusading spirit did not in fact gain much from the Rushdie affair, some in the West saw it serving to reaffirm Christian values. In the words of L. A. Siedentop: "The unintended consequence of the Rushdie affair may be, and probably should be, to make the West conscious of how Christian it remains" ("Liberalism: The Christian Connection," *Times Literary Supplement*, March 24, 1989, p. 308).

all the worst stereotypes of the Muslim world."[39] Rushdie wrote a book about cultural misunderstanding—and succeeded beyond his wildest dreams. The irony of Rushdie's novel setting off this clash goes deeper yet. *The Satanic Verses* has been called, with good reason, "the first major novel of the new England, an England with more than two million immigrants, one in which it is no longer clear, exactly, what 'English life' comprises, what 'being English' means."[40] How strange that, of all stimuli, this book was the spark to ignite the new Englishmen and Englishwomen to take to the streets, to organize, and to find their voice in opposition.

Thus, the Rushdie incident simultaneously confirmed deep Western fears about Muslims and marked the first time Muslims in the West flexed their muscles. This unhappy combination augured further troubles to come.

NOTES

[1]For the parallels between the Fazlur Rahman and Rushdie affairs in Pakistan, see Khalid Durán, "Woher kommen die Verse denn nun wirklich?" *Frankfurter Allgemeine Zeitung*, February 27, 1989.

[2]John R. Weeks, *The Demography of Islamic Nations* (Washington, D.C.: Population Reference Bureau, 1988), pp. 52-53.

[3]Durán Khálid, "Der Islam in der Diaspora: Europa und Amerika," in Werner Ende and Udo Steinbach, eds., *Der Islam in der Gegenwart* (Munich: Verlag C. H. Beck, 1984), pp. 459-62.

[4]*Jeune Afrique*, March 15, 1989; *Bild*, quoted in *Der Spiegel*, February 13, 1989.

[5]Islamic Revolution News Agency, July 8, 1989. See also *Tehran Times*, July 8, 1989.

[6]*The Independent*, June 3, 1989.

[7]*The Observer*, April 2, 1989.

[8]*The Sunday Telegraph*, March 19, 1989.

[9]*The Independent*, February 20, 1989.

[10]On this, see Andrea B. Rugh, *Reveal and Conceal: Dress in Contemporary Egypt* (Syracuse, N.Y.: Syracuse University Press, 1986), especially chapater 7, "Religion and Dress."

[11]Radio Tehran, March 1, 1989.

[12]Josette Alia, "Que veulent les musulmans de France?" *Le Nouvel Observateur*, March 23, 1989, pp. 52-53.

[13]*Le Nouvel Observateur*, March 23, 1989. A Beur is a Muslim born in France.

[14]Jane Kramer, "Letter From Europe," *The New Yorker*, January 30, 1989, p. 82.

[15]'Adil Darwish and 'Imad 'Abd ar-Raziq, *Al-Ayat ash-Shaytaniya: Bayn al-Qalam wa's-Sayf* (London: Editest-Kamel, 1989). A 73-page pamplet, *Ayat Shaytaniya am Ahqad Shaytaniya* ["Satanic Verses or Satanic Hatreds"] ([London: n.p., [1989]) was published about the same time.

[16]Ian Davidson, "Why British Diplomacy Cuts a Poor Figure in Iran's Holy War," *Financial Times*, March 9, 1989.

[17]Centre for the Study of Islam and Christian-Muslim Relations, Birmingham, *Newsletter*, May 1989, p. 22.

[18]"Limits to Mutual Tolerance," *The Independent*, February 18, 1989.

[19]Anthony Burgess, "Islam's Gangster Tactics," *The Independent*, February 16, 1989.

[20]*Sunday Sport*, February 19, 1989.

[21]Quoted in Gerald Marzorati, "Salman Rushdie: Fiction's Embattled Infidel," *The New York Times Magazine*, January 29, 1989.

[22]Anthony Hartly, "Saving Mr. Rushdie?" *Encounter*, June 1989, p. 74. *Daily Mirror*, February 15, 1989 referred to Khomeini in a banner headline as "that Mad Mullah."

[23]*The Independent*, January 16, 1989.

[24]Press Association, February 22, 1989; *Sunday Times*, February 19, 1989.

[25]*Le Monde*, March 2, 1989.

[26]Henri Tinco, "Un mauvais coup pour l'Islam en France," *Le Monde*, February 28, 1989.

[27]*Le Monde*, February 28, 1989.

[28]André Pautard, "Les versets de la République," *L'Express*, March 10, 1989, p. 9.

[29]*The New York Times*, March 5, 1989; *Le Monde*, February 28, 1989.

[30]Peregrine Worsthorne, "The Blooding of the Literati," *Sunday Telegraph*, February 19, 1989.

[31]*Times Educational Supplement*, February 24, 1989.

[32]*The Times*, March 11, 1989.

[33]*Jordan Times*, March 5, 1989.

[34]*The Economist*, March 24, 1989.

[35]Yusuf 'Aqid, "Raha'in Salman Rushdi," *Al-'Arab*, August 4, 1989.

[36]*The Independent*, June 3, 1989.

[37]*The Guardian*, February 27, 1989.

[38]Centre for the Study of Islam, *Newsletter*, May 1989, p. 20.

[39]*The Observer*, January 22, 1989.

[40]Marzorati, "Salman Rushdie."

13.

CONCLUDING THOUGHTS

When 'Ali Akbar Hashemi Rafsanjani, speaker of the Iranian parliament, observed that the Rushdie affair is "one of the rarest and strangest events in history,"[1] he for once got it right. Several aspects of the Rushdie incident were unprecedented. Never before had a government picked a fight with a private individual in a foreign country. Never had a book been the cause and the source of an international diplomatic crisis. Never before had censorship driven a conflict between states.

Never before had there been a human rights case across boundaries. To be sure, state terrorism had often reached long distances (for example, Stalin's having Trotsky killed in Mexico), but never against a novelist and never with a "sentence" against him proclaimed by a head of state. Never before had the very notion of exile been jeopardized in this manner. As Eliot Weinberger explained: "Rushdie is the first outlaw of the global village: the man for whom exile is not possible."[2]

In a strange reversal, governments waited on the statements issued by a private citizen. Never before had this happened. Nor had an individual's choice of words ever borne so directly on the course of international relations. The situation was especially anomalous in Great Britain, where the authorities at one point felt compelled to deny that they had cleared a pronouncement made by Rushdie. As a news item reported it, with reference to his February 19 apology,

232

Whitehall sources said the Foreign Office had not asked to see the statement in advance. It was volunteered by the publishers. The Foreign Office had not taken any initiative or tried to influence the publishers in any way, nor was there any question that the Foreign Office had "cleared" or "approved" the statement, or taken any view about it.[3]

The absurdity of the situation was caught by a cartoon in *Le Monde* which showed Rushdie at his typewriter, surrounded by fifteen harried bobbies all keeping an eye on him; one of the policemen barks into the walkie-talkie, "Close the airports!! He wants to write volume two!!!"

Caprice and Irony

As this cartoon suggests, a deadly serious incident contained its share of whimsy. In an almost comical reduction of the conflict between civilizations, the mayor and archbishop of Ravenna received threats to the effect that the monument to Dante Alighieri in their city would be blown up. The reason, they were told, was that *The Divine Comedy* "offends Muhammad." A previously unknown group, the Guardians of the Revolution, complained that Dante had placed Muhammad in the ninth circle of Hell (see Canto 28), and while nothing could be done about this literary crime of the fourteenth century, they demanded that the mayor disassociate himself from the work and that it not be read in public again. The mayor speculated that the letter might be "a poor joke," but he did step up security for Dante's tomb.[4] It turned out that the threat was in fact a hoax, perpetrated by an Italian, Vincenzo Strocchi. The fact that it was taken seriously enough to increase security around a memorial spoke volumes about the temper of the times.

The enormous attention paid to a demanding novel like *The Satanic Verses* inevitably led to the book being lampooned for its obscurity. There was said to be an informal Club of Thirty in London, made up of people who started Rushdie's novels and never got beyond page thirty. In *Iranian Nights*, a spoof written by Howard Brenton and Tariq Ali and produced at the Royal Court Theater, the Caliph asks Scheherazade, "What was the blasphemy?" "No one knows," she answers, "it was a book that nobody could read."

Then there was the battle in Los Angeles. As Richard W. Stevenson of *The New York Times* put it,

> When Southern California enters a battle, it does so with its own style, and so it is with the uproar over the novel *The Satanic Verses*. The newest twist is the contribution of a radio talk show host who has declared as the enemy not the novel's author, Salman Rushdie, nor his antagonist, Ayatollah Ruhollah Khomeini, but a rock singer, Cat Stevens.

The talk show host, Tom Leykis of KFI-AM, was so affronted by Cat Stevens' endorsement of Khomeini's death edict, he called for a mass burning of the singer's music albums (subsequently changed, for environmental reasons, to a mass steamrolling). The radio station management was delighted by the idea and spurred the cause by promoting it throughout the broadcast day. This had two unexpected consequences. First, one of the other KFI talk show hosts, Geoff Edwards, found the destruction of any artistic materials offensive and refused to air promotions for the mass burning during his program. As a result, he was suspended from his job by the station. Eventually, Edwards and the station's management agreed to a termination of his contract. Second, the brouhaha pleased Cat Stevens himself. Having converted to Islam, he wanted to retract his old music, but until this point had been unsuccessful in his efforts. "Only a few weeks ago," he announced, "I wrote to the record companies asking that they [withdraw my records], but they refused because it would not be commercially viable for THEM! God works in mysterious ways."[5]

Similarly, WNEW-FM in New York City offered to exchange a copy of *The Satanic Verses* with the first hundred listeners who sent in Cat Stevens albums, which the station planned to melt.

Within two days, WNEW had been deluged with over 500 albums.

Some in the West fantasized about putting a price on Khomeini's head, just as he had done to Rushdie. In case Salman Rushdie "is unnaturally and prematurely silenced," Wole Soyinka declared that "the creative world will launch its own Jihad" (righteous war).[6] Joseph Brodsky, the poet, commented:

> As for Khomeini himself and what he has under his turban, I'm quite surprised that nobody thus far has put a price on that as well. It would be the only comparable response. If men of letters feel so indignant about the whole affair they should have pooled their resources and come up with the price. Mind you, it shouldn't be too big.[7]

Brodsky proposed this idea only as a fancy, but Robert Maxwell, the British publisher, did offer a counter-reward of £6 million to anyone who succeeded in civilizing "the barbaric Ayatollah" by having him publicly recite the Ten Commandments.[8] A British sports paper offered £1 million to anyone who brought Khomeini "to face a fair trial in this country."[9] Needless to say, no one won either prize.

The confrontation over Rushdie proved an irresistible subject for columnists and satirists. Andrew Rawnsley of *The Guardian* drew one of the cleverest parodies of Tehran-watchers in the West. Noting the toing-and-froing of the British government, he asked:

> Did Sir Geoffrey [Howe]'s latest statement mean that the pragmatists or the fundamentalists within the London regime were in the ascendant? Which of them now has the ear of the country's ageing absolute ruler, Ayatollah Thatcher? Was Britain serious about opposing Iran or was that just propaganda to divert the attention of the population from the once oil-rich regime's ailing economy?[10]

Eliot Weinberger described the Rushdie affair as Rushdie himself might have done in a one-paragraph *tour de force*:

After the thousand and one magical realist novels, with their daffodils falling from the sky and ancient crones giving birth to pig-faced children—novels desperate to recapture from the movies some small piece of the art of narrative by creating imagery that cannot be adequately represented on the screen—the genre has finally produced its masterpiece. Yet, as might be expected, it is not a novel at all, not even a book, but a tale that exists only in bits and pieces in the newspapers and on radio and TV, in oral transmission and cocktail party chatter. It is a plot that is still unfolding, and strangely, or not so strangely, it is the story of a magical realist novel: Once upon a time there was a man who wrote a book which a billion people didn't like. They tried to kill him for it, and ended up killing each other. Few of these people had even seen the book, yet all, friend and foe alike, found that it revealed their own worst natures... [11]

It is hard to imagine a more brilliant or succinct synthesis than this of a complex controversy.

The incident led to a host of ironies. The strongest opinions on all sides came from those who had not even seen the book. Salman Rushdie first savaged the British government, then sought its shelter; he renounced police methods, then gratefully accepted an around-the-clock police bodyguard. Rushdie forcefully denounced the shah's government and supported the Islamic Revolution, and ten years later found himself persecuted by the latter. Similarly, he condemned the U.S. raid on Tripoli in 1986 and found himself threatened by Mu'ammar al-Qadhdhafi in 1989. Prime Minister Benazir Bhutto of Pakistan was lampooned in one of Rushdie's novels, then found her government under fire because she was associated too closely with another of his books. Muslim leaders in Britain once considered commissioning Rushdie to write a play about the Muslims of Britain, then initiated steps which eventually jeopardized his life. Conversely, the first major work of art about the new England of immigrants stimulated them to find a voice to protest the status quo. By taking liberties with Islam, *The Satanic Verses* became the preeminent vehicle by which true believers of several faiths could cooperate.

Repercussions

Javier Pérez de Cuéllar, secretary-general of the United Nations, tried to put the Rushdie affair to rest by saying that it was time to drop this war of words and concentrate on the world's real problems. In saying this he was, like many others, impatient with the international furor over a novel, seeing this dispute as so much hot air—a battle which could be avoided and which was not terribly consequential. But Pérez de Cuéllar, and anyone who thought like him, was wrong: the Rushdie incident had real importance, partly because of its direct consequences, partly because it brought key issues to the fore.

To begin with, the controversy affected individuals. Twenty-two people lost their lives, many others feared for their safety, and hostages remained in captivity. It also affected states, especially Iran, where the authorities made the Rushdie affair their top political priority from mid-February to mid-March 1989. This decision led to the loss of billions of dollars in trade, diplomacy turned head over heels, and domestic political life veering in a new direction.

Since Iran's isolation had been a major reason why the war with Iraq had to be called off in August 1988, the high price of pursuing a revolutionary agenda abroad forced the Iranian leaders to temper their dogmatism. Through months of diplomatic spade work, Tehran's foreign relations had improved dramatically in the half year since the ceasefire with Iraq, only to be undone by the repercussions from Khomeini's *fatwa*. The need for good relations was apparently forgotten in February 1989, when the Iranian government lapsed back into its customary isolation, half-repudiated by Muslims and stigmatized by Westerners.

The Rushdie incident did more than reverse efforts to improve ties with the West. It also finally convinced a number of observers that there were no moderates to be found in the Iranian government; or, in the metaphor favored by the Mojahedin-e Khalq, the cobras of the Khomeini regime cannot give birth to doves. Editorialists at *Le Monde* concluded, for example, that "there should be no illusions about improving relations with Tehran, at least so long as Imam Khomeini is in charge."[12] This reading seemed to be confirmed when several officials who had sought better relations with the West, including Deputy Foreign Minister Mohammed Javad Larijani and U.N. Ambassador Mohammed Ja'far Mahalati, were forced in part to resign because of their having adopted the wrong views on *The Satanic Verses*.

The incident had major economic consequences. Several Western countries reduced their purchases of Iranian oil, and the Japanese government directed oil companies to cut their intake from 300,000 to 200,000 barrels a day. Just after months of negotiations had led to the establishment of new credit lines to Iran from the West, the Rushdie affair led to a West European ban on loans to Iran. In all, the Iranians were deprived of some $3 to $4 billion in credit and the Europeans of about the same amount in exports. In addition, nearly every West European government cancelled at least one official visit, loan or trade agreement with Iran, further delaying a resumption of economic relations. For example, negotiations for an Iranian purchase of three Airbus passenger planes from a European consortium took several months more than was expected.

In the weeks preceding Khomeini's *fatwa* it had appeared that the Western hostages held in Lebanon would finally be released, but this too was upended in February 1989. *Newsweek* reported an "almost-done deal" in which the British government would have secured the release of its hostages by paying money to the Palestine Liberation Organization, which in turn would pass the funds to Iranian proxies in Lebanon.[13] But this complex arrangement fell through when the hostage-takers blamed London for sheltering Rushdie and linked the hostages' fate to the Western governments abandoning their support for him. The Iranian press subsequently endorsed this position.

The Satanic Verses caused Tehran's relations with all but one of its neighbors to deteriorate. Erratic and bellicose behavior from Iran buttressed Iraqi arguments about the impossibility of reaching a reasonable agreement with the Iranians, thereby strengthening Baghdad's hand in the United Nations-sponsored negotiations to end the Iraq-Iran war. International pressure on Baghdad to show more flexibility, which had been strong for half a year, simply vanished in February 1989. Iranian efforts to get *The Satanic Verses* banned in Turkey, then to reverse a court decision in the headscarf controversy caused relations with Ankara to slip to their lowest point in decades. Iranian incitement of fundamentalist Muslims in Pakistan against their government was deeply resented in Islamabad. Only in the case of the U.S.S.R. did the confrontation enhance relations; just twelve days after issuing the Rushdie *fatwa*, the ayatollah himself received the Soviet foreign minister in a televised meeting. In ten years of diplomacy, through revolution and war, no other foreign politician had been thus honored.

In domestic Iranian politics too, the *fatwa* appears to have ended the half-year of moderation which followed the cease-fire with Iraq. With some exceptions (notably the executions of Mojahedin-e Khalq members), Khomeini seemed to tolerate more pragmatic policies. This trend came to an abrupt halt on February 14. In the months that followed, he condemned liberals in Iran, displaced Ayatollah Montazeri as his successor, and redoubled efforts to impose a strict Islamic order within Iran ("misveiled" women, for example, found themselves subject to up to seventy-four lashes for wearing the wrong color veil or allowing some hair to show in public).

The Satanic Verses had an impact in other countries too. In India it inflamed the always delicate relations between Hindus and Muslims. In Pakistan, the incident provided the opposition forces with ammunition against the leftist government of Benazir Bhutto; riots that protested the book were intended for her as well. The authorities responded to this challenge by banning public meetings in Islamabad, the capital, thus taking a large step backwards on the path to martial law.

These developments, significant as they were, tended to be either personal tragedies or transient matters. The West European governments could not bring themselves to abandon the Iranian

market for long, just because a British writer remained se-
questered. The European Community's withdrawal of ambassadors, after all, lasted just one month. Even the British posture
quickly changed. On February 21, Sir Geoffrey Howe indicated
that normal relations with Iran could not be restored until Tehran
renounced the use or threat of violence against citizens of other
countries. Though nothing much had changed a month later,
William Waldegrave announced on March 22 that "Britain is not
in conflict with Iran."[14] It was inevitable that ambassadors would
quickly return to their stations and the outside world would once
again patiently tolerate Iranian misbehavior.

From a long-range point of view, probably the most important
consequences of the Rushdie affair have little to do with eco-
nomics, politics, or diplomacy, but bear on the attitudes of
millions of individuals around the world. The incident raised a
wide array of issues—freedom of speech in India, race relations
in Britain, the role of bookstore chains in the United States, even
the nature of the secular state. But two issues stood out, one
having to do with Islam and the West, the other with censorship.
By making all parties more aware of those controversies, the
incident clarified differences and deepened the awareness of
cultural distance.

Images of the Other

The Rushdie incident prompted a confrontation of Christian
and Islamic civilizations the likes of which had not been seen in
centuries. Confronted by a largely united Muslim world, Westerners did something remarkable: they stood together in their
disapproval of Khomeini's act. (Only three "Western" governments broke ranks, it bears noting, and banned the book: South
Africa, Japan and Venezuela.) The issue encouraged solidarity on
both sides because it transcended foreign policy and touched on
issues of basic domestic values in each civilization. In the West, it
was a matter of possibly the single most important principle of
modern liberal ideology, freedom of speech. In the Muslim

world, it was the dignity of Islam. The controversy made it painfully clear that what the West holds sacred easily conflicts with what is holy to Muslims. Despite many efforts to find common ground, the conflict did not lend itself to reduction, for matters of principle resist compromise and negotiation. One side had to win, the other had to lose.

By similar token, the Rushdie case exactly confirmed some hoary stereotypes. No event in previous decades had delineated cultural lines with such clarity and along such well-established lines. In calling Khomeini "a joyless, glowering fanatic," editorialists at *The New York Times* were clearly invoking old notions about Muslims behaving like maniacs; so too did the French magazine *L'Express* when it announced that "fanaticism is exploding."[15] The normally calm *Independent* called Khomeini "a bloodthirsty medieval bigot."[16] A letter to *Le Monde* summed up this attitude:

> Simple questions. Which offends Islam more, a novel or an assassin? Writing on paper or a bloody crime? Disprovable deaths or deaths without appeal? Who? The alleged satan or the avowed fanatic?
>
> Is man authorized to kill man in the service of God? To serve God! Is that Islam? Where is such a satanic verse written?
>
> Who will offer three million prayers so that Khomeini can just venerate his God? In a silence of fanaticism.[17]

For the first time in memory, the Western press described Europe and America as the "the civilized world,"[18] and Muslims were clearly seen as living outside the borders of this world. According to one poll, 66 percent of the French public wished to see *The Satanic Verses* published in France, while 74 percent saw fundamentalist religion as a danger of global proportions. In another survey, 60 percent saw fundamentalist Islam as a serious danger, with its Jewish and Catholic counterparts worrying, respectively, only 35 and 32 percent of the public.[19] Bernard Oudin concluded from the Rushdie controversy that "the [Muslim-Western] dialogue is dead."[20]

Some very peculiar ideas about Muslims came out of the woodwork. Norman Stone wrote about "those beards, those absolutes, that dreadful unconcern with obvious sentiment," calling these "parody-masculine attributes, and the Ayatollah, to perfection, has them in old-man form."[21] Arnold Wesker, the playwright, waxed lyrical, describing Khomeini as "a bigoted, medieval throwback...whose perpetually angry demeanor told anyone perceptive enough to read expressions that here was an old-fashioned religious zealot whose petulant and tortured heart, so obviously engraved in his eyes, was about to wreak destructive and revengeful havoc."[22]

If the mainstream saw Islam as hopeless, the fringes seized the moment to spread an anti-Muslim message to a wider audience. Thus, the Fighters of the Greek Islands took the occasion to distribute a document in the capitals of Europe which, referring to the building of a mosque in Rome, asserted that, "as Christian Europeans, we do not accept the erection of a minaret and the recitation of the Islamic call to prayers in front of the Vatican."[23]

Reading Muslims out of the civilized world is, of course, flat wrong. Even if freedom of speech is the ticket of admission, a good number of Muslims, some of them in positions of authority or prominence, have the credentials to enter. For all the battering they have taken, liberal ideas remain alive in the Muslim world; not all is submerged under the darkness of fundamentalism. Admittedly, it is easy to forget this, given the impoverished leadership, the political turmoil, and the violence that prevail in the Middle East and beyond. In terms of perceptions by the outside world, perhaps the key problem lies in the fact that the most prominent representatives of Islam—the Khomeinists, the Wahhabis of Saudi Arabia, and Mu'ammar al-Qadhdhafi of Libya—are all extremists. In Western eyes, their eccentric and distasteful behavior overwhelms the religion as it is practiced daily on an individual level by hundreds of millions of the faithful. It is no wonder that Westerners, watching such outlandish leaders, find it hard to perceive the many attractive qualities of Islam.

Some Muslims recognized this problem at the time of the Rushdie affair, and fretted over it. According to Coskun Kirca, a retired Turkish diplomat, "Iran is behaving barbarically, and its behavior has belittled all Muslim countries in the eyes of the Western world."[24] Many Muslims in the West fretted in private about Khomeini's *fatwa* making life a lot more difficult for them, and some went so far as to believe this was intentional on Khomeini's part. But Kirca and the anti-fundamentalists found themselves nearly powerless to challenge the unholy trinity in Tehran, Riyadh and Tripoli; a combination of oil wealth and ideological fervor endowed those regimes with an unrivaled might in Islamic affairs. The older bastions of a more moderate vision of Islam had all declined, and their interpretations had suffered grievously in an era of fundamentalist enthusiasm. The secular experiment in Turkey, the attempts at a reformist compromise in Egypt, and the steps toward adjustment to minority status in democratic India had not come to an end in the 1980s, but they had been seriously weakened. Only when the oil boom ends entirely and the vitality of fundamentalist Islamic ideas dims will their chance come again. This is, however, thin consolation in a time of zealotry.

Given the simplifications that seize the imagination, Westeners all too easily assumed that all Muslims endorsed Khomeini's intolerance and bigotry. Even when dimly aware that this was not the case, they were tempted to forget this fact. This left non-fundamentalist Muslims not only with their radical brethren to combat, but also the prejudices of Westerners, which lumped them together with their rivals. No wonder that moderate and liberal Muslims despised Rushdie, even if their real disagreement was with the fundamentalists.

As is always the case, a few figures in the West found a way to apologize for Khomeini's behavior. Two arguments recurred. In one, it was pointedly recalled just how many blasphemers in the West had lost their liberty or their lives at the stake. True enough: but this ignored the West's achievement, which lay precisely in leaving this stage behind and moving on to a more sophisticated and humane treatment of religious differences. Conversely, the tragedy in Iran lay in the fact that its leaders renounced what the West had so arduously achieved, and insisted on returning to the older, cruder approach.

The other argument noted that Islam, being less than fourteen centuries old, is now at a comparable state of development to Christianity in its fourteenth century. In other words, this is a religion yet to experience its Reformation. The assumption behind such a calculation is that "major religions, involving as they do deep-seated webs of philosophy, emotion and politics, require a millennium to shake themselves out."[25] But this is nonsense. The notion that religions share patterns over millennia is almost too crude to require refutation; suffice it to note that Judaism and Hinduism, which have almost nothing in common, and never have, are about the same age, as are Mormonism and Christian Science. Further, the connection between Muslim intolerance and the relative youth of Islam is directly refuted by the fact that Islam had sheltered a more tolerant ethos in its earlier centuries. Rather than looking the calendar to understand the bigotry of figures like Khomeini, the Wahhabis, and Qadhdhafi, an explanation should be sought in the predicament of modern Islam and the deep feelings of inferiority among some Muslims toward the West. The many conspiracy theories circulating among Muslims confirm how close old fears remain to the surface.

The Satanic Verses had special importance for the millions of Muslims living in the West. The controversy helped them find their voice, and they are unlikely to allow it to be silenced in the future. The organizing and excitement of early 1989 gave Muslims in West Europe a first taste of power. In the short term, this should spur political ambitions. In the longer run, it will probably translate into an enduring aspiration to bring the Middle East to Europe, perhaps even to the United States. If this happens, Muslims are likely to place less emphasis on the limited efforts of past years (single-sex schools, Islamic forms of divorce) in favor of something much deeper—the assertion of Muslim values in society at large.

The logic of numbers points to such developments. The West has by far the lowest birth rate in the world, so low that it will soon not be replacing itself. Today, only Poland, Ireland and Malta have naturally growing populations. In contrast, the Muslim countries have the hightest rate. Demographically, the two groups complement each other so well that the continued migration of Muslims to the West seems unstoppable. Rightists in Europe may resist the idea of letting such aliens in, fundamentalist Muslims may shudder at the thought of taking up residence in a land of blasphemy and lewdness, but the two are almost fated to join each other. Indeed, there are probably cases already of neo-fascist German employers hiring fundamentalist Muslim workers, with both parties hating the relationship, but accepting it nonetheless. Much more of this is likely to come, and it will be fraught with difficulties for the two sides.

Unfortunately, the presence of Muslims in the West encourages the worst in each camp: ugly nativistic reactions from those who resent the growing numbers of dark-skinned, poor foreigners with strange eating habits and less-developed notions of hygiene; and arrogant fundamentalist Islamic ambitions among emigrants culturally unprepared for immersion in an alien civilization and therefore prone to insist on the most dogmatic version of their faith.

By giving both sides a foretaste of problems to come, the Rushdie incident offered an important lesson. Christians and Muslims will presumably wish to live together in harmony if they are fated to live side-by-side. This means breaking a millennial tradition of mistrust and hostility that can only be achieved by changing a number of attitudes. Europeans must accept the fact that their societies are about to become multi-racial and multi-ethnic; that their cultures are to include new languages, religions and ways of life; and that their politics are to be subject to new influences. Clinging to visions of Ye Olde England is not just futile but profoundly reactionary, and the same goes for the like pastoral visions that exist in most other countries of West Europe. Instead, the British and others need to accommodate the new reality of an immigrant society.

As this adjustment takes place in Western Europe (and, one day, perhaps Japan too), it may be helpful to learn something from Europe's daughter countries—the United States, Canada, Australia and New Zealand. Grudgingly and haltingly, the leaders of all immigrant countries gave up the vision of racial or cultural purity and adopted a more open attitude. Initially, this meant accepting the Irish in America and the Greeks in Australia; more recently, it meant welcoming Vietnamese and Chinese. In the future, it will almost surely mean assimilating large numbers of Muslims.

Historically, these four immigrant societies absorbed new peoples through three mechanisms: idealism, education and secularism. Ideals such as the pursuit of happiness and freedom of speech have been vital to all immigrant societies, making up for the absence of shared ethnic bonds by providing the population with a common purpose. For Muslims to live harmoniously with their Western neighbors, they must adopt the ideals of the host society.

Education of children is critical, for even if the adult immigrants cannot understand the ideals of their adopted country, it is imperative that these be communicated to the next generation. Ideals provide a substitute for lineage. Indicative of this, George Washington is in the symbolic ancestry of every American child, even if his parents arrived at the time of his birth. If the European states are to absorb the Muslim (and other alien) immigrants, they must move in this direction. It will not be easy for old societies, but the tradition has to stress ethnicity less and principles more. The glorious history of France, for instance, needs to concentrate less on the victories over others and more on efforts to attain liberty, equality and fraternity.

Secularism has particular importance in the case of Muslims. It needs to be given pride of place in the pantheon of civic virtues, for only secularism makes it possible to transcend the historic Christian-Muslim conflict and treat the other as an equal. Only if Muslims accept secularism can they fully integrate into society. But secularism has its costs; it means having to give up all notions of molding Western countries in the Islamic image. Instead, Muslim leaders in the West must push their followers to integrate into the larger society. This means, for instance, no pressure on the government to pay for Muslim schools, no attempts to get Islamic law accepted in courts, and no extension of blasphemy laws to cover Islamic topics. To integrate into the West, Muslims need not forego their faith, but they must accept the supremacy of civil law—and freedom of speech is a critical element of that law.

As anti-Khomeini Muslim politicians, intellectuals, and even religious leaders made clear in the course of the controversy over *The Satanic Verses*, Muslims need not stumble over the premises of modern life. The problem lies not with Islam as such, but with the fundamentalist strain of Islam—the one which holds literally to the archaic rules of Islam and refuses to accommodate to the realities of modern life. In the fundamentalist reading of Islam, principles of the faith frequently contradict those of the West and the usual response to this dilemma is to undo the modern world. Thus, fundamentalist Muslims rail against international law and the Universal Declaration of Human Rights. At other times, they redefine Western precepts to the point that they are no longer recognizable: Freedom of religion means the freedom for a Catholic to become a Protestant or for a Shi'i to become a Sunni, not conversion out of Islam; non-interference in the internal affairs of other countries does not restrict Iranian efforts to spread its notions of Islam. By similar token, when fundamentalists say that "blasphemy is definitely against freedom of expression,"[26] freedom of expression essentially means the freedom to make statements which offend no political, religious or sexual sensibilities. The Rushdie incident makes clear that such self-serving interpretations will not do if the experiment of Muslims living in the West is to succeed.

Freedom of Speech

The other key issue concerns freedom of speech, both in the Muslim countries and in the West. For Muslims in the Middle East and elsewhere, Khomeini's attack on Rushdie served as a reminder of just how seriously personal liberties are lacking, and especially that of freedom of speech. As Amir Taheri has explained, Khomeini forced a debate on the long-deferred question, "can a man speak his mind without risking death or imprisonment?"[27] If no, then there is every reason to fear that Muslim countries will remain in the world's rear guard. As Muslim critics are the first to admit, their coreligionists fare poorly almost without regard to the index one chooses. Whether one considers material well-being, social equity, military power, public hygiene or cultural originality, Muslims have done badly compared to others. While this array of problems is obviously too complex to be cured by a single solution, it is also clear that the severe limitations on personal freedom under which most Muslim peoples toil has crucial importance. As Communist regimes are learning around the world, you can only go so far with repression and imposed ideologies. Only when the answer to Taheri's question becomes yes, when the autocrats are forced to loosen the fetters, only then will it be possible for the Muslim countries to make real progress.

Rushdie was correct when he portrayed his enemies as rulers seeking to control new domains. "I think the real issue is the power over the story. What these people are saying, the Mullahs and the Saudis, and God knows who, is that they are the only people who have the power over the story and that's because they have power: financial power, political power, and the power of the pulpit."[28] If the authorities can even control fiction, it is hard to see how the Muslim countries will ever progress.

It is true that most Muslims approved of the *fatwa* and most Westerners abhored it, yet opinions counted more than affiliation. Some Muslims did condemn the edict, just as some Westerners apologized for it. In the final analysis every person could freely choose sides, and almost every one did so. This said, differences of opinion in the West tended to be tactical, while those in the Muslim world reflected disagreements over first principles. The cultural crisis prompted by *The Satanic Verses* had less to do with East and West, or Muslims and Europeans, and much more to do with the direction of Islam. Would there be freedom of speech or not? Would the rulers have an exclusive prerogative to interpret the Islamic saga? Would fundamentalists prevail, squeezing out secularist Muslims? The debate was really about competing visions of society—closed or open, religious or secular, bigoted or tolerant.

As such, the controversy over *The Satanic Verses* continued an already long-running and bitter debate between Muslims. The key actors—Rushdie, Khomeini and their followers—were all Muslims, and the elemental issues all concerned Islam. What made this argument different was not its terms of reference but that it took place on a Western stage, and so was witnessed by a global audience.

As for the West, Khomeini achieved something remarkable with his edict; in Europe and North America (and in other regions too), he created an unprecedented climate of worry. Concerned for their personal safety, writers, publishers, booksellers, book-buyers, faculty and students watched what they said. In a temporary and partial way, then, Khomeini succeeded in imposing his will on the West. His success raised the possibility that other dictators and extremists would resort to similar forms of intimidation to prohibit the discussion of their pet subjects, with a similar chilling effect. Why should they not emulate him, and ban books and kill authors wherever they may be? In the Middle East alone, Saddam Husayn, Hafiz al-Asad, Mu'ammar al-Qadhdhafi and Yasir 'Arafat have writings and writers they fondly would wish eliminated. It would make good sense for them to emulate Khomeini and place a bounty on their opponents' heads. In this way, the *fatwa* may have altered the rules.

The whimsically named League for the Spread of Unpopular Views, a West German organization, saw Khomeini's edict as a direct challenge to a central feature of Western civilization. "The Rushdie case is a deadly earnest probe to see what freedom of expression in the West is worth. Should Rushdie be killed, it would be the first burning of a heretic in Europe in two centuries. The West would then carry the full responsibility, for it would have failed to have protected with all available means Rushdie and with him freedom of expression!"[29] Though a shade alarmist, the League's point is worth pondering.

At the same time, the ayatollah's accomplishments must not be exaggerated. The global fear of early 1989 is not likely to be soon repeated. Khomeini was a unique ruler and the furor surrounding *The Satanic Verses* is likely to remain without match. In theory, while many of Khomeini's tactics can be imitated by anyone, Iranian prototypes tend rarely to be imitated, so this incident may well turn out to be a one-time affair. The Iranians institutionalized and systematized the recruitment of suicide bombers, but few states availed themselves of this powerful tool. Seizing the U.S. embassy in Tehran proved to be a brilliant tactical innovation by the Iranian radicals in 1979, but it has not been emulated even once. Taking such a step requires a radicalism, an ideological devotion, and a personal commitment as deep as that of Khomeini and his followers. In the Rushdie case, Khomeini managed to impose an unprecedented form of trans-border censorship precisely because no one is like him. No other leader challenged the existing order in so profound a way or had a vision of the just society that differed so fundamentally from the prevailing models. Accordingly, conventional dictators typically find that following in the ayatollah's footsteps is beyond their capabilities.

Moreover, even his achievement was less than complete. It should be remembered that it was the Saudis who got the book banned in most Muslim countries; Iranian efforts to extend censorship to the West failed. For all the fear Iranians created in the West, their attempts at intimidation turned *The Satanic Verses* into a spectacular commercial success. Despite and because of the Muslim efforts, *The Satanic Verses* became the book of the year. Boastful claims that protests would continue until the book was recalled and the author and publisher apologized came to naught. The controversy caused many Westerners to feel a highly unusual sense of solidarity, seeing themselves again as the only civilized people and recalling old animosities toward Islam. In many ways, the ayatollah not only did not get his way but he stirred up antagonisms that will harm his cause for years to come.

Is the power that Khomeini achieved an aberration or the beginning of a subtle shift in norms? While it is too early to say, it is clear that the answer depends far more on the West than on Khomeini and his ilk. The West has to make it clear that the fundamentalist Muslims will gain nothing through threats and intimidation. "The only acceptable way to end *The Satanic Verses* affair is to go on repeating that until the message is heard and believed."[30]

NOTES

[1]Radio Tehran, March 10, 1989.
[2]Eliot Weinberger, "The Month of Rushdies," *Boston Review*, August 1989.
[3]Press Association, February 18, 1989.
[4]Associazione Nazionale Stampa Associata, March 7, 1989.
[5]*The New York Times*, March 8, 1989.
[6]*The African Guardian*, February 23, 1989.
[7]*The New York Times Book Review*, March 12, 1989.
[8]*The Bookseller*, February 24, 1989.
[9]*Sunday Sport*, February 19, 1989.
[10]Andrew Rawnsley, "Howe's Many Hands Make Short Work of the Iranians," *The Guardian*, March 9, 1989.
[11]Weinberger, "Month of Rushdies."
[12]*Le Monde*, February 16, 1989.
[13]*Newsweek*, March 13, 1989.

[14]Press Association, February 21, 1989; *Al-Qabas*, March 22, 1989.

[15]*The New York Times*, February 10, 1989; *L'Express*, February 24, 1989.

[16]*The Independent*, February 21, 1989.

[17]Letter from G. Abeille, *Le Monde*, March 4, 1989.

[18]For example, *Handelsblatt*, February 22, 1989.

[19]*Journal du Dimanche*, March 5, 1989; *La Vie*, March 15, 1989.

[20]Bernard Oudin, *La Foi qui tue*, 2d ed., (Paris: Éditions Robert Laffont, 1989), p. 15.

[21]*Sunday Telegraph*, February 19, 1989.

[22]*The Independent*, February 17, 1989.

[23]*Milliyet*, February 20, 1989.

[24]*Milliyet*, March 26, 1989.

[25]Gregg Easterbrook, "Behind Moslem Fury at 'Satanic Verses'—The West's Enduring Ignorance of Islam," *The Washington Post*, February 19, 1989.

[26]Habibollah Bi'azar Shirazi, ambassador to Greece, *Tehran Times*, March 18, 1989.

[27]Amir Taheri, "Pandora's Box Forced Open," *Index on Censorship*, May 1989, p. 8.

[28]Ameena Meer, "Interview: Salman Rushdie," *Bomb*, Spring 1989, p. 36

[29]Bund zur Verbreitung unerwünschter Einsichten [Hamburg], "Der Fall Rushdie und die Feigheit des Westerns," pamphlet, p. 3.

[30]*The Times*, July 31, 1989.

APPENDIX

From Edwin McDowell, "Book Notes," *The New York Times*,
July 19, 1989:

A CONTRACT FOR "THE AYATOLLAH, THE NOVELIST AND THE WEST" IS CANCELED.

When the furor over *The Satanic Verses* by Salman Rushdie was at its
peak in February, publishers predicted that houses would think twice
before publishing other books that might be construed as critical of
Islam. Now a Middle East scholar says, despite a publisher's denial, that
he wonders if such caution led to the recent cancellation of his contract
for a book about the Rushdie affair.

The scholar, Daniel Pipes, the director of the Foreign Policy Research
Institute in Philadelphia, proposed a book that would explore why *The
Satanic Verses* has prompted such intense reactions. In April, Basic
Books, which had published one of Mr. Pipes's three books on the
Middle East, sent him a contract for the book, which it planned to
publish next spring.

In May, Mr. Pipes submitted the finished manuscript, titled "The
Ayatollah, the Novelist and the West." Three weeks later, he received a
phone call from Martin Kessler, the president and publisher of Basic
Books, telling him that the contract was canceled. "He indicated he was
not happy about the cancellation," Mr. Pipes said. "He said that while
he had initial concerns about the commercial viability of the book, he
had decided to go ahead with it, but that the corporate higher-ups had
turned it down." Basic Books is a subsidiary of Harper & Row, which is
owned by Rupert Murdoch's News Corporation.

Mr. Pipes said Harper & Row had allowed him to keep the advance
and to place the manuscript elsewhere. "In that sense, I'm not an

aggrieved author," he said. "But I'm appalled by the implications for general publishing." What added to his discomfort, he said, was that about that time, one of Mr. Murdoch's other publishing companies, William Collins Sons, canceled a book in Britain called *The Rushdie File*.

George Craig, the chief executive of Harper & Row and Collins, said Mr. Kessler made the decision alone to cancel the Pipes contract after Harper's marketing department convinced him the book would not be profitable. Mr. Craig said the decision to cancel *The Rushdie File* was made by the Collins managing director, also on commercial grounds. Mr. Kessler did not return telephone calls yesterday or Monday.

Mr. Craig denied that Harper & Row and Collins had any prohibition against books about Islam or the Rushdie incident.

GLOSSARY

Allah: Arabic for God.

Ayatollah: Highest level of religious official in Iran.

Caliph: Political successor of the Prophet Muhammad.

Fatwa: An opinion on relogus doctrine or law delivered by a mufti (or some other Muslim religious authority).

Fundamentalist Islam: A variant of Islam which demands application of the Islamic law in its every detail and holds that Islam contains all the answers to modern life.

Gharaniq: Birds; the tag by which the Satanic verses incident of Muhammad's life is known in Arabic.

Hizbulluh: Party of God; the name of pro-Khomeini groups in many countries, most notably Iran and Lebanon.

Imam: For all Muslims: (1) Prayer leader; (2) Honored religious leader. For Shi'is only: (3) Caliph; (4) Intermediary figure between man and God.

Islam: Faith in one God and in the Qur'an as the literal Word of God.

Islamic Revolution: Overthrow of Shah Mohammed Reza Pahlevi by Ayatollah Khomeini in 1978-79.

Jahiliya: The society of Arabia before Islam.

Jihad: War by Muslims in conformity with the Shari'a; righteous war. More generally, any war by Muslims against non-Muslims.

Majlis: Parliament (in the Islamic Republic of Iran).

Mojahedin-e Khalq: Iranian opposition movement based on a blend of Marxist and Islamic ideas.

Mufti: A Muslim religous authority with the authority to deliver *fatwas*.

Muhammad: Prophet of Islam; also known as Mohammed.

Mullah: Iranian religious figure; comparable to a rabbi.

Muslim (noun): An adherent of Islam; (adj.): Pertaining to Muslims. Also known as Moslem.

Qur'an: The Word of God, made available to humans by Muhammad; also known as the Koran.

Shari'a: The sacred law of Islam.

Shi'i: Second branch of Islam, comprising about 10 percent of Muslims; also known as Shi'ites.

Sunni: Majority branch of Islam, comprising about 90 percent of Muslims; also known as Sunnites.

POSTSCRIPT
THE RUSHDIE AFFAIR'S LEGACY

Koenraad Elst

In the thirteen years since the publication of *The Rushdie Affair*, Salman Rushdie's name has become a byword for the persecution of free speech by the forces of militant Islam. Ironically, although Rushdie himself is very much alive—writing well-received books, popping up among the literary jet-set, and even acquiring a new girlfriend—the same cannot be said of many other critics of Islam, both Muslim and not.

In retrospect, the lasting importance of the edict by Ayatollah Ruhollah Khomeini sentencing Rushdie to death was to open the door for Islamist terror against Muslim freethinkers and non-Muslim critics of Islam—what Daniel Pipes has dubbed the "Rushdie rules." Given how much the frequency of attacks has increased on them since 1989, it seems fair to conclude that this edict served as a catalyst. The assault on September 11, 2001, made this taboo on criticism of Islam all the more apparent and public, even as it broke it down in select ways. At the same time, there are some grounds for optimism that the killings and persecution are growing less common.

The following essay updates *The Rushdie Affair*; it has benefited from input and review by Daniel Pipes.

MUSLIM-MAJORITY COUNTRIES

Rushdie-Related Violence

Tehran has steadily upheld the Islamic correctness and permanent validity of Ayatollah Khomeini's edict, even as it declared its lack of intention in sending out its own hit men to prosecute the death sentence. Sayyed Husayn Musavian, an Iranian envoy who downplayed the whole controversy in his talks with Western leaders in the hopes of renormalizing Euro-Iranian relations, made this point explicitly: "The fatwa was merely a statement of something that has been part of Islamic law for 1,400 years."[1] Though some elements in the government profess no longer to back these efforts, Ayatollah Hasan Sanei'i's Khordad Foundation still has a standing offer of $2.8 million for anyone who slays Salman Rushdie and many mullahs have pledged a month's salary as contribution to the award.

The Iranian regime gave added credibility to its continued threat against Rushdie by executing dissidents within the country and assassinating dozens of Iranians living in exile, such as the musician Fereydun Farokhzad in Bonn[2] and the columnist Mustafa Jehan in the Christian sector of Beirut.[3] One count, by the exiled former prime minister Abol Hassan Bani Sadr, has the regime killing thirty-three exiled opponents between 1980 and 1996.[4]

Violence most directly related to Rushdie includes several attacks on his translators. Two of them, the Italian Ettore Capriolo and the Norwegian William Nygaard, were seriously wounded in knife assaults. (In defiance, Nygaard declared at the 1994 Book Fair in Frankfurt that the only correct reply to the terrorists was to stand firm for freedom, and that his way to do this was to translate and publish yet another blasphemer's book, Taslima Nasrin's *Shame*.)[5] More alarming yet was the lethal attack on Hitoshi Igarashi, a Japanese professor of literature and translator of *The Satanic Verses*, right on the campus of Tsukuba University in 1991.[6] To the indignation of the Japanese public, Japanese Muslims applauded this killing and declared that "even if the murder was not committed by a Muslim, God made sure that Igarashi got what he deserved."[7]

But the most murderous consequence by far took place in July 1993 in the town of Sivas, Turkey, at a cultural conference commemorating Pir Sultan Abdal (ca. 1480-1550), a poet sometimes called "Turkey's first socialist."[8] Participants included Aziz Nesin, the translator of *The Satanic Verses* into Turkish and a Marxist author in his own right who had declared that "an end should be put to the millennial tyranny of the Qur'an" and that Muslims "should not be guided by such an antiquated book."[9] Most conference participants were Alevis, members of a Shi'i sect widely seen by Sunni Muslims as beyond the pale of Islam. To protest the meeting, a mob destroyed a statue of Abdal and demanded Nesin be handed over for summary execution. Failing this, the crowd stormed the conference hotel, set the building on fire, and prevented firefighters from extinguishing the blaze. As a result, thirty-seven conference participants died. Although Nesin himself escaped death, state attorney Nusrat Demiral accused him of behaving "provocatively," and thereby being the prime culprit for the deadly riots.[10]

In 1996, a Pakistani Christian named Ayub Masih was accused by his Muslim neighbor of encouraging him to read *The Satanic Verses*. Under Pakistani law, the testimony of a single Muslim suffices in blasphemy cases, and Masih was sentenced to death on April 28, 1998. When the Court failed to order his immediate execution, he was attacked in the courthouse itself but was saved. In a subsequent Christian protest march, attacked with stones by Muslim bystanders, Bishop John Joseph shot himself in a spectacular act of desperation (some Christians allege he was murdered). In Masih's village, all the Christians fled and their houses were occupied by Muslims.[11]

One prominent Muslim who suffered for *The Satanic Verses*, notably for protesting against the ban, was Mushir-ul-Hasan, pro-vice-chancellor of Jamia Millia Islamia, the Muslim university of Delhi. He told an interviewer, "I think the ban should be lifted. I think every person has a right to be heard and to be read."[12] In his view, the ban "qualifies as an indefensible move," though he took care to deny any sympathy for the book's contents. Overnight, he became the object of a vicious campaign by most students and some professors at Jamia Millia. Though he buckled, apologizing and saying he never meant to demand the lifting of the ban, he had to stay away from his own university. The day he showed up again, he was severely beaten up and had to be hospitalized.

The result of this terror is clear: critics of Islam feel constrained to apply self-censorship or accept a life of living in fear.

Select Countries

Rather than provide a survey of the Rushdie rules being applied globally, here is a closer look at three countries, Turkey, Egypt, and Algeria.

Turkey. Islamist militants killed journalist Cetin Emec (1990), Turan Dursun (1990), exiled Iranian dissident Ali Akbar Gorbani (alias Mansour Amini, 1992), and leading leftist journalist Uğur Mumcu (1993). These murders were probably committed by the Islamic Action Group, whose members were arrested in 1993 and the murders stopped.[13] Toktamis Ates, a left-secular columnist for the daily *Cumhuriyet*, escaped death when the police discovered a time bomb fixed underneath the table in an Istanbul bookstore where he was to sign autographs.[14] A Turkish bartender, Oğuz Atak, had the name "Allah" tattooed on his shoulder; in 1997 he was shot dead for defiling God's name.[15] On 21 October 1999, prominent secularist academic Ahmet Taner Kislali died after picking up a parcel left on the roof of his car in an Ankara street.[16]

Turks responded robustly; for example, a quarter million Turks marched against radical Islam ("Turkey will never be

Iran") in the mourning procession for Uğur Mumcu.[17] None-theless, as Islamist pressure rose, the government began ban-ning books critical of Islam, such as Ilhan Arsal's *Stories about the Shari'a*, a volume that tells about the historical basis of Islamic law, questioning whether modern behavior should be based on ancient and sometimes even comical incidents. This was deemed insulting to Islam and the Prophet Muhammad. Arsal replied that he had wanted Turks to know more about the Shari'a and had simply brought authentic Islamic materials to public attention: "Most quotations have been taken from pub-lications by the Ministry for Religious Affairs."[18] Thus did Atatürk's successors prohibit a faithful rendering of Islam's own traditions for the crime of insulting Islam.

Egypt. Egypt has a history of Islamist violence that has af-fected even the country's most renowned writer, Nobel Prize winner Naguib Mahfouz (b. 1911), who was stabbed in the neck and seriously wounded in 1994. Farag Foda, a Muslim liberal and long-standing critic of the fundamentalists, was murdered in June 1992; his son and other bystanders were se-riously wounded. During the trial of several suspects in the Foda murder, expert witnesses defended the execution of apos-tates and blasphemers. As a newspaper report put it,

> Those accused of killing Farag Foda were defended in court by Sheikh Muhammad al-Ghazali, one of Egypt's most senior theologians. He is an official at Al-Azhar [University, a theological academy] and thus a government em-ployee. Mr. Ghazali testified in court that Mr. Foda and 'secularists' like him are apostates who should be put to death. He added that if the government failed to carry out that 'duty', individuals were free to do so.[19]

As Ghazali's testimony suggests, censorship has become a joint venture of the Egyptian state and the guardians of ortho-doxy. A fundamentalist member of parliament, Jalal Gharib, demanded in 1994 and won an assurance from Culture Minis-ter Faruq Husni that a committee of Islamic scholars from Al-Azhar University would henceforth screen (and possibly re-ject) ministry books scheduled for publication.[20] This agreement merely confirmed a privilege that Al-Azhar had already exercised many times in the past, most notably, by banning Nagib Mahfouz's 1959 novel, *Children of Gabalawi*,[21] which it claimed contained "insulting" references to God and the prophets.[22]

Sheikh Muhammad Sayyid at-Tantawi, the head of Al-Azhar, in 1996 called *A Psychological Analysis of Prophets* by journalist 'Abdullah Kamal, a blasphemous book on the grounds that "Islamic doctrine does not permit description of the divine messengers in terms which erode their religious position. It is the task of Al-Azhar and other religious institutes to correct such sinful thoughts." The government dutifully imposed a ban on the book and confiscated all unsold copies.[23]

Egyptian courts have tried to steer a middle course between purely Islamic verdicts (death sentence for apostasy) and showing an amiable face to the outside world. For this reason, 'Ala' Hamid, a civil servant and author of a Voltairian essay,[24] was not sentenced to death but to eight years' imprisonment for blasphemy.[25] His publisher, Muhammad Madbuli, a critic of Islam who has dismissed religion as "a fabric of myths," got the same sentence, along with the printer of Hamid's book.[26] Hamid hadn't expected this much trouble: "My only crime is that I allowed myself to think."[27] Likewise, Nasr Hamid Abu Zayd, a reformist Muslim professor of literature, was not sentenced to death for apostasy, but found his marriage dissolved on the Shari'a grounds that a Muslim woman may not be married to a non-Muslim man.[28] Fortunately for the couple, the University of Leiden in Holland invited both to teach, permitting them to escape Egypt.

Islamists have killed Western tourists to Egypt in many incidents, most notoriously in an assault in Luxor in late 1997. This campaign of violence not only reduces the Egyptian government's vital tourist income but it punished those who visit Egypt to see the Pharaonic "idol temples." (Though less well known than the Taliban destruction of the Buddha at Bamiyan, the famous Karnak temple was bombed in 1992, giving teeth to Islamist calls for demolishing the Sphinx and other antiquities.)[29]

Even living in the West does not guarantee safety for Egyptian dissidents, however. After the Mecca-based Council of Religious Scholars declared Rashad Khalifa, an Egyptian emigrant to the United States, to be an "infidel," he was killed in Tucson, Arizona. Unknown assailants shot Makin Morcos in Australia after a radio station broadcast his criticism of Islamists for harassing and murdering Coptic Christians in Egypt.[30]

Algeria. From freethinking journalists to women in Western dress, many alleged enemies of Islam have lost their lives in Algeria, where the death toll from an Islamist insurgency numbers over 100,000. The year 1993 alone counted the following victims. Berber writer Tahar Djaout, shot dead as he walked out of the Algiers office of the secularist weekly *Rupture*; political scientist Mohammed Boukhobza, his throat cut; sociologist and poet Youssef Sebti, his throat also cut;[31] and political scientist Djillali Lyabès, writer Hafidh Senhadri, and doctor and writer Laadi Flici.[32] Newsreader Tayeb Bouterfis was shot dead near his residence in Baraki outside Algiers in October 1994.[33] Playwright Abdelkader Alloula was shot in Oran.[34] Said Mekbel died on December 4, 1994 from his bullet wounds, the twenty-fourth journalist killed by the Islamists since 1992; his final article was found in his computer, describing some of the stratagems he used to deceive the terrorists about his whereabouts.[35] Film director Ali Tenki was among sixty-five civilians killed west and south of Algiers in a particularly bloody week in August 1997.[36] Terror by the mysterious Groupe Islamique Armé (GIA) struck unveiled schoolgirls, working women, and entire villages, as well as targets outside the country. The GIA continues its policy of carrying out massacres in undefended villages to the present.

The Berber singer-songwriter Lounès Matoub had described himself as an apostate ("ni Arabe ni musulman," "neither Arab nor Muslim"); in June 1998, he was murdered.[37] Though some insiders to the Berber autonomist movement sought to blame the Algerian government,[38] the GIA claimed responsibility,

explaining that Matoub was among the fiercest enemies of religion and of the *Mujahidin*, as did another Islamist organization, the Groupe Salafiste pour la Prédication et le Combat.
Consequently, the murder remains shrouded in mystery.[39]

The Islamist terror campaign extends to Westerners in Algeria, secular and religious. Notable among the latter: A bomb
killed Bishop Pierre Claverie of Oran in 1996, along with his
chauffeur,[40] making him the nineteenth Catholic priest killed
since 1992. Other victims included Father Charles Deckers, a
Belgian pioneer of Muslim-Christian dialogue, one of a group
of seven White Fathers murdered in a single attack.

Miscellaneous and Unreported Cases

The Rushdie rules apply to fashion and the arts as wells in
other places. In several cases, utilizing the name "Allah" (or
any of its many derivatives in personal names, such as
'Abdallah) on clothing has lead to protests and apologies. The
model Claudia Schiffer wore a dress with Arabic letters in Paris
but the resulting protests led to the fashion house withdrawing
the dress. Several similar cases of protest occurred in Bangladesh
and elsewhere because manufacturers allegedly defiled the name
"Allah" by imprinting it on something as lowly as a shoe. More
bizarre yet was a case in the United States, where the sports-
apparel firm Nike, threatened by a global Muslim boycott,
agreed not only to recall 38,000 pairs of shoes bearing a logo
that some Muslims claimed resembled the Arabic spelling of
the word "Allah," but also to apologize for the incident, provide "sensitivity training" on Islam for all Nike employees,
and donate $50,000 to an Islamic school in the United States.[41]
By contrast, the Israeli-Arab fashion designer, Fida' Na'amna,
though deemed a blasphemer and unbeliever by some imams,
refused even to apologize for using the calligraphy "Allah" in
one of her creations.[42]

In instances like these, the offending artists have a fairly
good case in denying any commission of an act of blasphemy.

In this register of "blasphemy," people are making ritually improper references to Allah or Mohammed but without any hostile or even skeptical intent. Thus, in the 1999 case of Christian singer Marcel Khalife in Lebanon, Judge 'Abd ar-Rahman Shihab demanded his imprisonment for up to three years for insulting religious rituals by using a chapter of the Qur'an in his song lyrics. But the trial got postponed and derailed thanks to the singer's friends in high places. Druze leader Walid Joumblatt and even Prime Minister Salim Hoss came out in his support. Shi'i leader Mohammed Hasan al-Amin said that the use of Qur'anic quotations is a common practice in Arabic poetry. Another Shi'i leader, Muhammad Mahdi Shams ad-Din, considered the use of a Qur'anic text to be blasphemous but rejected the idea of putting the singer on trial.[43] This ritual impropriety was enough to raise some frowns from clerics but not sufficient to provoke the anger needed for a real persecution.

This list of victims of the Islamist book-banners and blasphemy-avengers is, however, far from complete. In many cases, lighter forms of suppression take place and do not attract international attention. Bassam Tibi, a Syrian professor based in Germany, has noted the many cases of "critical Muslims in Algeria, Egypt or Turkey who are persecuted or even killed by fundamentalists and about whom world opinion never gets informed. In a fundamentalist environment, being both Muslim and intellectual is a risk, because the Shari'a's big stick tolerates no freedom of opinion."[44] Likewise, Rachid Boudjedra of Algeria remarks that the international media reports only selected cases: "When Farag Foda fell, they were briefly persuaded [to report] but even before Foda many intellectuals in Cairo and Alexandria have been killed by fanatics."[45]

Some examples: In the United Arab Emirates, eleven Indians were sentenced in May 1992 to six years' imprisonment for staging a play, *Shavamtîni Urumbukal* (Malayalan: "Ants feasting on a corpse"), which contained allegedly blasphemous passages.[46] This award-winning play, written in 1981-82 by Karthikeyan Padiyath and frequently staged and applauded throughout Kerala, "is a social comedy on the followers of Christ, Prophet Muhammad and Karl Marx."[47] In other cases, no judicial prosecution nor physical violence occurs but people are threatened with financial or career consequences for smaller "offences." For example, a Muslim school principal in India was forced to resign because she had allowed pupils to stage a play depicting scenes from the life of a Hindu family.[48] In this case, the mere expression of sympathetic interest in heathen neighbors amounts to a deviation to be punished.

Even more serious cases go unreported. Islamists shot and killed in October 1997 the Pakistani High Court judge, Arif Bhatti, who had acquitted two Christians on blasphemy charges. In Saudi Arabia in 1992, young poet Sadiq 'Abd al-Karim Milalla was beheaded for having declared that Islam is a false religion, the Prophet a charlatan, and the Qur'an Muhammad's own creation.[49] That same year, a Christian preacher from the Philippines was sentenced to death in Saudi Arabia for trying to convert Muslims.[50] In 1997, two Christian Filipinos from in Saudi Arabia were sentenced to death, ostensibly for common crimes, but according to witnesses it was in fact because they had tried to preach their religion as preferable to Islam.[51] Media interest in all these events was minimal.

Some Muslim intellectuals complain that their culture has still not produced a Voltaire.[52] But the truth seems rather to be that there are quite a few Muslim Voltaires, only they are working under more difficult circumstances than the French satirist: some of them are in exile, many are being very cautious, and others have been silenced for good.

THE WEST

Intimidation

The traditional Muslim countries may be where the Rushdie rules are most often applied, but they also extend now to the

West as well. In March 1989, French singer Véronique Sanson performed a song titled *Allah* in a show at the Paris Olympia Hall, which begins with the story of a Lebanese female suicide-bomber, then implores God:

> Allah, why the fire and thunder?
> Why do you wage this war? . . .
> It is you whom they are using.
> It is in your name that they are fighting. . . .
> If I were you, I wouldn't be proud.[53]

Sanson received death threats after just one performance of this song, so she immediately removed it from her program. "I am not so much afraid for myself," she explained. "But I cannot run the risk of endangering the lives of my musicians and of the thousands of people in the audience."[54]

Mostly, however, the main brake on critical discussion of Islam in the West results not from physical threats but from subtle and not-so-subtle forms of censorship. Westerners who have critical things to say about Islam render themselves unemployable. The French civil servant Jean-Claude Barreau, head of the administration for the integration of immigrants, was sacked in 1991 for publishing a book in which he questioned the "golden legend" of the "great Islamic civilization" which is only believed because "man's capacity for self-deception is enormous." He called the spread of Islam "one of the great catastrophes in history," pointing out that agriculture collapsed where peasants converted to Islam, a city-based religion: "The Muslims are not the sons but the fathers of the desert."[55] Strong language, certainly, and critics discovered a number of errors of detail in the book, but Barreau was right to point out that similar criticism of Christianity would never have caused his dismissal. Barreau called himself a victim of the taboo on critical discussion of Islam.[56]

In France, the late bishop Marcel Lefebvre, leader of the traditionalist Catholics, was sentenced to pay a fine of 5,000 French francs (about $900) for his "racist" statement, to a non-

Muslim audience, that when the Muslims presence becomes even stronger, "it is your wives, your daughters, your children who will be kidnapped and dragged off to a certain kind of places as they exist in Casablanca [Morocco]."[57] That a prominent bishop can be brought before a court for evoking the historical fact of European slavery at the hands of Muslim slavers is a sign of a new power equation. (In contrast, British Muslim leader Kalim Siddiqui was not prosecuted for blaming European civilization for all the evils of the modern world, nor even for breaking the law by publicly calling for the murder of Salman Rushdie.) And Lefebvre got off lightly, the judge having ruled that he had not "actively incited to discrimination," in which case he would have received a prison sentence plus a fine of 300,000 francs. Fines of this magnitude have recently been imposed twice on actress and animal-rights activist Brigitte Bardot for comparing Muslim settlement in France to the Nazi occupation, and for saying, "Tomorrow, the Muslims who cut the throats of innocent sheep to celebrate Eid, may well cut the throat of human beings, as is already being done in Algeria."[58]

In 1994, the city government of Geneva organized the performance of all of Voltaire's theatre plays to celebrate the famous freethinker's 300th birthday. However, the Muslim community (not Islamists, but state-subsidized cultural foundations) objected to the staging by director Hugues Loichemol of Voltaire's play, first staged in 1742, *Mahomet ou le fanatisme*, an attack on religious intolerance based on the Muslim biography of Muhammad in which he orders the murder of his critics.[59] The city government withdrew funding for the play and no one dared come forward in response to Loichemol's plea for private sponsorship, so the performance was cancelled.[60]

Those in the West who speak out critically in their own name sometimes must live underground. This is the case for Steven Emerson, the American journalist researching Islamist networks in the United States,[61] and 'Abd al-Qadir Yasin, a Palestinian writer and ex-assistant of Yasir Arafat, now living in Sweden. Yasin comments,

Rushdie has written what we wanted to say. He has told the world that we exist. He ended our isolation. But at the same time he has isolated us again. He has freed us only to put us in chains again. Now it has become entirely impossible to see anything in the Qur'an except a sacred and unassailable book of God.

> Yasin also testified from personal experience how difficult and dangerous it is to speak one's doubts about Islam even with friends, always knowing that "when we declare ourselves separated from the faith, it is the duty of the faithful to put us to *justice*."[62]

A number of books on Islam, even serious and important works, are now published under pseudonym. Thus, the apostate Muslim author *Why I Am Not a Muslim*, a well-argued secular-humanist critique of Islam, felt compelled to hide his identity behind a false name.[63] So did the nationalist French author of *Islamism and the United States: An Alliance against Europe*, which sees a conspiracy in America's pressure on the European Union to admit Turkey and its all-out American support for the Bosnian Muslims.[64] Then there is the case of the book published in 1990 by a Muslim who called himself "Mohamed Rasoel,"[65] *The Impending Ruin of the Netherlands, Country of Gullible Fools*,[66] which deserves special attention.

Warning that the Dutch are mistaken to tolerate the establishment of Islamic institutions and the mushrooming growth of their Muslim population, *The Impending Ruin of the Netherlands* predicted this would lead to a civil war and the country's partition. Significantly, the author's first warning to this effect was an unsolicited guest column in a Rotterdam daily during the heat of the Rushdie controversy.[67] Many progressive intellectuals reacted to the book in a vicious way. For example, the Hindu-born secularist Anil Ramdas equated its author with Khomeini, saying that he was "revealing himself as an intentional murderer."[68] A number of bookstores refused to sell the book.[69]

Unwilling to reveal his whereabouts, the author did grant media interviews, prompting the Dutch press frantically to try to uncover his real identity. A television talk show host tried to grab his passport and pull off the shawl with which he covered his face; a Muslim politician was ostensibly willing to talk to him, only to pass his teacup onto the police for the finger-prints. After a few months of cat-and-mouse, this effort finally succeeded; the author turned out to be a Pakistani cabaret artist living in Edam who was known to the public only as "Zoka F."

Rendering his last name with only the initial reflected the fact that by the time he became known, the author had become a suspect in a court case; the Anne Frank Foundation, of all things, then controlled by the far left, had brought charges of racism against Rasoel. During the course of the trial in 1992, the Dutch public beheld the remarkable spectacle of a dark-skinned immigrant shouted down by the press and sentenced to a heavy fine by white judges, while his white collaborators – the publisher and translator (from broken English to Dutch) of his book – were acquitted. The judge decided that Rasoel had made "unjustified generalizations" by contrasting "soft Dutch-men" with "crude, cruel, corrupt and bloodthirsty Muslims."[70] Although the verdict left Rasoel with a large debt, he felt vindi-cated by it:

> It proves that the general thrust of my book is correct, that Dutch society is changing and becoming less tolerant. Freedom of opinion is already being sacrificed. I don't blame this state attorney, he is a nice man but rather dumb and naïve like most Dutchmen. . . . Muslims are allowed to shout: kill Rushdie. . . . When Muslims say on TV that all Dutch women are whores, it is allowed. . . . It is ridiculous and scandalous that I have to justify myself in court for discrimi-nation of Muslims.[71]

Rasoel's case points to the fact that the proliferation of anti-racist legislation offers a mechanism to punish critics of Islam; in addition to the Netherlands, it has already been used to this effect in France and Belgium. This is doubly ironic, for one, there are plenty of critics of Islam by not-so-white people, es-pecially former Muslims.[72] For another, real racism, that is, belief in the inequality of races, is now definitely at its lowest ebb in centuries. Still, the highly charged accusation of racism is now used for an ever-widening spectrum of non-racist opinions, from xenophobia (which is indeed on the rise) to legitimate criticism of cultural expressions associated with immigrant groups. The anti-racism laws also include the creation of a legal category of "opinion crimes" that can be used to suppress opinions having nothing to do with racism.

Who are the Censors?

Governments. It need not be Muslims who put pressure to prevent criticism of Islam or punish its authors; in a number of instances, Western governments have attempted to thwart, or at least refused to support, criticism of Islam. The British government banned a demonstration in support of Salman Rushdie on the thousandth day of his underground life, fearing that this would endanger the negotiations to release Terry Waite, a British hostage in Lebanon.[73] Lufthansa, the German airline, refused to let Rushdie on to one of its flights; as recently as March 2002, Air Canada banned Rushdie from its flights for six months.[74] A public reading from *The Satanic Verses* in a Muslim-dominated suburb of Brussels was prohibited; when questioned, the City Council and the Home Ministry held one another responsible for issuing the ban. When the European Parliament invited Bangladeshi author Taslima Nasrin to come and receive the Sakharov Prize in Strasbourg, the French government initially wanted to grant her a visa for a single day, pleading an inability to guarantee her safety for any longer period than this utmost minimum.[75]

Despite the American tradition of tolerating even the most repugnant speech, the State Department in mid-1997 publicly demanded the punishment of an Israeli woman who had distributed a poster depicting the Prophet Muhammad as a pig. And an Israeli judge did its bidding, sentencing her to two years' imprisonment.

Intellectuals. On several occasions, university authorities in Belgium have cancelled permission for lectures and debates expected to be critical of Islam. A Brussels weekly published a cover story titled "Will the Belgium of Our Children Be Islamic?" that was filled with sober references to human rights violations against Christians in Turkey and Egypt, plus an excerpt from a speech by a Belgium-based imam: "Soon we will take power in this country. Those who criticize us now, will regret it. They will have to serve us. Prepare, for the hour is near."[76] In response, the Belgian Human Rights League filed a suit on the basis of the anti-racism law—and not against the imam but against the journalist. The palace contacted the editor to protest the issue's cover, which showed King Albert II wearing an Arab headdress. The editor had advertisements of the issue removed; soon after, he himself was sacked.[77]

Pressure is sometimes applied in private. A well-known Belgian psychologist, Herman Somers, published a book, *A Different Muhammad*, that contains a detailed analysis of the words and acts of the prophet and concludes that his prophethood is a typical case of paranoid delusion nourished with sensorial hallucinations.[78] The psychiatrists and specialists on Islam who helped Somers do his research, it bears noting, did so only on condition of strict anonymity. Somers also wrote best-selling studies of Jesus, Biblical prophets, the Jesuit order, and Jehovah's Witnesses, all of which were widely discussed in the media. This time, however, his book met with a deafening silence. Reviewers looked the other way, scholars of religion strictly avoided mention of the book, and even the publisher failed to publicize the book. It sold poorly and quickly became unavailable. Without any law being violated or any ban issued, Somers' thesis was effectively prevented from entering public discourse. These cases contain not a hint of Islamist threat, nor government pressure.

In some cases, Western intellectuals who wish to stand by Muslim-born critics of Islam simply can't get a grip on the problem. In November 2000, a theater in Rotterdam was forced to withdraw from its program a play called *Aisha*, written by Dutch playwright Gerrit Timmers but manned entirely by Moroccan-born actors. After persuasive interventions by some imams, the actors pleaded that they couldn't be a party to an enactment of scenes from the life of the Prophet and of his favourite young wife 'A'isha.[79] There was some commotion about the matter (even in the Dutch parliament), with the general conclusion being that non-Muslims just have no clue to Islam and the Muslim community, and that freethinking Muslims would just have to sort matters out for themselves.

Political authorities at least have the excuse that they have other concerns (financial, diplomatic, security) beside the cause of intellectual freedom. Intellectuals, however, have no such excuses. Nor can they point to personal danger; there have been practically no attempts on the lives of Western critics of Islam, the most conspicuous exception so far being Steven Emerson, who has indeed been threatened. Muslims dislike it when a non-Muslim articulates his non-acceptance of Islamic doctrine, but they find this much less shocking than when a born-Muslim does the same thing. After all, a non-Muslim by definition does not believe in Muhammad as God's messenger, so theories about Muhammad being a fraud and the like merely make explicit the skepticism common to nearly all non-Muslims. So, fear of physical violence probably does not account for the silence of Western intellectuals. Rather, it is a matter of careerist calculations. Criticism of Islam is easily associated with a retrograde Christian fanaticism or anti-immigrant xenophobia—and being tagged with such labels is disastrous publicity, whether or not they accurately apply.

Islamist organizations. Now that Islamist organizations have taken root and are prospering in the West, they have shown skill at turning the laws of their host societies against its supposed high valuation of freedom of expression. Islamist groups had an important role in the case of the Voltaire play (above) and Michel Houellebecq (below).

Some Muslim organizations, all while treading the legal path themselves, obliquely support or applaud the actions of their more militant brethren, at times even openly. This happened in two cases concerning Muslims who critique their coreligionists who gave Islam a bad name by their intolerance and violence. The Washington-based Council on American-Islamic Relations, an organization with an entrée to the White House, brought about an edict against Khalid Durán for his allegedly misrepresenting Islam in his book on Islam; then CAIR pretended that the edict had not taken place but was made up by the publisher in an effort to stimulate sales.[80] In July 1998, Professor Ebrahim Moosa and his family narrowly survived when a bomb blew up their house in Cape Town, South Africa; to this, the Islamic Unity Convention publicly rejoiced.[81]

The Impact of September 11

The events of September 11, 2001, slightly shifted but did not fundamentally change the publicly stated Western opinion landscape regarding Islam. Debate about the need to limit immigration or to pursue energetic policies of assimilation rather than pampering isolationist structures in the immigrant Muslim communities could finally break through the limits imposed by political correctness. It suddenly became acceptable to mention and discuss the higher crime rate among Muslims, as in the epidemic of gang-rapes from Sydney to Paris and Copenhagen. Even so, it remains risky to take liberties with the Islamic religion. People have felt emboldened to express their misgivings about the increasing Islamic assertiveness, but the (generally well-meaning) enforcers of the taboo on criticizing Islam have not disarmed.

The Netherlands was typical of many Western countries. There, the freedom to discuss Islam increased after September 11 – up to a point. The flamboyant homosexual sociology professor Pim Fortuyn drew the logical anti-Islamic conclusions from his ultraliberal views. Single-handedly, he broke the taboo on non-deferential discussion of Islam, which he saw as "backward" and threatening to modern values. Out of the blue, the party he founded cornered twenty-six of the 150 seats in parliament in the elections of May 2002, but he himself was murdered a week earlier by a Green-Left activist. All the same, his party joined the new center-right government, which immediately broke with the earlier routine of pampering the mushrooming Islamic establishment, at least at the verbal level. Though the party soon lost credibility because of its political ineptitude, even leading to the early fall of the government in October 2002, much of its agenda was absorbed by the mainstream parties. Fortuyn was against demands of sending immigrants back to where they came from, but he insisted on their gradual assimilation on the pattern of earlier waves of immigrants. Even this was enough to earn him al kinds of hate labels ("Mussolini," "Milosevic,," etc.)[82] but after September 11, the tide of public opinion had clearly turned in his favor.

After September 11, it became much easier openly to question the virulent sermons given by imams in some Dutch mosques, without incurring the "racism" indictment that had struck Mohamed Rasoel a decade earlier; but the taboo on criticism of Islam did not disappear. It had merely receded to protect Muslims as a whole, if no longer their more embarrassing extremist spokesmen. Muslim-born critics of Islam still run a more serious risk than the non-Muslims, who can get away with a mere verbal reprimand from the multiculturalist opinion hegemons. "For me as a non-Muslim it is easier to criticize Islam than for Muslims," noted the Arabic scholar Maurice Blessing.[83]

In the course of 2002, writer Hafid Bouazza and jurist Afshin Ellian, a refugee from Iran, received death threats after criticizing Islam. In September 2002, Ms. Ayaan Hirsi Ali, Somali-born political scientist working for the Dutch Labour Party, was threatened from several quarters after uttering criticism of Islam on television. Inside the party, she had launched the debate on the emancipation of Muslim women, a debate that the

Dutch socialists had been avoiding for too long. In a talk show, she had conceded that, "measured by certain criteria," Islam is indeed a "backward" religion.

Muslim author and prison chaplain Ali Eddaoudi, who had angrily walked out of the television debate with her, explained afterwards that Muslims are enraged with her "dilly-dallying with the Dutch" who embrace her as their "model immigrant."[84] Imam Abdullah Haselhoef, who had emerged after September 11 as the government's favorite liberal Muslim, lambasted her as a "coconut": brown on the outside, white within.[85] Ali went underground for a while and cancelled her lectures and publications, for the police took the threats very seriously. Muslim members of the Labour Party protested, for example: "I am a liberal Muslim and I am boiling with rage, so you can imagine how conservative Muslims feel about this and what they may do."[86]

These incidents spelled out the ultimate Islamic principle that underlie the controversies over freedom of expression: the prohibition on apostasy from Islam. "Apostasy is the biggest taboo in Islam," noted Maurice Blessing. "It is a frontier you cannot cross." Blessing became worried when he saw the reactions of Muslim panel members in the television debate with Hirsi Ali: "Accusing someone on TV of apostasy, as Muslims did to her in this TV programme, is nasty. If you do that as a Muslim, you know how serious the allegation is and what the consequences can be."[87] Arabic scholar Fred Leemhuis explained,

> Every Muslim who executes the death sentence on an apostate, does work pleasing to God. So this is freedom of religion. This is Islam. In Egypt the highly authoritative imam Muhammad al-Ghazali confirmed before a court of justice that apostasy is punished with the death penalty. If the state doesn't implement it, doing so himself would be the duty of every Muslim. Those are statements which can inspire people. And fundamentalists don't feel restrained by national borders or legislation.

One limitation does exist, however: "It must really be established with certainty that the accused is an apostate," according to Leemhuis, and this can be deduced from his or her words and actions.[88]

Cases of quiet apostasy are relatively common, typically during the student years under the influence of secularized or (more rarely) firmly Christian natives. But going public with apostasy, even if only implicitly through criticism of Islam, is not tolerated and requires great courage. That is why columnist Sylvain Ephimenco congratulates Hirsi Ali: "Your participation in this type of debate in the last few weeks has meant more for the emancipation of Muslim women in this country than a whole decade of deafening silence from the Dutch feminists."[89]

In the immediate aftermath of September 11, it was striking how seemingly the entire political and intellectual class hurried to assure the Muslim community that it would not be targeted with suspicions of collective guilt. This cuddly goodwill offensive included a visit by Prime Minister Wim Kok to a mosque. While this was not bad in itself, and may even have saved a few Muslim lives by nipping a possible wave of anti-Muslim anger in the bud, it remains hard to imagine such an attitude in case of violence by other groups, such as autochthonous nationalists. In such a case, there would be an outcry about how "this event shows the ugly true face of nationalism," and there would be no goodwill missions of politicians to the beer halls of the nationalists.

But claims that Osama bin Laden incarnated "the true face of Islam," or even "a legitimate *part* of Islam," remained confined to an extremist fringe in Holland, while everyone of some standing came out to affirm the opposite. For example, in a collection of articles on 9/11 published in the highbrow daily *Trouw*, not a single author links these acts of terrorism to any Islamic doctrine. One contributor says the events were proof of "nihilism," another puts them down to "Third-World frustration," the next one accuses "economic inequality," but all are in effective agreement to deny and smother the Islamic motive explicitly invoked by the suicide terrorists themselves.[90]

Looking quickly at other countries: In November 2001, the Danish people elected a government promising to curb the perceived advances and increasing arrogance of the growing Islamic establishment. The new government's policies regarding the integration or assimilation of Muslim immigrants and the creation of hurdles in the way of mass immigration were widely criticized as being too "xenophobic" by some—but as too tentative and timid by others. This aptly sums up the power equation after September 11: an acknowledged desire to "take no more nonsense," but also a sense of restraint so as not to veer from one extreme (starry-eyed multiculturalism) to the other, combined with a fear of criticism from the left.

In Italy, the contradictory reactions can be seen in two prominent cases. In autumn 2001, the media's cries of "racism!" forced Prime Minister Silvio Berlusconi to retract his description of Islam as "backward" and "inferior to European civilization." But other voices critical of Islam became bolder, and especially the shrill critique of Islam by the veteran leftist journalist, Oriana Fallaci, in her *La Rabbia e l'Orgoglio* (*The Rage and the Pride*). Not surprisingly, Fallaci herself received lambasting reviews of extraordinary ferocity.[91]

In France, a petition seeking to ban Fallaci's book for alleged racism narrowly failed; but more important was the late 2002 trial of postmodern novelist Michel Houellebecq, for anti-Islamic utterances in his novel *Plateforme*, published in August 2001, and in subsequent interviews.[92] In the book, after the protagonist's beloved is killed by a Muslim in a bombing, he applauds the killing of a Palestinian militant. Professionals of the French race relations industry joined hands with Islamic organizations (the mosque foundations of Paris and Lyons, the Saudi-based World Islamic Council) to file a court case against Houellebecq for "incitement to racial hatred."

The trial became an arena where the core questions of the whole debate on the Rushdie rules found expression. Dalil Boubakeur, rector of the Paris mosque, made the basic case: "Freedom of expression ends where it can hurt .... I think that my community has been humiliated, my religion insulted, and I want justice to be done."

The court also heard representatives of a group of writers and journalists (including Philippe Sollers, Michel Braudeau, Josyane Savigneau, Francisco Arrabal) who came out in support of Houellebecq and freedom of expression. They were mostly celebrities of second rank, for the really big names chose to remain aloof. Pierre Assouline, editor of the magazine *Lire,* which had published the offending statements, even came to testify that Houellebecq had displayed a crude "aversion for Arabs" and that he had transgressed the boundaries of literary provocation to lapse into a frenzy of pure "vengeance."[93] Interestingly, the public prosecutor demanded Houellebecq's unconditional acquittal: "His statements are admittedly shocking, but we are not here to moralize, only to determine penal guilt. And on those terms, I must request his release."[94]

Interrogated by the court, Michel Houellebecq explained that he had the right to criticize the "monotheistic religions," adding some detail of what he considered wrong and "hate-mongering" in the Bible as well as the Qur'an. He stood by the utterances he had made in the offending interviews, that between the two scriptures, he considered the Bible superior, as it had been written by many writers, some of them "worthless as excrement" but others "true men of genius" and "Jews, who are good at writing." By contrast, the Qur'an was produced singlehandedly by an Arab businessman who was a "rather mediocre" writer. Summing up, he found the Qur'an a "devastatingly depressing" book and Islam "the most stupid religion" as well as "a dangerous religion since its very beginning."

The core of Houellebecq's defence was, firstly, that criticism of a religion cannot fall under the legal category of "racism" because Islam or the Muslim community is not a race; and secondly, that criticism or even "hatred" of a religion doesn't imply hatred of its adherents. He also expected people to understand from the tone of his statements that his position regarding Islam was clearly not one of "hatred" but one of contempt. To the question of one of the prosecuting lawyers whether he "considered the Muslims stupid," he clarified that he didn't think so, that he had never made such sweeping generalizations about the Muslims, but that Islam as a belief system did indeed remain "stupid" in his opinion. In particular, he felt it was time to pinprick the claim that "Islam preaches peace." [95]

This record illustrates two major developments. Apologetic claims on behalf of Islam, engaged in by governments and the media in hopes of smoothing the transition to the multicultural society, are making way for a hard look at what Islamic teachings really say, even as Islamist institutions develop a foothold in Western societies.

CONCLUSION: A RAY OF HOPE

We conclude this update with a ray of hope. Firstly, it is rare and getting even rarer that Muslim-majority states, including declared Islamic *Shari'a*-based states, dare to openly implement the whole procedure of arresting a "blasphemer," sentencing him to death and effectively executing him.

In Pakistan with its draconian anti-blasphemy law, many people (mostly from the Christian and Ahmadiya minorities) have been arrested on blasphemy charges, many of them have been sentenced to years in prison, some have been sentenced to death, some have been murdered in custody or at large, but in no case has the state dared fully and formally to implement the whole course of its legal provision of a death sentence. Thus, in 1995, two Christians were sentenced to death for blasphemy against the Prophet Mohammed: Salamat Masih, an illiterate fourteen-year-old, alleged to have written blasphemous words on the wall of a mosque, and his uncle, Rehmat Masih.[96] However, local and international support helped finance a High Court appeal and they were acquitted of the charge. The authorities kept an eye closed when the Masihs were smuggled out of Pakistan to find refuge in Germany,[97] relieved to be rid of a source embarrassment in its relations with what it perceives as "Christian" America.

Ayub Masih, the Christian who had been sentenced to death in 1998 on charges of propagating Salman Rushdie's offending book, was still alive in February 2002 when he was allowed a retrial. This was not coincidentally at a time when Pakistan's leader General Pervez Musharraf was critically dependent on American support and greatly embarrassed by regular attacks on Christian churches by Islamist militants eager to thwart his alliance with the United States. Ayub Masih was acquitted in August 2002 and immediately released from prison.[98]

Other Muslim countries likewise try to steer a middle course between Islamist demands for heavy penalties and a more progressive international image. In Egypt, as noted above, sentences demanded against and imposed upon religious offenders typically amount to a few years in prison, or to some personal harassment such as an enforced divorce. In Indonesia, Permadi Satrio Wiwoho, who had called Muhammad a "dictator," was taken to court for "demeaning the Islamic religion" and sentenced to seven months' jail: unsecular and unpleasant, certainly, but not the end of the world either.[99]

Iranian government support for the Rushdie edict has been gradually declining and the trigger-happy days of executing dissidents at home and abroad seem to be over. In the last weeks of 1998 the writers Majid Sharif, Mohammad Moukhtari and Mohammad Ja'far Pouyandeh were killed, as were the elderly couple Dariush Forouhar and Parvaneh Eskandari. Instead of celebrating the death of these "apostates," the government announced on 6 January 1999 that "rogue elements" in its own ranks, notably in the security forces, had been arrested for the killings.[100]

On October 6, 2002, American televangelist Jerry Falwell asserted on the CBS news programme *Sixty Minutes* that Mohammed was "a violent man, a man of war." Citing studies "by both Muslims and non-Muslims," he specified, "I think Mohammed was a terrorist." Apart from triggering Muslim rioting in Sholapur (near Mumbai, India) killing five, this statement provoked stern protests from Iranian clerics. Hossein Shariatmadari, editor of the hardline evening paper *Kayhan*, threatened Falwell and his colleagues Pat Robertson and Franklin Graham: "In accord with Islam, it is imperative to kill the three priests linked to the Zionists because they have insulted Islam and the Prophet." He hoped that "Muslims oppressed by the powerful USA would have the honour to carry out this act" and called on them to exercise their "right to attack US embassies."[101] In Tabriz, Imam Mohsen Mojtahed Shabestari denounced Falwell as a "mercenary" who "must be killed," just when Falwell himself was trying to quell the storm by apologizing and retracting his statement.[102] But note that the Iranian government stayed aloof from the controversy, and a cleric close to the regime, Ayatollah Hossein Nuri-Hamedani stopped short of issuing a threatening fatwa, even while lambasting "the priests linked with the White House who stand against the Prophet."[103]

With its extreme dependence on foreign aid, Bangladesh is understandably concerned about not offending Western sensibilities too much. Its government did not insist on implementing the prison sentence pronounced by a court against feminist author Taslima Nasrin for her 1994 book *Shame*, much less the death sentence pronounced by individual Muftis. Instead it preferred to send her into exile and be rid of the whole controversy. In 1998 it even allowed her briefly back in to visit her dying mother under strict security cover. Her latest book, *Wild Wind*, is the object of yet another ban by the Islamist-leaning government of Khaleda Zia, the reason given being that it "destroys the socio-political amity of the country" and "contains anti-Islamic statements."[104] But book-banning is not the same thing as a death sentence or an assassination.

Non-governmental Islamist forces are also becoming more circumspect. In Great Britain, after thousands of Muslims openly shouted "We will kill Satan Rushdie," the next death edict, against Pakistani-born Anwar Sheikh in 1995, was much more restrained.[105] Unlike the novelist Rushdie with his oblique and ironical challenge to Islam, Sheikh very formally renounced and criticized Islam in a bilingual English/Urdu quarterly, *Liberty*, and in a series of erudite books.[106] When news of his critique reached his homeland Pakistan, at least fourteen clerics there issued death sentences against him. A Pakistani daily reported,

> All Pakistani clergy demand extradition of the accursed renegade Anwar Shaikh from Britain to hang him publicly. ... renegade must be murdered—this is a fundamental rule of the Islamic Law—Anwar Shaikh must be called back, some lover of the Prophet is bound to kill him. ... If he is not eliminated, more Rushdies will appear. He is an apostate for denying heaven, hell, revelation, Koran, Prophet and angels. The Muslims of the world are ready to behead the accursed renegade to defend the magnificence of their Prophet.[107]

But the Pakistani authorities never demanded Anwar Sheikh's extradition and the powerful Pakistan-originated Islamist groups in Britain never seriously threatened the offending author. Britain-based muftis explained that Sheikh deserves the death sentence but that it should not be carried out except by a duly constituted authority in a proper Islamic state. Again, no attempt was made to abduct the author to such an Islamic state for standing trial.[108] Shaikh continued to live discreetly but without police protection in suburban Cardiff.

A pattern seems to be emerging in the Muslim world: after a number of sensational murders or death threats against "blasphemous" authors in the early 1990s, life for freethinkers has become slightly safer again, with an unmistakable downward trend in the murder and execution statistics. Could militant Islam have grown wary of the negative publicity that comes from threatening writers for their thoughts? If so, then the main reason would be the increased interconnectedness of the world, especially with satellite-based television and the Internet.

Publicity can save lives. This was already evident in the Soviet Union: whereas unknown local activists for religious freedom or human rights were unceremoniously carted off to the Gulag camps, high-profile dissidents with fan clubs in the West were not physically eliminated, only thwarted in their careers. The same applies with Islamists and explains why in Egypt or Lebanon, where the Western presence is palpable through media, tourists and an American university, judges award (and even prosecutors demand) sentences which fall far short of the death sentence demanded by Islamic law for blasphemy and apostasy. With the world media reporting within hours on the fatwa issued against Taslima Nasrin, the government of Bangladesh simply couldn't risk incurring the opprobrium of the world by leaving the author to her fate, let alone by executing the death sentence on its own authority.

Today, stepping out of their cultural isolation, even militant Muslims now have a strong feeling of being watched and evaluated by the rest of the world. Governments concerned about good trade relations with the West are highly sensitive about foreign opinion, but even radical movements are increasingly PR-conscious. To some extent, they feel forced to live up to their own rhetoric about how advanced and civilized and humane the Islamic religion really is.

One practical implication is that non-Muslim governments and intellectual circles should maintain or increase their involvement with the situation of intellectual freedom in the Muslim world. It does make a difference.

At the same time, Western sympathizers should see their role as auxiliary. Like the West itself in the past few centuries, the Muslim world is bringing forth its own circles of freethinkers who are presently groping around for ways of communicating in reasonable safety with their fellow born-Muslims. Arab, Iranian, and Pakistani dissidents (as yet typically residing in Western countries) have set up websites where texts critical of Islam are made available, and where all the latest information about particular cases of persecution is centralized.[109] This way, the authors can spread their message and the interested Muslim-born seekers can read it without anyone much noticing, thus silently but irrevocably changing the opinion climate in ever-wider enclaves of Muslim society. Voltaire is not dead, he's only being discreet somewhere in the Orient.

NOTES

1. *Sunday Times* (London), June 3, 1990.
2. *Le Figaro* (Paris), August 10, 1992. In the 1940s, Khomeini denounced the modernist historian Ahmad Kasravi, who was subsequently assassinated.
3. *India Times* (Washington, DC), February 1, 1992.
4. *De Morgen* (Brussels), August 24, 1996.
5. *Gazet van Antwerpen* (Antwerp), October 7, 1994.
6. *De Standaard* (Brussels), July 13, 1991.
7. "Radio Trottoir," BRTN Radio-1 (Brussels), August 3, 1991.
8. *Elsevier* (Amsterdam), July 10, 1993.
9. *Elsevier*, July 10, 1993.
10. *De Morgen*, August 12, 1994.
11. "Persecution of Christians in Islamic countries," *Left Shoe News* (www.hraic.org); "Religious intolerance in Pakistan" (www.ReligiousTolerance.org).
12. Quoted in Arun Shourie's discussion of the affair: "The Point We Always Evade," *Observer of Business and Politics* (Delhi), May 18, 1992; included in his book *Indian Controversies* (Delhi: ASA, 1993), pp. 363-370.
13. *De Standaard*, February 5, 1993.
14. *De Morgen*, September 9, 1994.
15. *De Standaard*, May 7, 1997.
16. "Breakthrough in Kislali murder investigation," *Kurdish Observer*, January 21, 2000.
17. *Observer of Business and Politics*, January 29, 1993.
18. Interview in *Cumhuriyet*, cited in *De Morgen*, August 9, 1996.
19. *International Herald Tribune* (Paris), February 4, 1994.
20. *International Herald Tribune*, February 4, 1994.
21. *De Morgen*, October 18, 1994. Some characters in Mahfouz's *The Children of Gabalawi*, as in Rushdie's *The Satanic Verses*, are transparent allusions to the Prophet Muhammad and his companions, which is why an Egyptian imam is quoted commenting: "If only we had behaved in the proper Islamic manner with Naguib Mahfouz, we would not have been assailed by the appearance of Salman Rushdie. Had we killed Naguib Mahfouz, Salman Rushdie would not have appeared." Quoted in this book, p. 148.
22. *International Herald Tribune*, February 4, 1994.
23. *De Standaard*, July 15, 1996.
24. 'Ala' Hamid: *The Distance in a Man's Mind* (1990).

25. *Newsweek*, January 27, 1992.
26. Tahar ben Jelloun in *De Morgen*, February 1, 1992.
27. *The Economist* (London), January 25, 1992.
28. *Gazet van Antwerpen*, August 7, 1996.
29. *Der Spiegel*, 1992/40.
30. Robert Burns, *The Wrath of Allah* (Houston: A. Ghosh, 1994), dedication.
31. Reported by Hassouna Moshabi in *Die Zeit*, February 11, 1994.
32. *Newsweek*, July 19, 1993.
33. *Gazet van Antwerpen*, October 17, 1994.
34. *De Standaard*, Mar. 12, 1994.
35. The article was printed in *De Morgen*, December 15, 1994.
36. "Algeria: A Few Days in August," *Left Shoe News Archive* (www.hraic.org), August 25, 1997.
37. Hassane Zerrouky, "Matoub Lounès assassiné," *L'Humanité* (Paris), June 26, 1998.
38. Vide Ferhat Mehenni: "Communiqué du Mouvement Autonomiste Kabyle en mémoire de Matoub Lounès," www.kabyle.com, June 24, 2002.
39. Farid Alilat reviews the evidence in "Matoub: le dossier qui fait peur," *Le Matin* (Algiers), December 21, 2000.
40. *Gazet van Antwerpen*, August 3, 1996.
41. *The American Reporter*, June 24, 1997.
42. Celean Jacobson: "Arab fashion designer under fire," The Associated Press, August 26, 2002.
43. "Singer denounces blasphemy charge," *BBC News*, October 3, 1999; "Blasphemy trial adjourned," *BBC News*, Nov. 3, 1999.
44. Bassam Tibi, "Wie Feuer und Wasser," *Der Spiegel*, September 20, 1994.
45. Rachid Boudjedra speaking to *Libération*, quoted in *De Morgen*, July 22, 1992.
46. *Times of India*, October 29, 1992.
47. *Times of India*, December 6, 1994.
48. *Times of India*, October 29, 1992.
49. *Die Zeit* (Hamburg), February 11, 1994.
50. *The Statesman* (Calcutta), December 23, 1992.
51. "Two Filipino Christians Beheaded in Saudi Arabia," *Left Shoe News Archive* (www.hraic.org), July 27, 1997.
52. *De Morgen*, July 13, 1991.
53. *'t Pallieterke* (Antwerp), Mar. 23, 1989.
54. *Wereldwijd* (Antwerp), July 1989.
55. Jean-Claude Barreau, *De l'islam en général et de la modernité en particulier* (Paris: Le Pré aux Clerics, 1991).
56. *Le Figaro*, Nov. 13, 1991.
57. *De Morgen*, July, 14, 1990.
58. *Le Figaro*, Apr. 26, 1996; *Le Monde*, January 21, 1998.
59. Voltaire, *Mahomet the Prophet or Fanaticism: A Tragedy in Five Acts*, trans. Robert L. Myers (New York: Frederick Ungar, 1964).
60. *The Economist*, July 2, 1994.

61. Emerson revealed his personal plight in "Foreign Terrorists in America: Five Years After the World Trade Center Bombing," testimony before the Senate Judiciary Subcommittee on Terrorism, Technology and Government Information, February 24, 1998. The same testimony also supplies extensive information on Islamist intimidation of writers and journalists in the United States.

62. 'Abd al-Qadir Yasin, *Göteborgs-Posten* (Göteborg), quoted in *Süddeutsche Zeitung*, Apr. 25, 1992.

63. Ibn Warraq, *Why I Am Not a Muslim* (Amherst, NY: Prometheus, 1995).

64. Alexandre del Valle, *Islamisme et les Etats-Unis, une alliance contre l'Europe* (Lausanne: L'Age d'Homme, 1997).

65. Recalling the many cries of "Death to Salman Rushdie," the author chose a pseudonym that means "Muhammad the Prophet," calculating that Muslims would find it difficult to shout "Death to Muhammad the Prophet."

66. Mohamed Rasoel, *Ondergang van Nederland, Land der Naïeve Dwazen* (Amsterdam: Gerard Timmer, 1990).

67. *NRC Handelsblad* (Rotterdam), Mar. 6, 1989.

68. "De kleur van Mohamed Rasoel," *Groene Amsterdammer*, October 17, 1990.

69. *NRC-Handelsblad*, October 19, 1990.

70. *NRC Handelsblad*, December 17, 1992.

71. *NRC Handelsblad*, February 29, 1992.

72. E.g. Ignacio Ramonet, "Islam contre Islam," *Le Monde Diplomatique*, July 2002.

73. According to Tariq Ali, interviewed in *Groene Amsterdammer*, Nov. 13, 1991.

74. Reuters, March 18, 2002.

75. *Gazet van Antwerpen*, October 7, 1994.

76. Alain De Kuyssche, "La Belgique de nos enfants sera-t-elle islamique?" *Télémoustique*, October 7, 1994.

77. *De Morgen*, October 5, 1994.

78. Herman Somers, *Een Andere Mohammed* (Antwerp: Hadewijch, 1992).

79. See interview with Gerrit Timmers, "Ik geloof in pragmatisme," *De Standaard*, May 24, 2002.

80. See Daniel Pipes, "An American Rushdie?" *Jerusalem Post*, July 4, 2001.

81. Ebrahim Moosa, "Muslim world reacts: silence of Islamic leaders harmful to great religion," *Atlanta Journal-Constitution*, October 14, 2001.

82. See Koenraad Elst, "De betekenis van Pim Fortuyn," *Vivat Academia* (Brussels), September 2002.

83. Yoram Stein, "Het vonnis voltrekken zou de plicht zijn van iedere moslim," *Trouw*, Sep. 19, 2002.

84. "Hirsi Ali bedreigd na kritiek op islam," *NRC Handelsblad*, Sep. 18, 2002.

85. Quoted by Sylvain Ephimenco in his column in *Trouw*, Sep. 19, 2002.

86. "Hirsi Ali bedreigd na kritiek op islam," *NRC Handelsblad*, Sep. 18, 2002.

87. Ibid. In contrast, Yassin Hartog, coordinator of the integrationist committee *Islam en Burgerschap* (Islam and Citizenship), thinks most Muslims in the

Netherlands don't make an issue of apostasy any more: "In the Dutch setting, it is seen as a personal choice. This is not a debate on apostasy. There is only an individual who has informed us that she has secularized. That has induced certain prejudices in her. Thus, she is fervently opposed to the creation of a separate Islamic school network. I think the Somali community is angry with her for explaining problems like the mistreatment of women as problems of Islam. Muslims as a community feel she has attacked them." Sylvain Ephimenco in *Trouw*, Sep. 19, 2002.

88. Yoram Stein, "Het vonnis voltrekken zou de plicht zijn van iedere moslim," *Trouw*, Sep. 19, 2002.

89. Quoted by Sylvain Ephimenco in *Trouw*, Sep. 19, 2002.

90. Peter Dekkers, ed., *Grenzeloze Haat* (Amsterdam: Trouw/Rainbow, 2001); reviewed by Koenraad Elst in *Punt*, February 12., 2002.

91. Bernard-Henri Lévy's column "Bloc-notes" in *Le Point*, 24 May 2002; P. Stouthuysen's review "De zonen van Allah" in *De Standaard*, 25 July 2002; Rana Kabbani's review "Bible of the Muslim Haters" in *The Guardian*, 11 June 2002, the review by Gilles Kepel in *Le Monde*, 30 May 2002, by Mona Chollet in *Périphérie*, June 2002, etc. Lévy's case is most peculiar: he promoted the Bangladeshi dissident author Taslima Nasrin on a tour in Europe and attacked militant Islam in his related book *La Pureté Dangereuse* (1994), yet he also worked as PR adviser to Bosnia's Islamist president Alia Izetbegovic.

92. Interviews with Michel Houellebecq in *Figaro Magazine*, August 2001, and in the leading literary magazine *Lire*, September 2001.

93. This apparently refers to the author's painful first experience with Islam: his mother had abandoned him when he was 6 and she, upon completing her wild hippie years, converted to Islam.

94. "Relaxe requise pour Michel Houellebecq," *Reuters*, Sep. 18, 2002.

95. "Michel Houellebecq admet son 'mépris pour l'islam' mais pas pour les musulmans," *Agence France-Presse*, Sep. 17, 2002.

96. "Pakistan Blasphemy Update," *Left Shoe News Archive* (www.hraic.org), February 20, 1995.

97. *Left Shoe News Archive* (www.hraic.org), Nov. 14, 1997.

98. Munir Ahmad: "Pakistani court orders Christian freed," *The Philadelphia Inquirer*, August 15, 2002.

99. "Blasphemy in Indonesia," Left Shoe News Archive (www.hraic.org), June 23, 1995.

100. *Index on Censorship*, January 1999, with reference to the revelations in the Iranian pro-reformist daily *Salam*, January 5, 1999, which forced the government to denounce and arrested the suspected culprits.

101. "Top Iranian cleric slams US pastor, paper calls for death sentence", Agence France-Presse, October 8, 2002.

102. "Falwell sorry for bashing Mohammed", CBSNews.com, October 14, 2002.

103. "Top Iranian cleric slams US pastor, paper calls for death sentence," Agence France-Presse, October 8, 2002.

104. "Shame," editorial in the *Hindustan Times* (New Delhi), August 29, 2002; interview with Taslima Nasrin in the *Times of India*, August 29, 2002.

105. Virendra Kapoor, "Another Salman Rushdie in the making?" *The Free Press Journal*, Sep. 2, 1996.
106. Mainly *Eternity* (1990), *Islam, the Arab National Movement* (1992), *Islam* (1994), and *Faith & Deception* (1996), all from Principality Publishers, Cardiff, Anwar Sheikh's private publishing outfit.
107. *Daily Sadaqat* (Lahore), October 21, 1995, quoted by Ibn Warraq, "Anwar Shaikh: The Autobiography of an Apostate," www.secularislam.org/skeptics/anwar.htm.
108. Tariq Ali, "The case of Anwar Sheikh," in *The Clash of Fundamentalisms* (London: Verso, 2002).
109. E.g. www.golshan.org, www.secularislam.org, www.hraic.org .

INDEX